Nordic Politics

KNUT HEIDAR (ED.)

# Nordic Politics

*Comparative Perspectives*

UNIVERSITETSFORLAGET

# Contents

# Preface

*Knut Heidar*

The Nordic countries are usually seen as a particular region within Northern Europe. Denmark, Sweden, Norway, Finland and Iceland have overlapping histories and are sufficiently homogeneous in terms of religion, language and politics to make them stand out as a distinct part of the European setting. Their close political cooperation, much of it organized under the auspices of the Nordic Council since the 1950s, underpins the image of a social and cultural Nordic-ness and a "Nordic model" in politics.

In this book we discuss how homogeneous these countries actually are in terms of institutional structures, political forces and public policies. What similarities do they share and what differences separate the Nordic countries from one another? Is there a special type of "Nordic democracy" or "Nordic welfare state" that marks these countries out from the continental European countries and the Anglo-Saxon world? We raise several "why"-questions. Like why did the Scandinavian countries handle their NATO and EU connections so differently? Can it be explained by reference to their individual histories, the contemporary character of Nordic societies and the geo-political order?

The book's contributors all address three questions, though from their own particular starting points of course. The book probes, collectively so to speak, 1) what unites the Nordic countries and what separates them; 2) the most likely explanations for the similarities/differences; and 3) how far the Nordic region can be said to differ from other countries and regions.

Although all chapters include a descriptive part, in terms of the analytical questions related to explanations and distinctiveness, however, emphasis will vary according to the perspectives that are central in the literature.

The book concentrates on three Scandinavian countries – Sweden, Denmark and Norway. Finland and Iceland are not excluded, but are only discussed when considered by the author to be of particular relevance to the

topic. We do this not only to make more room for a discussion of the three selected Scandinavian countries but also in view of the declining significance of
the regional, "Nordic" approach – both in politics and research – following
the end of the Cold War and the rising influence of the European Union.

The emphasis is on comparative perspectives. This means that we are not
interested *per se* in discussing recent political trends in the Nordic countries.
To take one example, the EU has had a major impact on political processes
throughout Scandinavia, and not only on member states. The EU itself is an
important political issue in all countries and developments of and within the
EU have a bearing on all topics under discussion. Still, our angle is first to
make descriptive comparison of some selected topics, then to suggest likely
explanations.

Most chapters build on lectures in "Nordic politics" given at Oslo University's Department of Political Science in the spring of 2004, a course offered as a
basic English-language introduction to Nordic politics for foreign students.
Our aim was not to cover every topic but to present basic information about
the politics of the Nordic countries to non-Nordic students. We also wanted
to introduce the students to central interpretations and relevant analytical
perspectives. It is our hope that the book will encourage further reading and
studies.

Svein Skarheim of Universitetsforlaget has guided the book through every
stage in a most professional way, and also offered very useful comments on
several chapters. Thanks also to Silje Trollstøl who assisted in the handling of
the manuscripts.

Finally, this book would not have been written without the political efforts
of former and acting Minister of Education, Trond Giske and Kristin Clemet,
to reorganise and implement reforms in higher education.

*Knut Heidar*

June 2004

# Chapter 1: State and Nation-building in the Nordic Area

*Knut Heidar*

Is *Norden* a culturally homogeneous group of countries, accidentally separated by history? Is it basically a landscape, a geographical region, a group of neighbouring countries? Can we speak about *Norden* as something more than the "Benelux" of the north, but definitely less than Switzerland?[1] To ask if *Norden* exists is to ask whether it is reflected in the identity and the institutions of the people living in these countries. An affirmative answer would point to a conception of *Norden* as based on shared historical experiences. Historians would, however, immediately point out that the Nordic identity is fragmented by separate national identities (Sørensen and Stråth1997:19).

Elements of a "Nordic" identity surfaced in the nineteenth century, primarily among educated elites and triggered by the impulses from romanticism that also influenced the nationalist movements at the time. Five nation-states emerged in the Nordic region during the nineteenth and twentieth centuries. In the second part of the nineteenth century the German and Italian nation-states were created – "united" and "constructed" – from a number of autonomous principalities and regions. The Nordic region did not converge, however, it diversified. Why was there no Nordic or Scandinavian state?

Well, it was "blocked" from above as well as from below (Østerud 1998:130). It was blocked from above since none of the established states were strong enough to orchestrate unification (like Prussia in Germany or Piemonte in Italy). Nor could a Nordic state emerge from below since national mobilization in Norway, Finland and Iceland was fuelled by the politics of independence. The independence movements wanted separation from the two old, imperial powers of Nordic politics, Sweden and Denmark. There was also a communication problem in that most Finns and Icelanders spoke languages that were very different from those spoken by their Scandinavian kin.

The Nordic identity – as far as it existed – remained a by-product of the nationalist movements of the nineteenth century. The belief in the greatness of the Viking era was a shared cultural trait. Dynastic rivalries in the Viking age, however, had led to battles for control, to different routes for trading and pillage, to separate kingdoms. The nineteenth-century nationalist movements were in part nurtured by these differences. It was an age of "nation–building",[2] a cultural and organizational process that created new identities and reinforced existing ones[3] – only one element of which were their grand, but separate pasts. Out of two medieval imperial states (Denmark and Sweden), five nation-states emerged (Denmark, Sweden, Norway, Finland and Iceland) and three home rule territories (Åland under Finland and Greenland and the Faeroes under Denmark).

The Nordic countries are sometimes presented as a particular political type – like "the consensual democracies" or "working multi-party systems" – with a fairly uniform set of political institutions, practices and policies. In the interwar years Sweden modelled the "middle way" between liberal democracy and the totalitarian fascism and communism. It was based on the "historical compromise" between capital and labour in the 1930s that brought social democratic governments to power in the Scandinavian countries. One of the purposes of this book is to explore and question the "Nordic model".

"Scandinavia" and "Nordic" are used interchangeably in the literature. In strict geographical terms, "Scandinavia" is limited to the three middle countries, namely Sweden, Norway and Denmark. The thrust of our discussion concerns the three Scandinavian countries; Finland and Iceland are discussed whenever relevant.[4] We look at state structures, parliaments, party systems, voters, regional and local politics, gender politics and welfare state regimes. We also look at their security policies and the Nordic–EU relations. Our aim is to set out the facts and discuss alternative interpretations, not to argue a particular thesis on Nordic or Scandinavian politics as a whole.

## The Northern Countries

In geographical terms, two countries, Sweden and Norway, are situated on the Scandinavian Peninsula. Denmark, by tradition, also belongs to the "Scandinavian" group. Norway was a Danish province before 1814, and the southern part of Sweden was part of Denmark until the seventeenth century. The languages of the three countries are similar in the sense that they are fairly mutually intelligible (Table 1.1). Their roots lie in the Old Norse of the Vikings. While this is still the language of Iceland, German had a strong impact on the

Scandinavian languages in medieval times and changed them substantially in the process. Finland is bilingual with Swedish as the minority language (about 5 per cent). Swedish is spoken on the west coast and on the islands while the majority language, a completely different tongue belonging to the Finnish-Ugric language group, dominates everywhere else.

Table 1.1 *The population, language and religion of Nordic countries*

| | Population in millions | | | Non-nationals 2003[1] % | Language | Converted to Christianity | Lutheran Reformation |
|---|---|---|---|---|---|---|---|
| | 1900 | 1950 | 2000 | | | | |
| Denmark[2] | 2.4 | 4.3 | 5.3 | 4.9 | Danish[4] | 10th–11th century | 1536 |
| Finland[3] | 2.7 | 4.0 | 5.2 | 2.0 | Finnish-Ugric (95%), Swedish (5%) | 12th century | 1527–1600 |
| Iceland | 0.1 | 0.1 | 0.3 | 3.5 | Icelandic (Old Norse) | 11th century | 1538 |
| Norway | 2.2 | 3.3 | 4.5 | 4.3 | Norwegian[4] | 11th century | 1537 |
| Sweden | 5.1 | 7.0 | 8.9 | 5.3 | Swedish[4] | 11th century | 1527–1600 |

Source: *Statistical Yearbook 2003*, vol. 41 (Nord 2003:1), Copenhagen: Nordic Council of Ministers.

[1]  Percent with foreign citizenship 1/1-2003

[2]  Exclusive of the Faeroes and Greenland. Greenland is a Home Rule territory and unlike the "home country" Denmark not a member of the EU. It has a population of about 56 000 – 90 per cent of which are Inuit-speaking Eskimos. The Faeroes have a population of about 46 000 and also enjoys home rule. The language is Faeroese.

[3]  Inclusive of Swedish-speaking Åland. The Åland islands are a demilitarised zone with home rule since a 1921 League of Nations ruling following Swedish–Finnish disagreements over their status. They have about 26 000 inhabitants.

[4]  The Danish, Norwegian and Swedish languages are similar in the sense that one can understand and read each other's languages without much difficulty, although some of the minority dialects are hard to follow.

About 24 million people live today in the five Nordic countries, less than the combined populations of the Netherlands and Belgium, more than a half of Poland's but less than one third of Germany's population. Sweden is close to twice as large as each of the three countries Denmark, Finland and Norway while Iceland has a very small population – less than that of Luxemburg. All the Nordics are affluent countries – also when compared to the rest of Western Europe and with North America/Japan – with a GNP per capita of around 25 000 US dollars (2001).

If we look at the Nordic region as consisting of a Scandinavian core with Finland and Iceland as outliers we are easily mislead. One could alternatively speak of the East and West Nordic regions, splitting the Scandinavian countries. Finland was part of Sweden for centuries – from when Swedish kings established control and Swedes settled parts of the territory in the twelfth and thirteenth centuries till the Russians took over in 1809 when the Swedes were punished for refusing to support the continental blockade during the Napoleonic wars. Finland won its independence in 1917 in the wake of the Russian Revolution. The Swedish-speaking Åland is an archipelago in the Baltic Sea between Sweden and Finland. It is part of Finland, but with home rule and demilitarised under an international treaty. Increasingly the Baltic countries have been included in the East Nordic circumference after they broke free from the Soviet Union, although they have not been invited to join the Nordic Council, an organization set up during the 1950s to encourage inter-Nordic cooperation (more of this later).[5] The East Nordic area – the Baltic countries included – is roughly contiguous with seventeenth-century Imperial Sweden around the Baltic Sea (See Kirby 1990 and 1995). The West Nordic countries face the Atlantic and include Iceland with Norway and Denmark. Iceland was settled from Norway in the ninth and tenth centuries and governed from Denmark since medieval times (independent since 1944). The Danish home rule territories of the Faeroes and Greenland also belong to the West Nordic group. Greenland, with its predominantly Eskimo population joined – as part of Denmark – the EU in 1973, only to leave it again in 1986 after a referendum (see chapter 14 for Nordic EU policies).

The Nordics are generally peripheral in European affairs. That does not mean they cannot periodically play an important part or that they are not affected by developments in European politics. Within the European political and cultural mosaic the Nordic region stands out with particular colour and shape, what the Romans referred to as the North European territories or Northern countries that bordered their empire (Østergård 1997:31, Lindal 1981). In the ninth and tenth centuries the Vikings raided, conquered and settled in territories, some of which would later become parts of the UK, France and Russia. During the Thirty Years War (1618–48), the "Nordic lion", Gustav

Adolf II, turned Sweden into a military power and the country was a major party to the Treaty of Westphalia in 1648. The Napoleonic wars (1796–1815) forced Sweden to surrender Finland, brought a French general to the Swedish throne, transferred Norway from Denmark to the king of Sweden. Denmark lost part of its southern territory (Schleswig Holstein) after a war with Prussia and Austria in 1864. In spite of agitation within the Nordic "movement", none of the other Nordics were prepared to stand up for Denmark. In WWII Denmark and Norway were occupied by German troops (1940–45), and during the Cold War (1949–89) all the Nordic states were deeply affected by the European – and global – standoff between Western and Communist atomic powers.

## Origins of the Nordic States

The origins of the Nordic states[6] lie way back in history. During the age of the Vikings three kingdoms emerged, roughly continguous with the territories Denmark, Norway and Sweden occupy today. In contrast to the current situation, the Danish king in periods held power in southern Sweden and Norway, while the Norwegian kings – particularly in the twelfth and thirteenth centuries – controlled the western islands from their capital on the west coast, Bergen. During the twelfth century Norwegian power declined and dynastic changes brought Norway into a union with Denmark. In 1397 a Nordic Union was formed. The Swedes, however, resisted Danish supremacy in the union, and in the sixteenth century the *Vasa* dynasty came to power after a war with the Danes. For the next three centuries Denmark and Sweden were the only independent powers in the Nordic area.

Why today's five Nordic states, five nation-states in peaceful cooperation? History tells us that relations used to be different. There were never that many Nordic states before, nor much peaceful coexistence (see table 1.2). The last war between two Nordic countries saw Sweden take arms against rebellious Norway in 1814. But for more serious fighting we have to go back to "the Great Nordic War" which lasted from 1709 to 1720 and ended a series of wars between the two imperial countries for dominance in the Nordic area. In the late 1650s the Swedish nearly occupied the whole of Denmark but failed in an assault on Copenhagen. The sabre-rattling between Sweden and Norway following the 1905 Norwegian declaration of independence apart, relations between the Nordic countries have been exceptionally peaceful for the last two centuries. Wars there have been, but with other European powers: Denmark with Austria-Prussia in 1864 and with Germany in 1940; Finland with the

Soviet Union 1939–40 and 1941–44 and Norway with Germany 1940–45. And there was the internal war between reds and whites in Finland in 1918.

Table 1.2 State building, wars and state economic impact

| | Home Rule | Independence | Wars | Taxes as % of BNP[3] | | |
|---|---|---|---|---|---|---|
| | | | | 1900 | 1950 | 2000 |
| Denmark | 9th & 10th century state formation | – | Napoleonic 1803–15, Austro-Prussian 1864, Germany 1940–45 | 11 | 19 | 49 |
| Finland | 1809/1905 | 1917 | Civil war 1918, Soviet Union 1939–40/1941–44 | – | 29 | 47 |
| Iceland[1] | 1904/1918 | 1944 | Allied occupation 1940-45 | – | 1960: 28 | 37 |
| Norway[2] | 1814 | 1905 | Sweden 1814, Germany 1940-45 | 10 | 28 | 40 |
| Sweden | 11th & 12th century state formation | – | Napoleonic 1803–15, Norway 1814 | 1920: 11 | 23 | 54 |

[1]  Self-governed from the tenth to the thirteenth century.
[2]  Ninth-century state formation. Fourteenth–sixteenth centuries under ever-widening Danish dominion. From 1536 basically a dominion under the Danish crown.
[3]  The figures are from different sources and not fully comparable. See Heidar, Knut and Einar Berntzen, Vesteuropeisk politikk, 3rd ed., Oslo: Universitetsforlaget, 1998 and Statistisk årbok 2003, vol. 122, Oslo: Statistics Norway.

Denmark was the dominant Nordic power in medieval times, with Sweden emerging as an imperial rival during the sixteenth and seventeenth centuries. Among the new Nordic states Norway was first to gain independence in 1905. The country had been ruled from Copenhagen from 1536 to 1814. The Danish King appointed officials and made laws. Before Norway got its first university in 1811, Norwegians had to go to Copenhagen to get a university education. Much of the elite were Danes or immigrants from abroad, although they and their families gradually integrated with Norwegian stock. In 1814 this national elite – inspired by the Enlightenment ideas, the American Constitution of 1787 and the French Revolution – seized a window of opportunity in the post-Napoleonic turmoil to write a Norwegian constitution and declare independence. The victorious European powers, however, forced Norway into a union with Sweden, where the Norwegians had to accept a king with strong personal power, but were allowed to retain most of the new constitution, which – along with numerous changes – is still valid today. During the nineteenth century the king lost much of his powers. His prerogative to veto constitutional changes was challenged by the Norwegian parliament, the *Storting*. In 1884, the newly created liberal party, which enjoyed a majority in the Storting, forced the King to appoint a government to the parliament's liking. Home rule with a strong Storting to make laws, budgets and control the government were effective in most areas apart from one: joint foreign policy was directed from Stockholm. Nourished by increased nationalist sentiments this last reminder of Swedish supremacy was unilaterally removed in 1905 when parliament declared Norwegian independence.

Finland became a grand duchy under the Russian tsar in 1809, with some measure of home rule, at least it was separate from the Russian state. The tsar appointed governors to manage Finnish affairs, and some of them governed rather despotically. Periodically during the nineteenth century Russian rule was liberalized. The Estates Assembly was reconvened in 1863 for the first time since 1809, and a Finnish currency established in 1865. Also a small Finnish army appeared during the 1870s. Finland got its own constitution in 1905 following Russia's defeat at the hands of the Japanese in the Russo-Japanese war. The period of Russian rule was not over, however, before the tsarist breakdown during WWI and the subsequent revolution of 1917. Finnish independence in 1917 triggered a civil war between the Red Guards, following the example of the Russian Bolsheviks, and the Whites, holding the majority in parliament. The civil war itself and its aftermath were bloody and split Finnish society well into the post WWII years. In 1919 the parliament adopted a new constitution making Finland a republic.

Iceland was part of Norway from the thirteenth century and was ruled from Denmark from the fourteenth. In 1843 a national assembly (Althingi) was created to council the Danish king on Icelandic rule and, after a prolonged struggle, Iceland got its own constitution in 1874. According to the constitution, the parliament was to make laws and budgets. In 1903/04 Iceland got its own government which sits in Reykjavik. During WWI, a new constitution was adopted that made Iceland an independent state in a monarchical union with Denmark. This was confirmed by both parliaments in 1918. Germany's occupation of Denmark in WWII led first to British and later American military bases in Iceland. In 1944 the Icelandic Althingi declared full independence and the establishment of the republic.

## Nation-building, Citizenship Rights and the Rise of the "Social Democratic State"

The Nordic countries have all (till now) been fairly homogeneous – ethnically, linguistically and religiously. The growth of a national culture and an identity that supported the state in the sense that the inhabitants felt part of the national collective meant that the Nordic nations rested more on embedded cultural elements, less so on state institutions – much like the US "flag nationalism" or Swiss "citizenship identity".

There are of course fissures in this age-old homogeneity. Finland has a mixed population, with a 5 per cent Swedish-speaking minority commingling with the Finnish majority. What variation there is in ethnic terms is largely represented by the Sámi people – who reside predominantly in Northern Norway (estimated to around 20 000[7] in Norway altogether) – and the Eskimos of Danish Greenland. Table 1.1 shows that non-national citizens today make up between 2 and 5 per cent of the Nordic population. In terms of "multi-culturalism" these figures are of course misleading. Many nationals may not feel part of the dominant national culture, just as non-nationals may be fully integrated. Statistics show that 6.9 per cent of the Norwegian population were born of foreign-born parents (3.1 per cent had parents from Asia or Africa) (Statistical Yearbook 2003). In Sweden, 13 per cent (2001) had themselves been born outside the country (Statistical Yearbook for Sweden 2003). So although immigration and multi-cultural issues have figured high up on the political agenda since the 1970s, ethnic diversity is still relatively limited.

Lutheran Protestantism is the dominant confession; since the Reformation in the sixteenth century, it has also been the state religion of the Nordic countries (Table 1.1). Non-Protestant confessions have always been small and politically insignificant, but religious tension has been significant between clerical hierarchy and the lay religious movement, particularly in Norway. Increasing secularisation has stirred renewed debates about the future of the established Church; Sweden officially severed the ties between state and Church in 2000. On top of secularisation, immigration has also been a pluralizing force, not only in religious terms but ethnically and linguistically as well.

A broadly homogeneous culture underlay the nation-building of the nineteenth century. The most explicit and conscious efforts to (re-)create a national identity were naturally most vigorous in the dependent countries of Norway, Finland and Iceland. Married to the political struggle was a cultural campaign to integrate the people into the state institutions and create a national identity. The age of absolutist rule ended in Sweden/Finland in 1809, Norway in 1814 and Denmark/Iceland in 1849. When Finland became a Grand Duchy under the Russian tsar the Estate Assembly had to accept the rule of Tsar Alexander, while the Tsar acknowledged Finland's constitution, its religion and the privileges of the estates and the burghers. After the overthrow of absolutism the Nordic estate assemblies, the nascent parliaments, came to play an increasingly important part, and in the nineteenth century national movements made themselves increasingly felt on the political arena. In the arts and sciences the old, the original, the national were rescued and recreated, debated and cultivated. The Norwegian nineteenth century composer Edvard Grieg based his music on the folk music of west coast rural Norwegians. The Finnish national epos, Kalevala, published in 1835, was based on the old stories and myths that lived on among the Finns. In Iceland, when literature was reborn after 1830, it pursued a program to purify the language and promote national sentiments. Political parties emerged in all three countries during the latter half of the nineteenth century. They campaigned against foreign powers and the state-sanctioned, "foreign" culture of the dominant elites. These national movements not only envisaged a unified, national identity, they advocated a political program where nationhood converged with national independence and a role for the citizen in a new polity. Nation-building and citizenship rights came together in the nationalist agenda.

Building national identities was one part of the nation building process, building citizenship was another. The political sociologist Stein Rokkan enumerates four thresholds for mass incorporation in democratic politics (Rokkan 1970). His argument is that nation-building is only completed when the whole adult population becomes part of the polity and a democratic system is established. Normally this process of integration takes the form of political opposition to an established elite, an opposition that needs to surmount several thresholds on its way to inclusion and – finally – to power. To pass the first threshold the opposition requires legitimacy, in other words, there must be freedom of expression. Second, the population must win the right to political expression in free elections, meaning universal suffrage. Third, the voters must be fairly represented in the political institutions. The institutional mechanism to secure fair representation, including a political say for minorities, was the proportional representative electoral system. Finally, the chain of citizen influence must extend to the executive. Incorporating the citizens ought to have executive consequence, so elected parliaments should decide the fate of governments.

*Table 1.3 Rokkan's thresholds for popular political participation*

|  | Legitimacy: Freedom of the  press | Incorporation: Universal voting rights | Representation: PR electoral system | Executive: Parliamentarism |
|---|---|---|---|---|
| Denmark | 1849 | 1915 | 1915 | 1901 |
| Finland | 1917 | 1906 | 1906 | 1917 |
| Iceland | 1849 | 1915 | 1959 (1942)[1] | 1904 |
| Norway | 1814 | 1913 | 1919 | 1884 |
| Sweden | 1809 (1766) | 1921 | 1909 | 1917 |

[1]   Starting in 1942, some of the places in the Althingi were elected by proportional representation. In 1959 proportional representation was expanded to every seat in the parliament.

In Table 1.3 we set out when each of the Nordic states passed the four thresholds. Many of the dates could obviously be questioned on grounds of historical veracity. Is it "correct" to say that 1884 was when parliamentarism came into effect in Norway? This was the year a belligerent parliamentary majority for the first time forced the king to appoint a new government acceptable to them. Did this mean the enactment of a new constitutional principle in Norwegian history? As an uncontested constitutional procedure, parliamentarism was not in place until well into the twentieth century. Likewise, although freedom of the press was established in Sweden in 1766, later setbacks make 1809 a more robust date. What the table does show, though, is how the Nordic polities advanced at more or less the same general pace, at least when it came to the passing of the final three thresholds to democracy; they were more or less all taken care of in a 20 year span from 1900 to 1920.

Turning now to more established, more confident nation-states, what defined politics in Sweden towards the end of the nineteenth century was the conflict between conservatives and liberals.[8] The conservative elite of aristocrats, landed gentry, and top civil servants fought against free trade, universal suffrage, and democratisation, policies favoured by the urban bourgeoisie, the peasants and various temperance and nonconformist religious movements. Industrialization came relatively late to Sweden, but within the first three decades of the twentieth century, working class politics made conspicuous headway. Universal suffrage came in 1921 after general male suffrage in 1909. Conservative and liberal groups founded parties just after the turn of the century, with the party system in the crucible between 1890 and 1920 (see chapter 3).

Denmark was closer than Sweden to the old European trade routes – the city-based trading followed the Rhine across Europe and the Danube to northern Italy, where commerce, trade and politics had shaped history since medieval times. Commerce gave rise in Denmark to powerful urban centres. Absolutist rule had been based on an alliance between monarch and urban bourgeoisie, with the landed gentry dominating agriculture and controlling the peasantry. The bourgeoisie, the farmers and the workers all created political parties of their own in the latter part of the nineteenth century. In the 1870s the liberals started to campaign for parliamentarism, though the conservatives held back, in defence of traditional elites. The social democrats won an electoral breakthrough just after 1900, but would never equal the success of their sister parties in Sweden and Norway.

Although Norway's union with Sweden was basically monarchical, foreign policy remained in the hands of the Swedes; towards the end of the nineteenth century it became a source of constant irritation in Norway. Norway's nation-building process had started as a reaction against Danish domination in language and culture; it expanded in protest against the influence of urban elites and ended up focusing on Swedish supremacy in the union. Like Sweden, Norway had a large free peasantry and was dominated economically by its seaboard centres of trade and commerce. It was also the first Nordic country to have a broad-based electoral system: by 1814 about 45 per cent of all male citizens over 25 had the vote. Universal suffrage came in 1913.

Finnish history is marked by her close relationship with Sweden and Russia. In cultural terms, Finland was the "outpost" of the Protestant West against the Orthodox East (Lindstrøm and Karvonen 1987). Throughout the nineteenth century the dominant cultural and urban elites were mostly Swedish-speaking. Following the Russian Revolution of 1905, the Finns (as noted earlier) wrote a new constitution and became the first European country to establish universal suffrage in 1906. They also changed their old, Swedish-style four-estate assembly into a single-chamber parliament. Language caused political dissension early on, with Swedish-speakers pitted against Finnish-speakers. More discord arose over how far to press national demands with the Russian authorities. The conservatives (the "Old Finns") tended to tread the more cautious path.

For centuries, the people of Iceland retained a strong sense of national identity, notwithstanding political subordination to Denmark. The Danish written language made no inroads, nor was political mobilization nurtured by internal cultural cleavages as in Norway. Religious differences were neither significant nor politicised. Universal suffrage came in 1915 and the first political parties had been organized around 1900 on the basis of demands for independence. Between 1916 and 1930 new parties started emerging out of the developing class tensions.

By about 1920 nation-building and democratization had come more or less to an end in the Nordic area, with the partial exception of Iceland, which lacked formal independence. State and nation had come together in four internationally recognized polities. All five countries had freedom of expression, free and secret elections, proportional representation and parliamentary-based executive government. National unity obviously did not preclude political divisions. Industrialization had spawned an uprooted, mostly urban industrial workforce opposed to the middle classes or bourgeoisie and split society down the middle. The Nordic countries were not only faced with class conflicts. Older divisions, like the urban–rural cleavage, continued to leave their mark, too. The Finnish civil war (1918) was the extreme manifestation of this type of class conflict, stoked in large part by the Russian Revolution. Norway's labour movement also went through a radical period, with the Norwegian Labour Party a signed-up member, for a brief period, of the Communist International (1919–23).

Class tensions fell in the interwar years, bringing social democratic governments to each of the Nordics: Denmark in 1924, Finland in 1926, Sweden in 1932 and Norway in 1935. In Iceland the Social Democratic Party formed a coalition government in 1934. During the 1930s all these mainly working-class parties took on new leases of life as reformist social democrats – the Danes and the Swedes had always been moderate – fully integrated in the political system. And they gained power. In Sweden and Norway, the social democratic parties remained in government long into the post-WWII period.

The interwar Fascist parties of the radical right were very weak in the Nordic countries. Finland's so-called Lapua movement, however, did win a wide following in the years around 1930. It managed to find support among a suffering peasant class and unemployed workers on an extremely right-wing, nationalist–peasant ticket, but it was short-lived and never exerted much influence in Finnish politics. In the other Nordic countries, the social democratic labour movement found an accommodation with the agrarian parties –

through what were popularly known as the "Cow Deals" or "Crisis Settlements" – which helped lower the political temperature and defuse the political threats the radical right were issuing during the turbulent 1930s. All this meant that the Nordic Fascist movements remained a minute and marginal phenomenon. That said, however, when Germany occupied Norway in 1940, the rump of the Norwegian Nazi Party managed to form – under the leadership of Quisling – a collaborationist government.

Scandinavian post-war politics saw a series of social democratic governments. Sweden had social-democratic prime ministers till 1976, Norway till 1965, and social democrat governments (alone and in coalition with others) held power in Denmark for most of the time until 1982. The Swedish party was the strongest in Norden, holding onto the reins of power continually from 1932 till 1976 – an unbroken record of 44 years. Between 1932 and 1991 the Swedish party never polled less than 40 per cent of the vote at parliamentary elections. During the years of the "social democratic state" – an expression coined when the ideological and political tide changed during the 1970s [9] – collective, state provisions expanded and public spendings rose steeply. In Table 1.2 we saw that taxes more than doubled from 1950 to 2000 in Sweden and Denmark (see also Chapter 12), though they actually declined in the 90s. We should also note that taxation statistics reveal the redistribution of wealth by the state budgets. These are not necessarily money used to hire new state employees as figures on direct state expenditures amount to far less (around 20 per cent). The major re-distributive items on the budget concern business subsidies (for example to the agrarian sector), social security and pensions. The Nordic welfare states are the main legacies of the social democratic governments of this period, although opposition to welfare policies among the other parties can easily be exaggerated. Actually, there was a fairly broad consensus behind most welfare provisions.

## Norden Today

Nordic cooperation is surviving, just, in the old institutional structures but outside the dynamic political environment of the European Union. The formal institutional framework is intact, but the disappearance of the Soviet threat and the advent of the EU have made the work of the Nordic Council (among others) less politically significant (Olsen and Sverdrup 1998). The Nordic Council was established in the early 1950s to bring together parliamentarians and facilitate wider Nordic cooperation. In 1971, similar cooperative institutions were created for government ministers. There are Nordic meetings at all political levels, and informal meetings between, for example, the political parties, remain important. However, although the Swedes, Danes and even Finns remain tactfully reticent about it, their main cooperative arena is within the EU. Norway and Iceland have no place at the table when policies affecting Nordic cooperation are decided. Sometimes – as in some trade negotiations – they are actually on the opposite side of the table, splitting the Nordic family. The old dream of an integrated, collaborating *Norden* today mostly survives as a regional aspiration to make an impact within the EU, the "Nordic dimension" as the Swedish (EU) chairmanship labelled it.

Even if the Nordic dream is dimmed, the Nordic countries still have much in common. Culture, economy, sociological and political characteristics share in a common sense of "Nordicness". The Nordics are described as having a "passion for equality" (Graubard 1986), they are affluent, their citizens are long-lived and their democracies are stable. How far should we take this commonality? Does it extend to the political institutions to make a unique "Nordic model"?

The Nordic region – regardless of whether it harbours a distinct political model or not – is anyway interesting as a comparativist's laboratory. What are the main similarities and differences? Our review of Nordic state and nation-building provides some indications. Starting with the differences Stein Rokkan placed the five countries in separate categories in his "conceptual map" of state-building in Western Europe (Rokkan 1975; Rokkan 1981). Although Denmark and Sweden were similar in that they were strong empire states they differed, however, in their distance to the city network and in their seawards versus landward capacities. As for the new states, Norway and Iceland were seaward peripheries, while Finland was a landward buffer (against Orthodox, autocratic Russia). Economically the countries also differed. Denmark emerged with strong trade capitalism and a competitive agricultural sector. Sweden developed a strong and competitive manufacturing industry. Finland traditionally had an industry tied to primary resources like wood, but have more recently become very competitive in electronic consumer goods. Norway had shipping and used its abundant hydro-electric power to process raw materials. Norway has lately also enjoyed the lucrative benefits of an offshore oil industry. Iceland has always depended on its fisheries. Nordic differences are also apparent in international cooperation. First, EU relations differ, with three members and two "European Economic Space" (EES) attachments (see Chapter 10). Second, in terms of security relations Denmark, Norway and

Iceland are members of NATO – while Sweden and Finland are not – although it is safe to say that it matters less and less with the end of the Cold War and the emergence of EU-wide security arrangements.

The similarities are nevertheless large in number and importance for political comparisons. Language is more uniting than divisive, in spite of the Finnish and Icelandic outliers. The state-espoused Lutheran religion has shaped cultural traits in all countries – despite present levels of secularisation and an established church in the balance. As noted, there are differences in economic structure, but the populations are all affluent. In terms of state intervention, the Nordic countries have tended to espouse a "mixed economy" and all have far-reaching state welfare arrangements.

# Chapter 2: Modern State Reforms

*Tom Christensen*

*New Public Management* (NPM) is a reform wave that has been important in most Western countries during the last two decades, but has also spread to developing and transitional countries (Pollitt and Bouckaert 2004). We can view NPM partly in terms of ideology, ideas, myths and symbols, connected to how political-administrative systems ought to be organized, and partly as more specific reform measures (Christensen and Lægreid 2001a, Self 2000). NPM was disseminated by a group of Anglo-American countries, the front-runners of the reform (Hood 1996), and by international organizations like OECD, EU, the International Monetary Fund and the World Bank as reform entrepreneurs (Sahlin-Andersson 2001). Nationally, there have also been actors in the central civil service or private actors like consulting firms that systematically have tried to further NPM. NPM was taken on board for mixed reasons. One was because political and administrative leaders thought that NPM could solve problems in a practical way, another because they wanted to be seen as modern and rational. It was therefore tempting to import reforms whose benefits were taken for granted by many.

The three Scandinavian countries tend to be ranged with the group of *reluctant reformers* or *laggards*, having adopted NPM-related reforms only slowly (Olsen and Peters 1996). This picture is mostly right for the last two decades, but there are variations. For instance, although the Scandinavian countries belong to a specific family of political-administrative systems, their NPM implementation trajectories were by no means identical. We would like to focus on both the similarities and differences in Scandinavia concerning state traditions and reforms. The five main questions discussed are: 1) What are the traditional features of the central political-administrative systems in Scandinavia? 2) What are the main features of the NPM-inspired reforms in the public sector? 3) What are the important reform similarities and differences among the Scandinavian countries, when they import, handle and eventually implement NPM? 4) What perspectives can be used to explain this similarity and variety? 5) Is it a distinct Scandinavian reform model? We shall attempt to answer these questions on the basis of comparative Scandinavian country studies and NPM studies in general.

## Historical Background

It might help us understand approaches to reform if we outline the development of the political-administrative systems in Scandinavia prior to the early 1980s when the reforms started. The *centralized* and *hierarchical state* in Norway was established in 1814, when Norway formed a union with Sweden (which lasted until 1905). Over the next 190 years this state model was refined on numerous occasions (Christensen 2003). The period 1814–84 is commonly referred to as the *Civil Servants' State* because the central administrative apparatus was dominated by a powerful group of legally trained top administrative leaders. The first challenge to their power came in the 1840s and 1850s from professional groups who wanted more professional autonomous administrative bodies. The campaign persuaded the government to set up several independent agencies. The second challenge came in 1884 with the introduction of *parliamentarism*. While the balance of power shifted from the civil servants, the agencies came under stricter control, and there was less willingness to establish new ones. The politicians did not want to see their authority or democratic control undermined.

The centralized state expanded further after World War II when several national interest groups acquired integrated organizational participation or formal participation rights in public decision-making processes (Olsen 1983). This could indicate the growing influence of interest groups, or a democratic addition in that interest groups furthered their own interests while participating in a collective, public effort to develop the welfare state. This period was also characterized by fresh moves to hive off the agencies from the ministries, fronted on this occasion by the political leadership rather the professional groups in a bid to solve capacity bottlenecks (Christensen 2003). These 1955 arguments are not unlike the reasons promulgated in favour of NPM a couple of decades down the line. The new administrative doctrine led to several new independent agencies, but lasted only until the early 1970s, when constraints were put on establishing new agencies again.

The development of the administrative apparatus in Norway after World

War II is characterized internally by strong and increasing vertical and horizontal differentiation; new hierarchical tiers and positions were installed and the structure furnished with a profusion of horizontal divisions. Staff numbers grew more steeply in the agencies than the ministries. After the war, lawyers dominated in the civil service, though this is no longer the case. In the 1950s national economists were in demand; from the 1970s preferences turned towards social scientists who now represent the largest group of civil servants. From the 1980s on, business economists were also recruited. So, overall, civil servants' training has become much more varied over time.

Sweden had a professional civil service already in the *"the early modern era"* (around 1500–1800), as distinct from the state governed by the personal powers invested in the king, which tended to be the norm in Europe (Premfors 1999). It was particularly during the Age of Greatness (1611–1718), as it is known, that the state was run by a powerful civil service. The first independent civil service was a judicial body, but was soon followed by several independent central administrative or non-hierarchical collegial bodies, which, although weakened, are still in existence today. Apart from their collegial form, they possessed certain Weberian ideal-typical features, which was rather advanced then. For instance, they were controlled by formal rules, had elaborate differentiation of functions, job security was high, with civil servants only liable for dismissal after a court hearing. Finally, hiring and promotion depended on a standardized civil service education. This Age of Freedom (1718–72) was important as it saw the birth of a dualistic form of central government in Sweden, with a strong monarch surrounded by a court of advisers (later cabinet) and a strong and independent central administrative wing consisting of several bodies/agencies.

Sweden's era of the modern civil service started around 1800 with a highly tiered civil service, internal organizational differentiation in the ministries and several new independent agencies, mainly in the communication sectors, a development found in Norway in the same period. Around 1910 state enterprises came into being, and enjoyed slightly more freedom than the agencies. Collegial bodies were formed as boards or councils connected to the enterprises and agencies. This was the start of what is known as administrative corporatism. It gave interest groups and associations an opportunity to participate in public decision-making processes, and led, later on, as in Norway, to strongly corporatist features overall and the development of an elaborate "society of interest groups". From the 1930s, the Swedes started to develop their welfare state and expanded and differentiated the civil service accordingly, particularly after World War II, with the two decades from 1960 on as the most expansive period.

Autocracy was introduced in Denmark-Norway in 1660 (Norway was subordinate to Denmark for 400 years until 1814) when a new constitution was drafted naming the king absolute sovereign. At the same time, a new central administrative system was introduced, based on a principle of total responsibility of the top civil servants who headed the administrative bodies. The period marked the start both of *the doctrine of ministerial responsibility* and the centralized civil service, which remains important to this very today (Foss Hansen 1999). The first central administrative bodies, the colleges, were comparable to those in Sweden and members were required to have formal qualifications. Denmark got its first democratic constitution in 1848–49 (parliamentarism was introduced in practice in 1901) when the system of ministerial rule and hierarchical central administrative bodies was formally established. Denmark differed from Norway and Sweden here. The ministries often had two or three departments, each for a different policy area. They were in reality agencies integrated in the ministries, which offered the political leadership more control over them.

The period 1890–1914 was marked by expansion and differentiation in the central administrative apparatus, and several new ministries and agencies saw the light of day. While comparable to the expansion of the civil services of Norway and Sweden, Denmark was later off the mark. It was also a period when interest groups could call for and get whatever ministry they wanted, agriculture and trade and industry are two examples, and public colleges or councils were appointed, on which interest groups formally sat. These were the first corporate features. In 1920 the contours of the welfare state were evident with the establishment of the Ministry of Social Affairs, but the hard times of the 1920s and 30s prevented further expansion in Denmark as in Sweden and Norway. It was not until the end of World War II that new ministries and agencies were put in place. In the post-war period, particularly until the early 1970s, the central administrative apparatus grew substantially and became more *structurally differentiated*. Many collegial bodies, corporatist councils, boards and committees were also established. This was in fact a common trend in Norway and Sweden as well in the same period.

Table 1 sums up the historical differences among the Scandinavian countries concerning the structure of their central political-administrative apparatus.

Table 2.1 Historical differences in the central political-administrative structure in the Scandinavian countries

|  | Denmark | Norway | Sweden |
|---|---|---|---|
| Centralization | High | Moderate | Dual – strong cabinet and strong agencies |
| Responsibility base | Ministerial, individual | Ministerial, individual | Collective – cabinet-related |
| Agency structure | Integrated agencies in the ministries | Independent agencies mostly | Strong independent agencies |

## Main Features of New Public Management

To help understand the reception and implementation of NPM in Scandinavia, we need to know something about the 1970s and -80s wave of reform. But first, we need to understand what administrative policy means in theory and practice. There are different types of policies that are related to government activities and functions (Egeberg 2003). One type is the externally directed policy in different sectors, encompassing regulatory policies, general resource allocating decisions, decisions in single cases according to rules, etc. The other is the internally directed policy, often labeled *administrative policy*. This is a policy that consciously tries to change the governmental apparatus through systematic changes in the formal structure, personnel/demography, culture, etc, the logic being that administrative policy is supposed to influence indirectly the externally directed policy and therefore fulfill collective public goals. NPM belongs to this latter type of administrative policy.

Ideally, an active administrative policy requires several conditions to be met (Christensen, Lægreid and Wise 2002). Political and administrative leaders must be able to choose among different organizational forms when designing the civil service and supervising the implementation of the new structures. They must also have relatively unambiguous targets to which to tailor the means, reforms and structures. Different organizational structures must have different effects, and be assessed and evaluated in terms of given criteria and instruments, and facilitate a learning process related to the different organizational designs inhabiting the structure of government.

Central governments of many Western countries, particularly the Scandinavian ones, count as a vital part of the centralized state, combining a large public sector, structural centralization and homogeneity, strong state values and norms, emphasis on collectivity, equality and non-economic values (Christensen 2003). Added to this in the Scandinavian countries are elements of the corporatist state, which favour integrated participation of interest groups in government (Olsen 1983). NPM runs counter to many of these features; it represents a *supermarket state* or *fragmented state model* (Olsen 1988) and a *neo-liberal ideology*, often interspersed with anti-political or apolitical sentiments (Christensen and Lægreid 2001a). The basic ideology envisions a leaner state, as embodied in the catchphrase "roll back the state". NPM vaunts a dual theory, one part of which is a new institutional economic theory, favouring centralization and contracts; the other, a management theory that favours decentralization, delegation and the increasing autonomy of managers (Boston et al. 1996). The latter theoretical approach tends to dominate in most countries.

NPM has a core ideology and ideas, but has never been consistently applied: It offers instead a *"shopping basket"* of reform elements pointing in different directions (Hood 1991, Pollitt 1995). The inconsistencies are easily traced. In NPM, politicians are considered untrustworthy and inefficient, they promise and spend too much, partly because they are thinking about re-election. But politicians are also important when it comes to controlling subordinate administrative units and levels, and can as such be trusted. The administrative leaders are likewise often perceived as too expansive and inefficient in their desire for more resources and powers for their own administrative unit, a reflection of their self-interest, and as such need to be controlled. But they also should be delegated more accountability, influence and autonomy to increase their empowerment and efficiency in choosing among policy instruments to fulfill collective goals. And as such they can be trusted. These NPM inconsistencies is just one reason why NPM-related government reforms tend to be more, not less complex than promised, simply because contrary considerations need to be taken at the same time (Christensen and Lægreid 2002a).

NPM is relatively *one-dimensional* in its focus on *cost efficiency*, and most other essential elements of government such as political loyalty, professional competence, corporatist features, people's rights, etc. are subordinated to efficiency (Christensen and Lægreid 2001a). Emphasis on efficiency leads to a focus on *market principles, increased competition and competitive tendering* (where providers, whether public or private, compete), increased structural differentiation and fragmentation, focus on service provision to consumers and users, etc.

The most systematic structural part of NPM is the structural devolution of public organizations. Structural devolution consists of two dimensions, government's *vertical* and the *horizontal specialization* (Christensen and Lægreid 2001b). Vertical specialization is of two types. It can be *internal*, meaning that politicians grant more autonomy to (regulatory) agencies, while remaining ordinary public administrative bodies. Or it can be *external*, and concern the reorganization of former government enterprises or establishment of new enterprises in the form of independent state-owned companies. The main argument for the former would be the need for more professional autonomy in the agencies. The main reason for the second would be the need for more commercial freedom. In both types of vertical specialization the formal levers of control resting with the political executives are weakened, i.e. the distance between the politicians and the units is increased, providing a wider opportunity to subvert political control in practice. The difference between them is that the internally specialized agencies are relatively closer to the political executives than the state-owned companies and that the steering systems are different. The agencies are controlled through a formal letter of intent, specifying goals, resources and result expectations and a formal and informal steering dialogue, while the companies are supervised by a board and a director. Ministerial or political leadership can only decide on the most important principles and only then at the annual meetings of the companies, and their opportunity to exert control is constrained and related to economic issues. There has, however, been a tendency in many countries to put pressure on executive politicians to restrain from interfering with the state companies. Executive politicians can quite easily find themselves faced with a "double bind" under NPM. If they keep their fingers out of company business, they lay themselves bare to criticism from the opposition in the parliaments, the media and interest groups for being too passive. But if they try to intervene, they can be criticized for not acting in accordance with the formal structure and rules of the new autonomous companies.

Horizontal specialization in NPM is based on the principle of *"single purpose organizations"*, first exemplified in the reforms put in place by New Zealand (Boston et al. 1996). It was common to integrate different government functions and roles, but according to the new principle, that is wrong. It is much more useful to separate many of the different functions and roles, like ownership, administration, regulation, policy advice, service purchase and provision, etc. Not only should these functions not overlap, they should also be organizationally kept apart, for example having ownership functions in one ministry and regulations in another (Christensen and Lægreid 2003). It is argued that this new principle of horizontal differentiation will give less ambiguous control and activities and make it easier to reach goals, produce results and ensure accountability. One major argument against this is the danger of even higher levels of fragmentation in goverment, requiring more coordination, more resources at the top of the system, and more attention and capacity problems for executive politicians (Dunn 1997).

NPM also sees government mainly as a *service provider*. The argument is basically that it is a direct form of democracy, and that civil servants are thinking too little in service terms and need to change their culture, because their legitimacy should be more connected to how they serve the users or consumers (Pollitt and Bouckaert 2004). In defence, advocates regret the undermining of the citizenship role, and the more central status given to the role of a user or customer, because, they say, it is detrimental to democracy (Christensen and Lægreid 2002b). One thing is the principle of increased service orientation, another the practical aspects. Advocates of the service orientation in government say it would benefit efficiency and service standards, leaving more resources for unsolved societal problems and creating more satisfied customers. Opponents say that a lot of the new service-oriented programs are characterized by manipulation of symbols and that it is yet to be proven that this increases the efficiency and service quality.

Summing up, NPM is a one-dimensional reform mostly geared towards efficiency hiking. It spread more easily as ideology and ideas than as practice. There is a lot of variety and inconsistency in the practical implementation of NPM. Its main action appears to render an integrated state into a disintegrated state or government system.

## Similarities and Variety in Reform Profile in Scandinavia

The Scandinavian countries, like most other Western countries, have had their share of New Public Management over the last two decades. NPM soon ran up a public sector legitimacy deficit which many of the affected countries chose to address by institutionalising administrative policy. In the 1980s, then, the Scandinavian countries started to form government bodies with administrative policy as their particular remit, whether they were new ministries, agencies or other units (Lægreid 2001). The general advantage here was that questions of administrative reform and change could be dealt with more systematically and expertise on administrative policy would grow. It became easier to learn from one's own and others' experiences, and have the personnel in place to pursue reform agendas much more aggressively, both on the symbolic and practical fronts.

The second important institutionalization part was embodied in the Scandinavian-wide *reform programs* of the 1980s, which frequently resurfaced, often in conjunction with new governments. A common denominator of these programs as practised in most Western countries is the profusion of *reform symbols*, often pretty similar between programs. Studies of political leadership and reform programs indicate that such programs can serve different purposes (March and Olsen 1983). They can help get a political statement or political agenda/list of priorities across, and may lead to real changes. But they also serve symbolic functions. A political leadership will seldom miss the opportunity to boost its legitimacy by engineering symbols of rationality and modernity. The problem is how to balance symbols and real change. Political leaders have a tendency to lose interest in reform programs after a while, because they realize that they are unlikely to win the next election on administrative policy issues. Reform processes tend therefore to lose momentum. But there are many examples of reform programs that in the short run seem to be failures, but are long-term successes, because public opinion warms to the idea of practical reform, i.e. there is some kind of civic education at work (March and Olsen 1983).

When a country wants to put NPM into effect, they have a wide selection to choose from. What has been typical for the Scandinavian countries is that they have always chosen the less radical approaches (Lægreid 2001), or, in other words have gone mostly for the *Management by Objectives* (MBO) version and internal management reforms, much less for the more radical reforms involving downsizing and privatization, which have enjoyed more popularity among radical Anglo-Saxon reform countries. Scandinavian countries are therefore often characterized as *reluctant reformers*. Another Scandinavian idiosyncrasy concerns the close close collaboration with interest groups in programme execution, particularly the civil service trade unions. It goes without saying that negotiations with affected parties will tend to water down the most radical elements of the reforms and highlight their pragmatic capacity.

Even though the Scandinavian countries are broadly similar, there are some clear differences. Norway's reform profile throughout the last two decades is characterized by an *"incremental sector-based strategy"* (Lægreid 2001). It means that the driving forces pressing for pragmatic change in a rather reluctant climate have been the different sectors, ministries, agencies and companies, not a single, central political or administrative body. A fragmented government has therefore produced fragmented reforms. Ministries and agencies have been more concerned to push their own reform agendas than to join forces in a common reform strategy. This is basically because the lead ministry in charge of administrative policy and reforms – the Ministry of Labour and Government Administration – has always been one of the weaker sections of government. In a study of the top political and administrative leadership in Norway, around 70 per cent of the respondents said they were dissatisfied with the role of that ministry in reform processes (Christensen and Lægreid 2002a). It was seen as lacking a realistic or joined-up reform strategy, criticized for being too theoretical about the reforms and for lacking the requisite expertise. It was considered a roadblock, a reform obstructor rather than facilitator. The piecemeal nature of the reforms and weak reform entrepreneurship explain why Norway has the most symbolic reform profile of the Scandinavian countries.

During the last three years of the current center-right government, Norway has embarked on a more radical reform path, which may well challenge its image as a reluctant reformer (Christensen and Lægreid 2003). Although some reforms remain largely symbolic, perhaps even more than before, in reality we have seen more actual core NPM reforms than at any time over the last two decades. The emphasis in Norway is now on structural devolution of agencies and state-owned companies; indeed, some of the largest state companies have even been partly privatized. Regulatory agencies are to have more autonomy and 8–10 of them are being relocated out of Oslo, a widely controversial move in some quarters. Horizontal specialization in non-overlapping roles is also pursued more actively, related to agencies and regulatory agencies, but also connected to more competition and use of markets. Both individual and institutional contracts are used more extensively. Incentive systems are more actively used also, both at the leadership level and lower levels, like giving a higher salary to the best school teachers. The emphasis on service orientation and user choice is spreading to new arenas as well. While this does not put Norway in the forefront of reforming countries, it is now part of the reform mainstream.

Sweden has gone further than the rest of Scandinavia in embracing radical reform. It has been called a *"dual employers' strategy"* (Lægreid 2001), where duality refers to a system with a strong cabinet (Sweden practises collective government responsibility, not the individual ministerial responsibility of its neighbours), and strong, independent agencies with a long history. Two decades of Swedish reforms have been initated and supervised by the cabinet to a far greater extent than we have seen in Norway. It has also been more focused on rationality, efficiency and productivity than in either Denmark or Norway. But the Swedish reforms are also very much influenced and controlled by the independent agencies, and some of the regulatory agencies have achieved prominence thanks to structural devolution in the control of state-owned companies. Reforms have had a more local focus than in Norway. It is partly due to settlements with interest groups, making it seemingly easier to implement reforms in socialist-driven local authorities, and partly to the influence of and duplication by local private sector interests in solution development and service provision. Locally, market solutions and wider salary inequality have met with less resistance than in the other two Scandinavian countries.

Denmark's reform profile has been called a *"negotiated strategy"* (Lægreid 2001). It is primarily centered on the Ministry of Finance, which is the most important administrative policy body, a reflection of the generally more centralized structure of Danish government. The ministry has promoted reforms by insisting on efficiency measures while being willing to address the concerns of employees and their unions. In the early 1980s, reforms were rather ideological, at least as far as leading politicians were concerned, but became more technical for about a decade. They have returned to their ideological base camp in recent years. The negotiations with the unions were relatively idyllic for a long time, but dissention and controversy grew in the late 1990s. Interest groups remained uninvolved for many years, except for some negative reactions now and then, but have recently adopted a more activist approach in an effort to prevent more extreme devolution, downsizing and privatization.

The government's negotiation strategy has been to negotiate with different parts of its own civil service, and to encourage different ministries and agencies to become more committed to the reforms. So in this respect the reforms have become less centred on the Ministry of Finance. But the ministry has long insisted on an efficiency-focused reform strategy, and a precondition for such power sharing is that that the different ministries pursue the same reform implementation strategy. Overall, the reforms in Denmark have been more technical and less ideological than in Norway and Sweden, though this has changed over the last two years what with the recent center-conservative government's neo-liberalist ideological platform.

Table 2.2 sums up the differences between the Scandinavian countries concerning the reform processes.

Table 2.2  *Differences in the reform processes of the Scandinavian countries*

|  | Denmark | Norway | Sweden |
|---|---|---|---|
| Reform profile | Negotiated strategy | Incremental, sector-based | Dual employers' strategy |
| Leading actors | Ministry of Finance | Ministries, sectors | Cabinet and agencies |
| Long-term implementation of reforms | Rather reluctant | Reluctant, rather slow | In Scandinavian terms, the most radical sponsorship of efficiency and rationality-centred reform |
| Importance of reform symbols | Moderate – low | High | Moderate |
| Current reform situation | More radical reforms, ideology-driven | More radical reforms, ideology-driven, structural devolution | Consolidation, elaboration |

## Perspectives Explaining Similarities and Variety

The next question to be discussed concerns explaining what joins and what separates the reforming Scandinavian countries. We have combined three perspectives – the *environmental, the cultural and the structural* – to make a *transformative perspective* to help explain the different approaches etc. (Christensen and Lægreid 2001a). The environmental perspective sees national reforms as primarily driven by international and/or national environmental pressure. There are two different types of environment that can influence the reform processes in a country – the *technical* or the *institutional environment* (Meyer and Rowan 1977). The technical environment is that part of the environment that sees public organizations as instrumental systems that should provide specific services or products. Where problems arise in this respect, for example with the efficiency of service provision, strong pressure will be brought to bear on government to reform and restructure. It follows that there will be a clear relationship between technical elements in the environment and technical elements of public organizations.

The institutional environment is more connected to the development of myths. Because of complexity in the public sector and the need for simple guidelines, myths develop in the environment and spread fast from the private to the public sector, and between and inside countries (Sahlin-Andersson 2001). These myths consist of ideologies, ideas and symbols that take for granted that there are certain best ways to structure and organize government, that there are certain best procedures, rules, personnel, etc. Countries and national public organizations import these myths and produce look-alikes because they are good for legitimacy (Brunsson 1989). They give an organization a modern, rational appearance , without actually requiring much in the way of structural or behavioural change. Myths tend to be a surface phenomenon, and have little influence on actual behaviour. It is what Brunsson (1989) calls *hypocrisy* or *"double-talk"*.There is a discrepancy between politicians' symbol-speak, and their actions; and between the talk and the behaviour there is often only the most oblique of connections.

The difference between technical and institutional environment is not always clear and the two obviously converge on some points. For example, when a country is hit by an economic crisis, its severity is not always easy to measure objectively. Measurement therefore turns into a political process where it lends itself to different interpretations. In New Zealand in the early 1980s, several economically trained civil servants, university academics and business leaders were adamant that the economic crisis was extremely dangerous for the country and required substantial steps to reform the public and private sectors. Their arguments were often symbolic, typical of the institutional environment, the intention of which was to make it "self-evident" that something had to be done. When the Labour Party's Roger Douglas, the then minister of finance, started to reform the public sector after the 1984 election victory, the myth was already established to the effect that there was no alternative to the hard reform line, even though there obviously *was* from a technical point of view (Aberbach and Christensen 2001). The taken-for-grantedness shown here didn't last long after 1984, but was crucial for implementing the reforms.

Sweden was hit by an economic downturn around 1990, which seemed pretty severe from the technical point of view, though it is obviously difficult to compare it with New Zealand's. The political leadership, however, chose a different line of approach from politicians in New Zealand. While admitting its severity, the reform measures they put in place were much less dramatic. The situation was not milked for all its myth-making potential to create an image of a crisis-racked country, as was possibly the case in New Zealand.

The second perspective is the *cultural perspective* focusing on informal norms and values (Selznick 1957). The basic logic here is that political-administrative systems in different countries gradually develop over time through adaptation to internal and external pressures; in other words, they are institutionalized or they become institutionalized organizations. Along the way they develop informal norms and values, the building blocks of a distinctive culture or "soul", adding to their formal structure. Cultural traditions in public organizations change gradually through so-called *path-dependency*, meaning that the context or situation when they were established – *the roots* – later will have an impact on tradition development – *the routes* they are taking (Krasner 1988). So the conclusion, according to this perspective, is that different political-administrative systems in different countries develop different cultures.

The cultural perspective suggests that reforms like NPM have to face some kind of test of *compatibility* (Christensen and Lægreid 2001a). A crucial question is whether the norms and values of the reforms are compatible with the norms and values of the cultural traditions of a country's public sector. If they are incompatible, reforms could quite easily meet a wall of cultural resistance. If they are compatible, they should be easily implemented. And if they are only partly compatible, it stands to reason that only the compatible elements will be implemented.

The third perspective is the *structural perspective*, focusing on certain major polity features (Egeberg 2003, Weaver and Rockman 1993). What matters here is whether the country's constitutional constraints are solid enough to withstand reform efforts and whether the powers inherent in the political system are balanced, or whether some parts prevail over others. The form of government also plays a role, for instance whether it has a presidential system of some kind, a Westminster parliamentarian system or some other type of parliamentarian system, and finally whether the government is a majority or minority one. The last factor concerns whether the public sector is structurally homogeneous or heterogeneous, which refers to the level of fragmentation.

The relevance of these structural features should be obvious. Countries without constitutional constraints but with a dominant executive backed by a dominant party – often referred to as an *"elective dictatorship"* – and structural homogeneity, which is the case for several Anglo-Saxon countries, may find it relatively easy to introduce radical reforms. A fragmented presidential system or parliamentary system with a minority coalition government, as in Scandinavia, will clearly face an uphill struggle to effect the reforms.

The *transformative perspective* combines the three perspectives and emphasises that they represent different contexts – environmental pressure, cultural factors and structural constraints – that often is in a dynamic interaction concerning the leeway for political and administrative leaders to make reforms and implement them (Christensen and Lægreid 2001a). Dynamic processes often produce qualitatively fresh hybrid structures and cultures. They tend to occur more frequently than the outliers, which are generally countries under strong environmental pressures, with compatible, reform-facilitating cultures and instrumental structures, or, in contrast, countries in a low-pressure environment with incompatible, heterogeneous, non-reform-friendly structures.

## The Empirical Relevance of the Perspectives

We shall now test these perspectives on modern state reforms in Scandinavia. As mentioned above, none of the Scandinavian nations wanted to adopt NPM in its most radical incarnations. There was anyway little environmental pressure in any of the countries during the last two decades, whether of a technical or institutional nature, though the picture obviously is not without some gradation (Christensen, Lægreid and Wise 2002). There was also little compatibility between the cultural norms and values of the NPM reforms and those traditionally espoused by Scandinavian civil services. Scandinavia has long nurtured *a strong state tradition*, favoring centralized government and a large public sector. Equality is a leading value, along with high levels of trust between politicans and civil servants, as indeed between leaders and the general public. Governments have been willing to work with interest groups to implement the reforms, opting for peaceful coexistence and revolution in slow motion (Olsen, Roness and Sætren 1982, Premfors 991). And, the Scandinavian countries have all been structurally homogeneous, a reform-friendly factor, despite a profusion of political parties, frequent minority governments and extensive reform negotiations, none of which are particularly reform friendly.

While Norway and Denmark marched more or less to the same tune, Sweden followed its own. The explanation seems to be the economic downturn which hit Sweden around 1990, preparing the ground for a more radical reform approach than either Norway or Denmark were willing to contemplate. Sweden has also been more outward looking and aware of its international place than the other two, not least in its connection with some of the most important reform-disseminating international bodies such as the OECD and some of the Anglo-American countries (Sahlin-Andersson and Lerdell 1997). Sweden has also tended to be most efficiency and rationality centred, and set store by collecting and auditing public sector target achievement and performance levels with modern auditing techniques (Olson and Sahlin-Andersson 1998). What is more, Sweden has a dual structured executive political apparatus, a strong cabinet and strong agencies, all good for reform action. And lastly, corporatism in Sweden was showing signs of decay as far back as the 1980s, growing only more evident in the 1990s, which also may have removed reform obstacles (Micheletti 1991, Rothstein and Bergstrøm 1999).

The three Scandinavian countries have lately converged in their reform approaches; Norway and Denmark have both got rightist governments populated by entrepreneurs with a penchant for NPM-related reforms. The crucial question is, however, how much of this is symbolic and how much is real change. One should not dismiss too soon or underestimate the cultural and structural obstacles to reform still present in either country.

## A Distinct Scandinavian Reform Profile?

Looking at the Scandinavian reform effort with 20 years of hindsight, we see that the three Scandinavian countries belong to a family of reluctant reformers, so in this respect they conform to a distinctive Scandinavian or Nordic model (Dunleavy 1997, Pollitt 1997). The main reason seems to be cultural (Peters 1997). First, the Scandinavian countries were and remain relatively more preoccupied with *democratic values* than efficiency. Second, they are more preoccupied with *social responsibility and protecting the welfare state* from some of the adverse effects of NPM. Third, they tend to be more rule-centred and relatively less goal-centred. Fourth, they are relatively more caring of egalitarian and collective values and care less about competition, individualism and the market. Fifth, they nurture professional expertise in the public sector and discourage politicization of the civil service. Sixth, the Scandinavian countries are more likely to welcome interest groups in the reform processes, a reflection of their lengthy corporatist past, which gave non-public-sector parties an opportunity to work with government to promote collective values along with their special interests.

Recent pressure on some of these typically Scandinavian norms and values has caused a shift in balance. That said, the NPM reforms are still seen as an addition rather than a replacement. They are filtered, edited and redefined in a process of pragmatic adaptation.

# Chapter 3: Parties and Party Systems

*Knut Heidar*

Democracies are often grouped according to their party systems. The politics of two-party systems give different types of democratic linkage between elites and mass than the politics of multiparty systems. The two-party democracies present the voters with the option to kick the "rascals" out at the next election. The citizens know who to blame for the wrongdoings and they know the alternative available. That gives accountability to democracy. Multiparty democracies avoid the "adversarial politics" problem, the on-off, in-out logic of two-party systems that also denies broad sections of the population – the electoral minority – their legitimate influence. With more than two parties, the voters are presented with alternatives that presumably reflect their views more closely, and with government alternatives that are shaped by the search for broad-based and more durable compromises. That gives representative democracy. The two democracies purify different tendencies in the democratic tradition, often seen as a contrast between majoritarian and consensual democracies (Lijphart 1999).

Which is the best? Great Britain and the US are often showcases of "working two-party systems", while the Nordic countries exemplify the "working multiparty systems" (cf. Rustow 1956). The answer to this question does, however, in part depend on how democracy is conceived: Should representation or accountability be given priority? Both are clearly important, but it may be more profitable to discuss the right balance. It may also be that there is no theoretically "correct" answer to this question, as the democratic institutions must be tailored to fit the particular society. What works in one does not necessarily work in another. In the comparative politics literature there will be different interpretations of the extent to which the Nordic political systems "produce" democracy, stability, efficiency and the most desirable policies. Still, they will all – in comparative terms – be found high on the general ratings of system success (Lijphart 1999).

## Three Perspectives

In 2004 the parliaments in Denmark ("Folketinget"), Finland ("Eduskunta"), Norway ("Stortinget") and Sweden ("Riksdagen") had representation from seven or eight parties (cf. below, chapters 7 and 8).[10] They are traditionally persistent multiparty assemblies. Three approaches have been proposed to make sense of the Scandinavian parties and the multiparty systems of this region: cleavage analysis; the "five-party model"; and the two-bloc perspective.

Political cleavages are generally understood as recurring conflicts of interest that generate and sustain political parties. An example is the traditional conflict between work and capital that historically produced the socialist parties fighting the "bourgeois"[11] alternatives to the right. The cleavage structures of European societies in general are seen as products of the four "revolutions" that shaped their historical trajectories: the religious revolution of the sixteenth century (Reformation), the national (French) and the industrial revolutions – both basically nineteenth-century – and finally, the Russian Revolution of 1917 (Lipset and Rokkan 1967).

Stein Rokkan identifies in his socio-political history of the growth of mass politics in Western Europe similarities as well as differences in the resulting cleavage structures of the Nordic countries (on voters, see chapter 4). Variations in the cleavages gave rise to differences in the "initial alliance systems and later splits". For example, the party systems of the Nordic countries diverged "markedly in the expression of cultural protest" (Rokkan 1981:65–67). The Norwegian Christian People's Party was founded in the 1930s and the inter-war prohibition issue had a stronger impact on Swedish and Norwegian parties than in Denmark and Finland. During the Cold War years the four countries were exposed to different external pressures and opted for different security arrangements (Chapter 13). In the early 1960s this triggered left socialist splinter parties on "third way" platforms (around 1960 that meant "neither communism nor capitalism", not British Labour's "Third Way" of the 1990s) in Denmark and Norway, but not in Sweden and Finland. Finally, we may note the difference in the rise of right wing populist parties after 1970. These came to stay in Denmark and Norway, but failed to catch on in Sweden (apart from a brief spell in the early 1990s) or in Finland. The cleavage perspective leads Rokkan to *emphasise* the differences between the Nordic party systems –

both in terms of the parties' issue profiles and the multidimensionality of the systems – and only to *note* the similarities.

Sten Berglund and Ulf Lindstrøm presented their "five party model" in the 1970s. In moderate contrast to Rokkan, they *stressed* the similarities and *noted* the differences between the party systems (Berglund and Lindstrøm 1978; Berglund et al. 1981). First, they found that all four countries (not including Iceland) had parties belonging to the same five party families – although of varying size and importance – namely the Conservatives, the Liberals, the Agrarians, the Social Democrats and the Communists. Second, in political debates and in the process of government formation these parties fell into two blocs, suggesting a major socialist – non-socialist cleavage (1978:16). The Swedish party system was taken to be the paradigmatic case with exactly these five parties represented in the *Riksdag* and with two-bloc competition along the left–right axis for government power. The five party model gave priority to the logic of electoral competition and government formation. In was described as basically a "Downsian two-party system tempered by PR" (1978:169). The Downsian perspective prescribed a one-dimensional competitive space – in the Nordic countries focused on class issues – that generated two major (alliance) groups in competition for political power (Downs 1957). With the electoral system of proportional representation (PR), however, the two blocs were divided into several cooperating party alternatives.[12] The five party model is very much a product of the 1970s, and the authors also at the time found the model's fit to be imperfect "at best" (1978:169). Still, it has been a useful benchmark for discussions of the Nordic party systems.

The nature of party competition makes an impact on the democratic qualities of a political system. Giovanni Sartori grouped (democratic) party systems with more than two parties in three main types: the "predominant party" system where one party predominantly controlled government formations; the "moderate multiparty" system with 3–5 parties; and the "extreme multiparty" system with more than five parties. Moderate and extreme multiparty systems varied not only in the nature of the party competition but also in the direction of that competition. In the moderate system parties competed for the voters in the centre; in extreme multipartism they sought to mobilize the voters at the extremes or in special segments (ethnic, linguistic, religious) of the electorate. Sartori found extreme multipartism an unhealthy affair in democracies as it generated extremist, non-cooperative parties and gave little voter choice in terms of electable governments. This third perspective highlighted the "mechanics" of party system competition and how that affected democratic attributes. But as we shall see, it also became quite essential how one counted the number of parties.

Almost continually from 1970, all the Nordic countries have had more than five significant parties in the parliaments. The cleavage perspective opens for multidimensional competition and for more than two political blocs, while the five party model points to the dominance of a two-bloc, one-dimensional competition. But Berglund and Lindström also noted that Nordic politics had more than one operative dimension shaping party politics and their strategies for power — like agrarian and district opposition to the economic and political centres and the Christian segment's religious and family values.

In this chapter we discuss the best way to describe the current Nordic party systems. Which are the major significant party alternatives, and how many of them are there? Can we identify a common "competitive system logic"? We shall limit the discussion to the three Scandinavian countries plus Finland.

## The Parties

The major parties in these four countries are listed in Tables 3.1–3.4. The tables report their electoral support at selected parliamentary elections, including the two last elections in each country.[13] A challenge when presenting these tables is to group the parties in their proper "party family". Not only is this a problem for today's parties, parties may have changed over time. For example, the communist parties were fairly strong in early post-war Nordic politics; electoral results are therefore grouped with "other left parties". In Denmark and Norway, however, the communists later dwindled and the more moderate socialist people's and the left socialist parties have been included in this group. Both these parties advocated (in the 1960s and 1970s primarily) an anti-communist, but "left-of-social-democrats" type of political platform. In Sweden and Finland the old communist parties were politically reformed from within from about the late 1960s, and changed their names. So the reformed communists are the major vote catchers within the "Left Socialist" group in Sweden and Finland. The Danish/Norwegian "Left Socialists" clearly therefore have a different "family background" compared to the communist "Left Socialists" of the Finnish/Swedish party landscape. Within Nordic party cooperation today, however – for example in the Nordic Council – they are taken to be "party family". In 1991 they all also became members of the "New European Left Forum".

The tables leave no doubt that the Social Democrats are the strongest party family in the Nordic countries, though the selected elections do hide some electoral ups and downs (not to speak of fluctuations in the opinion polls). When other parties occasionally draw stronger support in the polls or at elections it is major news in the media. The exception is Finland where the Agrarians are a strong runner-up behind the social democrats. The social democratic parties cooperate closely through their Nordic, European and international party organizations. They were all historically anchored in the working-class movement and retain close – though weakened – ties with the trade unions. The Nordic social democratic parties all opted (in the end) for the reformist course when the Russian revolution split the international labour movement after World War I – although the Norwegian Labour Party took its time and the Finnish social democrats were severely weakened by a strong communist party. Since the interwar period the social democratic strategy has been to mobilize broad sections of the less privileged in the urban as well as in the rural areas. Increasingly, the social democrats also mobilized the public sector workers (see Chapter 4). Favouring a strong state, redistribution of wealth through taxation, equality of opportunities, social security and a wide reaching, "universal" welfare state, they fought attempts from the right to reduce taxes and shield the private sector from public interference.

Table 3.1  Parliamentary elections in Denmark, in per cent

|  | 1950 | 1971 | 1990 | 1998 | 2001 |
|---|---|---|---|---|---|
| Other left parties | 4.6 | 3.0 | 1.7 | – | – |
| Left socialists | – | 9.1 | 8.3 | 7.6 | 6.4 |
| Social Democrats | 39.6 | 37.3 | 37.4 | 35.9 | 29.1 |
| Greens | – | – | 0.9 | – | – |
| Christians | – | 2.0 | 2.3 | 2.3 | 2.3 |
| Social liberals | 8.2 | 14.3 | 3.5 | 3.9 | 5.2 |
| Liberal (agrarians) | 21.3 | 15.6 | 15.8 | 24.0 | 31.3 |
| Conservative | 17.8 | 16.7 | 16.0 | 8.9 | 9.1 |
| Populist right | – | – | 6.4 | 7.4 | 12.0 |
| Other parties | 8.5 | 1.9 | 7.7 | 9.4 | 4.8 |
| Turnout | 81.9 | 87.2 | 82.9 | 82.0 | 87.0 |

Sources: Heidar and Berntzen 1998, Qvortrup 2002:209

Table 3.2  Parliamentary elections in Finland, in per cent

|  | 1951 | 1970 | 1991 | 1999 | 2003 |
|---|---|---|---|---|---|
| Left socialists | 21.6 | 16.6 | 10.1 | 10.9 | 9.9 |
| Social Democrats | 26.5 | 23.4 | 22.1 | 22.9 | 24.5 |
| Greens | – | – | 6.8 | 7.7 | 8.0 |
| Agrarian | 23.3 | 17.1 | 24.8 | 22.4 | 24.7 |
| Other rural | 0.3 | 10.5 | 4.8 | 1.0 | 1.6 |
| Christians | – | 1.1 | 3.1 | 4.2 | 5.3 |
| Liberals | 5.7 | 5.9 | 0.8 | 0.2 | – |
| Swedish | 7.6 | 5.7 | 5.8 | 5.5 | 4.6 |
| Conservative | 14.6 | 18.0 | 19.3 | 21.0 | 18.6 |
| Other parties | 0.6 | 1.6 | 2.4 | 4.3 | 2.8 |
| Turnout | 74.6 | 82.2 | 68.4 | 68.3 | 69.6 |

Sources: Heidar and Berntzen 1998; Arter 2003:162; "Political Data Yearbook", European Journal of Political Research, 2000 (38), 3–4:374

Table 3.3  Parliamentary elections in Norway, in per cent

|  | 1949 | 1969 | 1989 | 1997 | 2001 |
|---|---|---|---|---|---|
| Other left parties | 5.8 | 1.0 | 0.8 | 1.8 | 1.3 |
| Left socialists | – | 3.5 | 10.1 | 6.0 | 12.5 |
| Social Democrats | 45.7 | 46.5 | 34.3 | 35.0 | 24.3 |
| Greens | – | – | – | 0.2 | 0.2 |
| Agrarian | 7.9 | 10.5 | 6.5 | 7.9 | 5.6 |
| Christians | 8.5 | 9.4 | 8.5 | 13.7 | 12.4 |
| Liberals | 13.1 | 9.4 | 3.0 | 4.5 | 3.9 |
| Conservative | 18.3 | 19.6 | 22.2 | 14.3 | 21.2 |
| Populist right | – | – | 13.0 | 15.3 | 14.6 |
| Other parties | 0.7 | 0.1 | 1.4 | 1.3 | 3.7 |
| Turnout | 76.4 | 83.8 | 83.2 | 78.0 | 75.5 |

Sources: Heidar and Berntzen 1998; Historisk statistikk 1994; Stortinget i navn og tall 2001–2005

Table 3.4  Parliamentary elections in Sweden, in per cent

|  | 1948 | 1970 | 1991 | 1998 | 2002 |
|---|---|---|---|---|---|
| Left socialists | 6.3 | 4.8 | 4.5 | 11.9 | 8.3 |
| Social Democrats | 46.1 | 45.3 | 37.6 | 36.3 | 39.8 |
| Greens | – | – | 3.4 | 4.5 | 6.1 |
| Agrarian | 12.4 | 19.9 | 8.5 | 5.0 | 4.6 |
| Christians | – | 1.8 | 7.1 | 11.7 | 9.1 |
| Liberals | 22.7 | 16.2 | 9.1 | 4.6 | 13.3 |
| Conservative | 12.3 | 11.5 | 21.9 | 22.9 | 15.2 |
| Populist right | – | – | 6.7 | – | – |
| Other parties | 0.1 | 0.5 | 1.2 | 2.6 | 3.0 |
| Turnout | 82.7 | 88.3 | 86.7 | 79.7 | 80.1 |

Sources: Heidar and Berntzen 1998; Mackie and Rose 1991; Madeley 2003:171

The green parties are newcomers to Nordic politics as in other countries. They are small, but have had a significant political impact in Sweden and Finland. The greens entered the Finnish parliament, Eduskunta, in 1983 and the Swedish Riksdag in 1988. In Sweden a referendum on the future of nuclear power in 1980 activated many environmentalists and voters, and the accident at the Chernobyl nuclear power station in the Soviet Union in 1986 helped their mobilization efforts. These green movements – they saw themselves as more than an electoral party – not only fought for environmentalist policies, they also expressed a general opposition to "politics-as-usual", as these sentiments were found in the peace movement of the 1980s, the women's movement and among voters demanding a revitalization of democratic practices. The same political tendencies also made an impact in Norway and Denmark, but in both countries existing parties – particularly the left socialists, but also the parties in the centre (in Norway the Liberals) – pre-empted the voter potential for the small green parties by adopting policies of a "post-materialist" nature (Chapter 4).

The Nordic Christian parties are rather different from the continental Christian Democrats. Further south in Europe these parties – like the Nordic ones – favour religious values and institutions (Catholic as well as Protestant). But in addition they are often the major conservative parties of their countries. The continental Christian Democrats emerged to defend establishment interests against the disruptive and secularising forces embodied by the rising liberal forces of the nineteenth century. The type of Protestant Christian party that originated in Norway during the 1930s was a different brand. This party grew out of groups previously linked through a wide people's coalition that had joined the Liberal Party to fight establishment forces – including the religion espoused by the state, i.e., the established Church. The Norwegian lay Christians' movement opposed all establishment interests – religious as well as economic and social. At first it was a regional party, based on the west coast of Norway. It was only after World War II that it expanded into a fully fledged national party. For the first decades it was a party of and for the religious lay movement – finding its members and voters within denominations outside the established Church. The Christian People's Party opposed the religious teachings and practices of the established religion; fought secularising forces in contemporary culture; opposed cuts in the teaching of religious knowledge in the (overwhelmingly state-run) schools and wanted to strengthen ethical standards in general. Later, the party succeeded in mobilizing large parts of the active religious segment of the electorate, including many at all levels in the established Church. The party grew to be a medium-large party, and a government coalition partner in the non-socialist bloc. Partly inspired by the success of the Norwegian party, similar Christian parties were founded in the other three Nordic countries in the 1960s and early 1970s. Their goals were the same: to fight secularisation, in particular the liberalization of pornography and abortion. In the 1970s and 1980s they also won representation in parliaments and were included in government coalitions in the other Nordic countries.

The liberal parties were among the first to emerge in the Scandinavian countries (not so in Finland). Party splits and the rising socialist movement subsequently weakened them. After a party split in Norway in the 1970s, the Norwegian liberals have struggled to keep their representation in parliament. In Sweden the liberals remained a medium-sized party for many years, despite several ups and downs, while in Denmark an early twentieth-century party split produced two viable parties, the largest of which included an agrarian wing, the smaller the more radical forces of social liberalism. Today the agrarian liberals and the social democrats are the major Danish parties.

The conservatives are traditionally the party of the right, mobilizing the voters first against the liberals and later against the social democrats. They defend the private sector interests and generally the freedom of individuals and businesses from state economic interference. In electoral terms the conservatives are all major parties, though of course, they too have experienced fluctuating fortunes over the years.

The populist right parties started out in Denmark, on the wave of a tax revolt in the early 1970s. The message and the party idea spread quickly to Norway. The two Progress Parties fought against increased taxes, unnecessary government red tape and for tough action against crime. Both were led by charismatic politicians, who came to embody the parties in the public eye. They advocated support for the "ordinary" voters against elites of all sorts. During the 1980s they pursued increasingly restrictive policies on immigration. After the Danish party split in the mid 1990s, a not too dissimilar "Danish People's Party" replaced the parent Progress Party. It adopted a slightly less personal and idiosyncratic leadership style than its forerunner. The Swedes had a brief encounter with a similarly constituted right-wing party when "New Democracy" stepped into the Swedish political arena in 1991. Infighting broke out among the leadership, however, and it disintegrated and vanished from the scene only three years later.

## A Five Party Arena?

The Swedish party system was the prototype for the "five party model" which, until the late 1980s, remained a fairly accurate description of the Swedish political landscape. The Social Democrats were the predominant party in Sweden during the entire post war period, in 1968 winning more than 50 per cent of the votes at the parliamentary election. Although smaller, they still attract electoral support in the high thirties and are still by far the strongest social democrats among the Nordics. The reformed communists – who changed their name in 1967 to the Left Communist Party, and in 1990 dropped the communist bit – were roughly a five-per-cent party until the last two elections. Thanks to a new popular party leader the party strode ahead on popular dissatisfaction with the social democratic government's austerity programme and pro-EU policies among leftist voters. The agrarian Centre Party fell from a 1970s electoral share in the twenties to about 5 per cent at the last two elections. The liberal People's Party attracted less than 10 per cent of the vote during the 1990s, though it more than doubled its support – to 13 per cent – at the 2002 election, one reason being its tougher, if controversial, stand on immigration. Finally, the conservative "Moderate Unity Party" competed in periods with the liberals as the strongest non-socialist party, but won that contest decisively in the 1980s. The conservatives have consistently gained around 20 per cent of the vote, though they experienced a setback at the last election when they appeared to lose votes to the liberals in particular.

Until the late 1980s these five parties dominated the Swedish electoral arena, and at the 1970 election they won 98 per cent of the votes. Although their joint support has declined during the 1990s, they still manage to capture more than 80 per cent of the vote. Three new parties have entered the Swedish political arena, changing its five-party format. First, despite official registration as a party in the 1960s, the Christian Democrats had to wait until 1991 to succeed with the electorate. This success was triggered by an announcement by the government to cut back on religious education in the state-run schools. Three years earlier the Greens had entered the Riksdag with 5 per cent of the vote. Their setback in the subsequent election left them without representation, but they reclaimed some of the seats in 1998. In the meantime, the low tax, anti-bureaucracy party "New Democracy" made a brief visit to the parliamentary arena, but failed to win representation following the 1991–94 electoral period.

If Sweden was the original prototype of the five-party model, Finland was the deviant case (Berglund and Lindström 1978:19). That said, its five parties did account for 84 per cent of the vote in the mid-1970s, and at the 2003 election won 78 per cent. A three-quarter fit is not bad for any model. The problem with Finland in a Nordic mould, however, was that the party system deviated from the start in several respects. These derivations had their roots in the particular history of Finnish nation-building (see Chapter 1). First, the social democrats did not make up the predominant party – as they did in the three Scandinavian countries – but were challenged by the agrarians, with the conservatives as runner-up. The social democrats scored fairly consistently between 20 and 30 per cent at elections, usually slightly more than the agrarian Centre Party. The Centre Party came neck-to-neck with the Social Democrats at the 1999 and 2003 elections with the support of 22 and 24 per cent of the votes. The conservative National Union Party came third with 21 and 19 per cent. The Liberal People's Party has, as mentioned, been a weak force in Finland and has basically been without representation in parliament for several decades. The Leftist Alliance (the old communists) experienced a decline throughout the post-war period. The communists started out in the 1940s and 1950s with between 20 and 25 per cent of the vote. After 1990 the reformed leftist party consistently scored about 10 per cent.

The second deviation from the five party model lies in the more complex cleavage structure of the Finnish parties when compared to the other Nordic countries. The Swedish People's Party is a language- and ethnicity-based party of and for the Finland-Swedes. It is also a regional party as the Finland-Swedes are concentrated on the west coast and the islands. Party support in electoral terms has tended to follow the decline of this group in Finnish society. Today they poll around five per cent of the vote. The agrarian forces were split in Finland; with a small-holder farmers' party present in parliament until the 1990s. Finally, the Green Alliance wielded substantial political clout in the 1980s, and from 1991 has polled around 7 per cent at elections. With ten parties in the Eduskunta in 1975, eight after 2003, all embedded in different cleavages, the five-party model gives a poor guide to understanding the "mechanics" of the Finnish party system today – in spite of the fact that the five parties represent three out of four voters.

The fit is better in Denmark, even though the number of parties at times has been far more than five. After the 1973 "earthquake election" – when the populist Progress Party made inroads in territory previously held by the Danish party establishment – the parties represented in the *Folketing* numbered eleven: Today there are eight. Still, the Danish party system is closer to the Swedish than to the Finnish. First, the Social Democrats have always been the largest party, surpassed only by the agrarian liberals at the election in 2001. Their electoral strength has not been as impressive as that of their Swedish brethren, but electorally they have remained fairly stable at about 30–40 per cent – again with the 2001 election excepted. Second, the other four "model" parties were all strong. The left parties were primarily active in the shape of the Socialist People's Party. This party was founded as an alternative to both the dwindling Communist Party and the power-holding Social Democrats in 1959. Its electoral showing has fluctuated between 15 and 6 per cent after the 1980s. The liberals are represented in the dual shape of the smaller Radical Liberals and the larger agrarian liberals of the Left Party. The agrarian liberals became the largest party in Denmark after the 2001 election with 31 per cent of the vote. The Conservative People's Party has traditionally alternated with the agrarian liberals as the second largest party after the Social Democrats, but the two last elections have been low points for the conservatives.

In 1971 – just before the "earthquake" – the six parties that made up the "five-party system" in Denmark (it is reasonable to include both liberal alternatives) won 93 per cent of the vote. In 2001, the figure was 81. Until the 1970s, the Danes talked about a four party system, as the left parties played only a minor role in the parliamentary arena. This system broke down at the 1973 election, when the number of parties rose – although the Danes have always had several small parties going in and out of the Folketing. The electoral system makes it fairly easy for small parties to enter parliament; they only need 2 per cent to pass the qualifying hurdle to win mandates (4 per cent in Norway and Sweden). A number of centre parties were among the new parties of the 1970s, reflected in the high figures for "other parties" in Table 3.1. The Christian People's Party entered parliament in 1973, but never won a large electoral following. The populist right Progress Party, however, at a stroke became the second largest party at the 1973 election, although it failed to maintain velocity. At the 2001 election a similar party (the Danish People's Party) – under a new name and new management – took its place on the populist right wing, with 12 per cent of the vote.

The Norwegian party system has tended to fit the five-party system relatively nicely, although there are significant deviations. The social democratic Labour Party consistently came out on top at elections and often won more than 40 per cent of the vote. After 1985, however, party fortunes have stayed in the 30s, dipping to a low of 24 per cent at the 2001 election. Not since the 1920s – when the labour movement was split in three after the Bolshevik Revolution – had the Labour Party done so poorly at elections. The Socialist Left Party attracted varying support throughout the 1980s and 1990s, but experienced its best result ever at the 2001 election, culling 12 per cent. Both the agrarian Centre Party and the Christians have inhabited "small to medium" electoral space, but at the last elections the Christian People's Party notched up about twice as many voters as the agrarians. The liberal Left Party has been a declining force in post-war Norwegian politics, and today are struggling to keep a toehold in parliament. Finally, the conservative Right Party, generally the major opposition party to the power-holding social democrats, has attracted votes in the 14–32 per cent range.

In 1969 the five "model parties" accounted for 90 per cent of the Norwegian vote; in 2001 that figure had sunk to 68. This is a rather steep decline in support. The Christian People's Party represents a deviation of its own. The split and decline of the liberals in the 1970s during the EU membership debacle also made this party a hesitant part of the model. Simultaneously, the populist Progress Party made gains that shocked the political establishment, as its sister party had done in Denmark. Despite the electoral swings and roundabouts, the Progress Party has remained a staying force in the party system, currently enjoying around 15 per cent of the vote. In surveys the party has even doubled that size, occasionally posing as the largest party in Norway, indicating a potential for increased support. It is now faced with the problem of institutionalising itself as an organization at a time when their popular and controversial leader has announced his retirement a few years hence.

## The Cleavages and Bloc Politics

It is not easy to fit the Nordic parties of today into the norm prescribed by the "five-party model". Table 3.5 shows the parliamentary strength of the major party families in the four countries at specific times. In the years since 1980, the Greens, the Christians, other centre parties and the populist right have all been parliamentary actors in at least two of the countries. The Christians, once an exclusively Norwegian phenomenon, now have parliamentary representation in all four countries. The other centre parties enjoy a more or less stable presence in Danish and Finnish politics. The liberal parties of Finland and Norway find themselves in a precarious electoral state. Today it seems more appropriate to speak about a "five plus" party system, if the actual number of parties in Nordic politics is the thing to go by. First, all four parliaments house five-party families, namely the left socialists, the social democrats, the agrarians, the Christians and the conservatives. Second, the "plus" rises from the fact that three party types have a major presence in two of the four countries. First, the old liberals have managed to cling onto a significant position in Denmark and Sweden, although the small Norwegian party actually was part of the coalition government 1997–2000 and again since 2001. Second, the Greens may be rather small, but they are significant parliamentary parties in Sweden and Finland. And third, the populist right has established strong parties in Denmark and Norway.

The five-party model stresses the one-dimensionality of the Nordic party systems. The "left" parties fought the "right" in the political arena over class issues: How to define the balance between state and society, how much redistribution over public budgets, how extensive a welfare state, etc., etc. In parliamentary terms this produced the two-bloc alternative for governments, with the socialists competing against the non-socialist (or bourgeois) bloc for power. We see from Table 3.6 on governments in the Nordic countries that only the Swedes managed to keep two-bloc politics going more or less as usual in the 1990s. Social democratic minority governments have actually been in position from 1982 to today, excepting the 1991–94 non-socialist centre-right minority coalition.[14] The non-socialist government had to negotiate with the populist right party to stay in power. The Social Democrats had to negotiate parliamentary majorities, but generally they had the support of the Left Socialists. From the mid-1990s the Social Democrats also collaborated with the agrarian Centre Party, which broke away

Table 3.5  Parliamentary strength of party families, in per cent

| | Denmark | | | Finland | | | Norway | | | Sweden | | |
|---|---|---|---|---|---|---|---|---|---|---|---|---|
| | 1980 | 1990 | 2004 | 1980 | 1990 | 2004 | 1980 | 1990 | 2004 | 1980 | 1990 | 2004 |
| Left socialists | 10 | 9 | 7 | 18 | 8 | 10 | 1 | 10 | 14 | 6 | 5 | 9 |
| Social Democrats | 39 | 39 | 30 | 26 | 28 | 27 | 49 | 38 | 26 | 44 | 40 | 41 |
| Greens | – | – | – | – | 2 | 7 | – | – | – | – | – | 5 |
| Agrarian | – | – | – | 18 | 20 | 28 | 8 | 7 | 6 | 18 | 9 | 6 |
| Christians | 3 | 2 | 2 | 5 | 3 | 4 | 14 | 9 | 13 | – | 7 | 9 |
| Liberals[1] | 19 | 21 | 37 | 3 | – | – | 1 | – | 1 | 11 | 10 | 14 |
| Other centre parties[2] | 3 | 5 | – | 9 | 11 | 6 | – | 1 | 1 | – | – | – |
| Conservative | 13 | 17 | 9 | 23 | 27 | 20 | 26 | 22 | 23 | 21 | 23 | 16 |
| Populist right | 11 | 7 | 13 | – | – | – | – | 13 | 16 | – | 7 | – |
| SUM | 98 | 100 | 98 | 102 | 99 | 102 | 99 | 100 | 100 | 100 | 101 | 100 |
| Number of parties/groups | 10 | 8 | 8 | 8 | 9 | 8 | 6 | 7 | 9 | 5 | 6 | 7 |

Sources: Heidar and Berntzen 1998; Skjæveland, 2003; Allardt et al. 1981; West European
  Politics; Stortinget i navn og tall 2001–2005.
[1]  Includes the Social Liberals and the agrarian Liberals in Denmark
[2]  In Denmark this group includes the Centre Democrats, in Finland the Swedish People's Party and the Rural Party.

from the "non-socialist fold". After the 1998 election the government remained
in power on support from the Left Socialists and the Green Party, an arrangement
which continued after the 2002 election (though only after the agrarians had turned down an invitation to join forces with the Social Democrats). Bloc politics
persisted, but in both (old) blocs tension was mounting throughout the 1980s
and 1990s. The Christians worked to highlight the moral issues in politics, the
agrarians stressed the centre–periphery resistance to increased centralization and
the Greens pursued environmental issues, advocating policies claimed to be beyond the "old right" and the "old left" axis. The centre-right governments of the
1970s to 1990s documented that the universe of important political issues was not
confined to the logic of traditional bloc politics.

Table 3.6  Parties in government 1990–2004

| Period | Parties in government | Parliamentary base % |
|---|---|---|
| Denmark | | |
| 1990–93 | Cons+AgrLib | 34 |
| 1993–94 | SD+SocLib+Centre Democrats+Christian | 51 |
| 1994–96 | SD+SocLib+Centre Democrats | 43 |
| 1996–98 | SD+SocLib | 40 |
| 1998–2001 | SD+SocLib | 40 |
| 2001– | AgrLib+Cons | 41 |
| Finland | | |
| 1990–91 | Cons+SD+Swedish | 61 |
| 1991–94 | Cons+Agrar+Swedish+Christian | 57 |
| 1994–95 | Agrar+Swedish+Cons | 53 |
| 1995–99 | SocLeft+SD+Swedish+Cons+Green | 72 |
| 1999–2003 | SocLeft+SD+Swedish+Cons+Green | 70 |
| 2003– | Agrar+SD+Swedish | 58 |
| Norway | | |
| 1990–93 | SD | 38 |
| 1993–96 | SD | 41 |
| 1996–97 | SD | 41 |
| 1997–2000 | Christian+Agrar+Lib | 25 |
| 2000–01 | SD | 26 |
| 2001– | Cons+Christian+Lib | 37,5 |
| Sweden | | |
| 1988–91 | SD | 45 |
| 1991–94 | Cons+Lib+Agrar+Christian | 49 |
| 1994–96 | SD | 46 |
| 1996–1998 | SD | 46 |
| 1996–2002 | SD | 38 |
| 2002– | SD | 41 |

Source: Heidar and Berntzen 1998; *European Journal of Political Research* (Political Data Yearbooks)

Danish governments were more balanced between the left and right, the blocs here not so "frozen" as far as the government formation was concerned. Denmark had a history of minority governments supported by parties in parliament. In 1993 the conservatives and the agrarian liberals ended a ten-year government partnership, which at times included the Christians, the Centre Democrats and the Social Liberals. The Social Democrats formed governments with parties from the centre for the next ten years, from 1993 till 2003, including parties which a few years earlier had been in government with the conservatives. After the 2001 election the agrarian liberals and the conservatives again formed a government, now with parliamentary support from the populist right. Although the blocs are more fragmented or "elastic" in Danish politics than in Sweden, the dimensionality of party competition is arguably less complex. The periphery's opposition to the national centre is less prominent, the Christians argue their case for morality and religion, but not from a position of much parliamentary importance, and the greens are not present – as a party alternative – in parliament.

Norwegian politics was never one-dimensional. The agrarians and the Christians made the political debate more complex than an argument over taxes and the state's role in the economy. When it came to government formation, however, the left and right blocs tended to fight it out, although the precise party composition of each bloc was increasingly a matter of post-election negotiations. Throughout the 1990s the Social Democrats represented a clearly defined government alternative on their own. Social Democratic governments succeeded a traditional centre–right coalition (Cons + Christian + Agrarian) run aground in 1990 on the rocks of the EU membership issue, repeating the events of the early 1970s. EU has always been a classical centre-right headache. In 1997, the first (post-war) "centre only" coalition appeared when a large parliamentary minority of Christians, agrarians and liberals joined hands in a minority government.[15] This broke down under a joint attack from left and right simultaneously, and a centre–right coalition appeared after the 2001 election, this time without the agrarians. Sensationally, the liberals were allotted three ministerial posts on the basis of two representatives in the parliament. It was a result of political imperatives rather than an expression of numerical strength. The Christians needed an ally to balance the Conservatives in government. In the run-up to the 2005 parliamentary elections, the social democrats are debating whether to include the Left Socialists, the agrarians and even the Christians in a centre–left alternative. These other parties are debating whether to accept the invitation, with divisions most apparent in the Christian People's Party, which has been part of the centre–right government since 2001. But all parties of the centre have concerns about the Labour Party's eagerness to reapply for EU membership during the next parliamentary period. If they pursue EU membership, the centre–left alternative is most likely dead. But so would the centre–right alternative be, as the Christians and the conservatives are on opposite sides of the EU fence.

The Finns spearheaded the rainbow coalition in Nordic politics. In 1987 the Social Democrats joined up with the conservatives in a coalition out of political necessity to get the dominant Agrarian Party out of office. This was (basically) the first time the conservatives had been in government, having been kept out to avoid offending Soviet Cold War sensitivities. Previous coalition governments had built largely on the agrarian and the Social Democrat tickets. During the 1990s social democrats starting alternating with agrarians – again with other parties added, but this time – until 2003 that is – they included the conservatives. Actually some parties stayed on whatever happened. The Swedish People's Party has been continuously in government since 1979. In 1995 the Greens entered government – making it even more rainbow-like in political terms. After the 2003 election the two old contenders for government – the agrarians and the Social Democrats – took the reins of government together, this time to keep the conservatives at bay. The new and complex pattern of the 1990s bore no resemblance to the old left and right blocs. The decline of classic left–right politics must not only be seen in view of the end of the Soviet threat, but also as a search for new coalitions made necessary by EU membership and the need for viable coalitions to bring the country out of the economic crisis caused by the breakdown of the trade with the Soviets.

No doubt the traditional left–right conflict still has validity in Nordic polities. But it is clearly less important than in the old days of bloc politics. The two-bloc competition never, of course, quite fitted the mould outside Sweden, and even in Sweden the agrarians represented rural communities regardless of left and right. After the 1970s, it became increasingly difficult to portray competition for government positions from a simple left–right basis in all of the four Nordic countries. We cannot find a predominant social democratic party – at the least not one commanding parliamentary majorities – and it is not very revealing to speak of two-bloc or even three-bloc competition for power. The "blocs" today are simply not sufficiently stable for this to make sense – instead, they are created or re-created in the post-election haggling for power. At most they are employed as rhetorical devices to appeal to voters and to other parties to remember old loyalties. On the other hand, the political power struggle in the Nordic countries is by no means disconnected from feuding over state power in the economy. Still, the centre is more open to collaborating with either side and the flanks are less loyal to their "next of kin". In other words, party concerns are no longer exclusively – or even (for parties like the Greens) predominantly – ordered along the left–right axis.

## The Nordic Party System(s) Revisited

As indicated earlier, party "counting rules" are central to discussions of party system types in democracies. Not all parties which put up candidates for election – not even all parties that succeed in getting their representatives elected to parliament – necessarily make an impact on the competitive logic of the party system. Some parties are simply irrelevant. When classifying party systems we need to "count intelligently" (Sartori 1976). Sartori argues that parties can be "significant" despite their low nominal strength, such as parties with only a five-per-cent parliamentary representation. They can exert influence either because of their "coalition" or their "blackmail" potential. To be "coalitionable" a party must have prior government experience or be needed for a potential government. For a party to have "blackmail potential" it must control the parliamentary votes necessary to present a credible threat to the life of the government or its potential alternative. If we employ Sartori's counting rules for the Nordic party systems today, we find that they all exceed the "five parties" type. The rules allow for qualified judgements, but a rough count shows that Denmark and Sweden have had eight (possibly nine) significant parties since 1990, Finland and Norway seven. We then count the government's allies in parliament, like the Greens in Sweden. Using Sartori's counting rules, therefore, we find no "five party system" in the Nordic countries today.

All of the Nordics follow this left–right cleavage pattern. Large parties like the social democrats, the conservatives and the liberals all used to espouse competing visions of the role of the state in society. Their programmatic core policies are still founded on particular perspectives on equality, redistribution and the "limits" of the state. The left-leaning socialist parties and the parties in the "centre" also position themselves along this axis – not the least to increase their coalition or blackmail potential. So far, the old model remains valid, up to a point. But as David Arter argues, apart from Sweden, the left–right cleavage approach failed to explain the "nascent party systems" (Arter 1999: 66). As the polarization between left and right loses much of its potency, the cleavage pattern grows in complexity. Post-World War II party politics was never very confrontational. Compared to the major European democracies, like the UK, politics in the post-war years stayed reasonably "consensual".[16] The political divide between the socialist and non-socialist blocs has narrowed over time, as seen in the parties' increasing propensity to break out of the two blocs and even to cross the bloc line to form government coalitions with old adversaries.

Other cleavages than the left–right cleavage make parliamentary politics less black and white. The old centre–periphery cleavage was a steadfast basis for the agrarian Centre parties even when these parties – in the 1950s – made an attempt (more or less successfully) to extend their electoral base to the urban voters. The moral–religious cleavage produced significant Christian parties in all four countries, and the post-materialist or environmentalist cleavage impacted existing parties and gave rise to new green parties. The populist right in Denmark and Norway – and its brief Swedish appearance – are rightist parties in the sense that they pursue lower taxes and less state interference in the economy. They do not, however, advocate the fiscal prudence of their conservative brethren when it comes to providing social services for the commoner and they are much less willing to consider humanitarian reasons when it comes to immigration policies. By and large, they are also more egalitarian than the conservatives in the sense that tax cuts should be for all, not only for "the rich". And, by the way, the elites should pay for their elitist culture themselves – the theatres and opera houses – and not through the public purse. The populist right are on the right wing in some issues and on the materialist end of the materialist–post-materialist cleavage in others. In short, the populist right parties are problematic "bed-fellows" for the old non-socialist bloc.

Returning to Sartori's distinction between moderate and extreme polarized party systems, the Nordic polities are still moderate systems, despite the profusion of parties and greater multidimensionality. This is because competition is for the centre ground of the ever-valid left–right cleavage. The parties compete for the median voter as defined by this old cleavage. But this only tells part of the party system story, and the two-bloc perspective will not carry far in predicting outcomes of coalition formations.

How similar are these four Nordic party systems? The Finns are the most difficult to fit into a common mould. The Finnish Social Democratic Party is smaller and the agrarian party stronger than the prevailing "norm". The Liberal Party is weak and the ethnic Swedish Party adds a different dimension to the system. The three Scandinavian countries still have strong, but no longer predominant, social democratic parties. Their position as the largest party is challenged in Denmark and Norway. A further difference between the Swedish–Finnish party systems on the one hand and the Danish–Norwegian ones on the other is that the former have small, but significant green parties, while the latter have medium–large, populist right parties. In spite of these differences, the Nordic party systems today converge on several points: they are multiparty systems; the social democratic parties have strong positions; they have – more or less explicithy – agrarian-based parties of varying strength; and small (by and large) Protestant Christian parties. Looking beyond the individual party, the Nordic systems are moderately multidimensional, dominated by left–right centripetal competition and shifting alliances in search of executive power.

Is this a distinctive brand within the European democratic family? There are a number of multiparty systems elsewhere with more than five significant parties, most of which include strong social democratic parties and most of which are dominated by left–right politics. Austria and the Netherlands are two examples. The social democrats do not predominate in these countries, but that is no longer the case in the Nordic countries either. Nor is the presence of the populist right and the green parties peculiar to *Norden*. The two countries mentioned have both party families present in their parliaments. What separates the Nordic party systems, however, is the *absence* of a strong continental type Christian-Democratic force and the *presence* of the agrarian party type. These specialities, however, do not arguably allow us to conclude on the existence of a particularly *Nordic* brand of party system, as neither gives them a particular parliamentary logic in the competition for government positions.

The particular Nordic characteristics could well be discussed with reference to historical background and institutional setting. But what is so special? In explaining the absence of Christian Democracy, Britain is equally interesting in a comparative analysis. Explaining the strength of social democracy, the comparative cases are legion. Perhaps the most notable and distinctive Nordic particularity – albeit moderately important – is the presence of the agrarian parties. We must add that these parties struggle hard to come over as more than single-interest farmers' parties: They are defenders of the peripheral communities and their cultural and economic interests; they favour equality in public services (wherever you live); they fight against administrative centralization and for a wider democracy, nationally and locally.

It is difficult to sustain the notion of a particularly Nordic or even Scandinavian party system. When we focus on formal aspects – like the number of significant parties, the cleavage dimensions and the nature of competition – we fail to discover reasonably important indications of party system exclusiveness.

# Chapter 4: Voters and Social Cleavages

*Oddbjørn Knutsen*

In this chapter we examine how and to what degree old and new cleavages have influenced voting behaviour in the Nordic countries over time. We will first discuss some important concepts and models related to social cleavages, and change in social cleavages, before addressing the established social cleavages which have underpinned the party system and how these have changed over time. Finally, in the last two parts we discuss the impact of new structural and value-based cleavages on voting behaviour of the electorate of the Nordic countries. Since extensive election survey data are only available for Denmark, Norway and Sweden, we shall concentrate on these three countries.

## Theories and Conceptual Framework

### WHAT ARE SOCIAL OR POLITICAL CLEAVAGES?

A traditional notion of social cleavage is that it reflects broadly based and long-standing social and economic divisions within society; the political cleavage structure is thought of in terms of social groups, the loyalties of individuals to their social group and how these loyalties influence party choice and political action (Franklin, Mackie, Valen et al. 1992: 5).

Cleavage as a concept, however, has been used differently by different authors. Some researchers see cleavages as deep-seated, persistent affairs, and include value orientations as an intermediate variable through which the impact of social structure is transmitted. Other researchers, focusing on changes in social cleavages after the 1960s, consider social structure and value orientations as sources of different cleavages or conflict lines and urge students to control for prior structural variables when analysing the new value-based cleavages.

## THE LIPSET/ROKKAN MODEL

In their seminal essay on the development of the conflict structure in western democracies, Lipset and Rokkan (1967) focused on the historical origins of the structural party conflicts (see also chapters 1 and 3 above). They saw the main political cleavages as direct products of two revolutions: national and industrial.

The two cleavages emerging from the national revolution were 1) the centre–periphery cleavage, which was anchored in geographical regions and related to different ethnic, linguistic and religious minority (confessional) groups, and 2) the conflict between the Church and State, which pitted the secular state against the historical privileges of the churches and, over control of the important educational institutions. This cleavage has more specifically polarised the religious section against the secular section of the population.

The battle lines which the Industrial Revolution gave rise to were marked by 1) the labour market cleavages, where owners and employers contended with tenants, labourers and workers, and 2), the commodity market cleavage between buyers and sellers of agricultural products, or, more generally, the urban and the rural populations (Lipset and Rokkan 1967: 15–23).

One important aspect in Lipset and Rokkan's work was the persistent impact of social structure on party choice. They called it the "freezing of party alignments". With few, if significant exceptions, the party systems of the 1960s reflected the cleavage structure of the 1920s. The party systems of the 1960s were more or less solidified by the 1920s, and the party alternatives had mainly tended to survive (Lipset and Rokkan 1967: 50–54). The freezing hypothesis is basically explained by the strong relationship between the socio-structural variables highlighted by Lipset and Rokkan and party choice. Lipset and Rokkan's "freezing" perspective is one of stable alignment – a force of stability in the party system and constancy in party support over time.

## CHANGES IN SOCIAL CLEAVAGES: DEALIGNMENT AND REALIGNMENT

From around the 1970s, the electoral behaviour of voters in the Nordic countries changed substantially. Instead of stable alignment, researches began talking about dealignment and realignment.

*Dealignment* means that the impact of the structural cleavages has become smaller. The increased instability in the party system is caused by the fact that voters do not vote according to their location in the social structure to the same degree as previously.

*Realignment* implies the eclipse of old cleavages and the rise of new ones.

There is first a dealignment from the old cleavages and then a new alignment related to the new cleavage structure. While Lipset and Rokkan focused on the national and the industrial revolutions, Dalton, Flanagan and Beck (1984: 455–456) talked for example of a third post-industrial revolution which might create a new basis of social cleavages.

Two kinds of new cleavages have received the most attention, new structural cleavages and value-based cleavages, both of which, according to some researchers, are more important in contemporary than industrial society. In this chapter we explore first sector employment and gender as significant new structural cleavages, followed by New Politics orientations, as the new value-based cleavages are termed.

Another type of realignment – *ecological* realignment – states that party support follows immediately from the changes in social structure. Ecological realignment not only affects the support of the various parties, but political agenda and party strategies, too. Parties try to appeal to the new, expanding social groups. Ecological realignment and subsequent changes in party strategies are discussed in relation to the changes in class structure and the growth of the new middle class.

## The Impact of Traditional Social Cleavages

### THE RELIGIOUS CLEAVAGE

The religious structure in the Nordic countries derives from their established Lutheran State Churches. The religious cleavage has had a specific character, between the secular and tolerant urban population and the orthodox and fundamental Lutheranism of large sections of the rural population. This was not only a secular/religious cleavage, but a division between the religious fundamentalists organised in various lay organisations within (and partly outside) the state church on the one hand, and the more tolerant government-appointed clerics (civil servants) and the more passive religious population on the other. These fundamentalists were active in various revival movements, evangelist/missionary organisations and non-conformist or free churches.

In their comparative discussion of the character of the religious cleavage, Lipset and Rokkan showed that the established churches in the Scandinavian countries (and in Britain) did not oppose nation-builders as the Roman Catholic Church had done, adding that "the 'Left' movements opposed to the religious establishment found most of their support among newly enfranchised dissenters, nonconformists, and fundamentalists in the peripheries" (Lipset and Rokkan 1967: 38). Christian parties were not among the first to emerge, which is basically why they are not part of the five-party model. They were born from an aversion to the secularisation of society and secular legislation on moral and religious issues (Karvonen 1994: 124–126).

Committed state church members have not tended to lend their backing to the pre-industrial left-leaning movements or the subsequent Christian people's parties in Scandinavia. The most vigorous support has always come from the non-conformist, fundamentalist groupings, some within and some outside the official Lutheran Church. For example, Swedish support for the Christian Democrats by the ordinary Lutheran church goer reached only 9 per cent, while 53 per cent of non-conformist adherents (who attended free-church services regularly) voted for the Christian Democrats in the 2002 election (Holmberg and Oscarsson 2004: 152).

The Scandinavian Christian parties deviated much more than their Continental sister parties. To be a Christian party voter in the Nordic countries has meant taking a stand which goes beyond conformist church membership or identification with general Christian values. The moral standards advocated by the Scandinavian parties on a variety of questions continue to be too demanding for the average voter (Karvonen 1994: 137–138).

THE FUNCTIONAL–ECONOMIC CLEAVAGES: LINES OF CONFLICT IN THE LABOUR AND COMMODITY MARKETS

The two functional–economic cleavages which sprang out of the Industrial Revolution are basic for any understanding of the Scandinavian party systems. Comparative analyses of voting by social class have shown that the incidence of class voting has been higher in the Scandinavian countries than in other democracies (Nieuwbeerta 1995: Chapter 3), reinforced by agrarian parties and urban–rural cleavages in particular.

Union density in the Nordic countries has been among the highest in the world. Denmark, Finland and Sweden have had the highest union density of all democratic countries. The Ghent system prevails in Denmark, Finland, Sweden and Belgium, where the trade unions administer unemployment funds, which naturally has provided a selective incentive to join unions or remain unionized following redundancy. Norway has the highest union density of the non-Ghent countries (Ebbinghaus and Visser 1999).

The high level of class voting is also due to the secular orientations of most people in the Nordic countries (Halman and Moor 1994). The religious cleavage cut across the class cleavage, with religious voters often voting for Christian parties independent of their class position. The widely secular nature of the Nordic orientation does, however, mean that class-crossing religious voting only concerns a small section of the population (Nieuwbeerta 1995: Chapter 4).

### ROKKAN'S TRIANGULAR MODEL OF ELECTORAL FRONTS

In the 1960s, Stein Rokkan (1966) formulated a model for these cleavages based on the Norwegian situation, but his model can be applied to the major social and economic cleavages of the other Nordic countries (Oskarson 1994: Chapter 2; Elklit 1984).

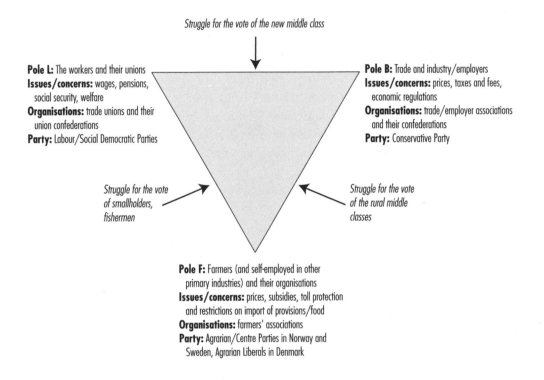

Figure 4.1 Rokkan's model of electoral fronts: The functional–economic axis

Rokkan saw the functional-economic lines of conflict as comprising three poles of electoral attraction. At each of the poles we find economic interests, issues, interest organisations and a major social class. They also comprise the major political parties in league with the economic interests and special interest organisations. Between the three poles we find voters espousing "contradictory" economic and social positions. According to Rokkan, the decisive electoral struggles took place in the space between the poles, and involved different political parties.

The "poles of electorate attractions" are shown in Figure 4.1. In the text below the figure we have indicated the various issues, peak interest organisations and parties located at the poles. Let us first examine the poles, and then go on to analyse the party competition between the poles.

The three interests are the labour unions and their peak organisation, the farmer organisations and the business community and their peak organisations. The three party families located at the poles are the social democratic, the agrarian and the conservative parties.

CHANGES IN VOTING BEHAVIOUR OF THE CLASSES AT THE POLES

This model is partly an institutional model because it is based on the organisational linkages between the interest organisations and their peak organisation and the three class parties which have developed historically. It is, however, also based on the assumption that most voters belonging to the various classes located at the three poles vote for "their own" parties. The most important types of class voting are the degree to which the workers support the Labour parties, the farmers (and other self-employed in the primary industries) the Agrarian parties and the employers the Conservative parties. Votes here are said to be for the classes' *core* parties. However, we also examine the tendency of the classes to vote for *party groups*, i.e., groups which broadly articulate the different class interests.[17]

For analysing change we use the election surveys from around 1970 from Denmark and Norway, various election surveys from the 1970s from Sweden, and surveys from the 1990s from all three countries.[18] Some of the data are set out below in Table 4.1.

In the early 1970s 72–75 per cent of the *workers* supported the socialist parties and 60–69 per cent the Social Democrats in all three countries. Support for the left socialists is highest in Denmark, and the Danish Social Democrats gained a somewhat smaller portion of the worker's vote compared with the other countries. Support for the Social Democrats in the 1990s varies between 50 and 59 per cent in most elections in all three countries, but is somewhat larger in Sweden than in the two other countries. Since the early 1970s support has declined most in Norway (17 percentage points [pp.]) and somewhat less in Denmark and Sweden (9 pp.). The decline in support for the Social Democrats is to some extent compensated by increased support for the left socialists. Support for the leftist parties declines among workers from 72–75 to 65 per cent in Denmark and Sweden and 57 per cent in Norway from the early 1970s to the 1990s. Again the largest decline is found in Norway (14 versus 6–8 pp.).

The *employers* should be strongly inclined to support the Conservative parties in the Nordic context according to Rokkan's model. More broadly, we would expect employers to vote for all non-socialist parties since all these parties emphasise "bourgeois" politics with private enterprises and few economic regulations.

In the 1970s only around 40 per cent of the employers support the Conservative parties in the three countries. Nearly 90 per cent support the non-socialist parties in Denmark and about 75 per cent in Sweden and Norway. The employers' level of class voting for the core party is stable in Sweden, but fluctuates widely in Denmark and Norway. In Denmark the Agrarian Liberals gain more votes than the Conservatives among employers in the 1990s. In Norway the vote of the employers are spread across all the non-socialist parties.

In sum, the absolute level of class voting for the core party among employers is fairly low. In Denmark and Norway, support for the core party has declined considerably, and in Denmark, another party has taken over as the "class" party of the employers – the Agrarian Liberals. On the other hand, employer support for the non-socialist parties has declined only slowly.

We find a fairly similar pattern with regard to the *self-employed in the primary industries* (called farmers below) and voting for the core, Agrarian parties (not shown in the table). In the 1970s, 58–66 per cent supported the Agrarian parties. By the 1990s, support for the Agrarian parties varies widely across the countries, ranging from 73 per cent in Denmark and 63 per cent in Norway to 48 per cent in Sweden. Absolute class voting for the core among farmers has increased in Denmark (11 pp.), remained fairly stable in Norway and declined in Sweden (19 pp.).

The other non-socialist parties get most of the other votes of the farmers, which are fairly evenly distributed among the rightist parties (Conservatives and Radical Right) and other centrist parties. Only about 10 per cent support the leftist parties in Denmark and Sweden and about 20 per cent in Norway. There is no change over time in this respect.

THE VOTING BEHAVIOUR OF THE VARIOUS STRATA OF NON-MANUAL WORKERS
The other aspect of the model concerns the electoral struggles between the poles (Rokkan 1966: 92–105):

At the L-F *front*, the competition has been for the votes of the declining population of subsistence farmers, smallholders, and fishermen. At the F-B *front* it has been for votes of managers and professionals at the intersections of the primary and the secondary–tertiary sectors of the economies. Finally, at the L-B *front* competition has been for the votes of the rising middle class of salaried employees in the private and public sectors. Since the competition along the two first fronts has become less salient over time due to urbanisation and the decline of the primary sectors, we focus on the competition on the third front (L-B).

Rokkan's own discussion of the competition on this front is important and still relevant. His point of departure was the political interests and values of the new middle class which – according to Rokkan – were on the one hand demands for explicit recognition of training and experience in a system of differentiated economic rewards, and, on the other, the concern for long-term security through the provision of collective and compulsory pension schemes.

The first claim ran counter of the equalitarian ideology of the labour movement and the policy of severe progressive taxation. The second claim implied opposition to the ideology of individual self-reliance and the belief in a beneficent free enterprise economy so strongly entrenched among conservatives. To meet these claims from the new middle class, the socialists moved closer to the recognition of a hierarchical structure of reward and the conservatives closer to the acceptance of the principles of collective solidarity underlying the welfare state. The result was a softening of class appeals and a greater emphasis on the role of the state as an arbiter between economic interests in Nordic party politics.

In newer research about social class in advanced industrial societies, the so-called Erikson/Goldthorpe class schema is frequently used (Erikson and Goldthorpe 1992). In the analyses below we use a slightly modified version of this class schema. The new middle class is named "service class" in this scheme, and includes administrators and managers, employed professionals, higher-grade technicians and supervisors. It is divided into a higher and a lower tier according to administrative responsibility and qualifications. Not all white collar workers belong to the service class. The lower-tier non-manual employees are called routine non-manual workers and comprise largely clerical personnel, sales personnel and other rank-and-file employees in the service sector.

*Table 4.1 Party choice according to social class in the early 1970s and in the 1990s*

| Denmark 1971 | | | | | | | |
|---|---|---|---|---|---|---|---|
| | Workers | Routine non-man. | Lower-level service cl. | Higher-level service cl. | Employers | Farmers | All voters |
| Left soc. | 13,1 | 10,1 | 11,5 | 7,4 | 2,3 | 0,0 | 10,3 |
| Soc. democrats | 62,1 | 47,2 | 22,1 | 14,8 | 11,6 | 4,3 | 42,4 |
| Centrist p. | 9,9 | 20,8 | 26,2 | 18,5 | 25,6 | 21,3 | 17,5 |
| Agrarian Lib. | 9,9 | 8,2 | 16,4 | 25,9 | 20,9 | 66,0 | 15,9 |
| Conservative p. | 5,0 | 13,2 | 23,8 | 33,3 | 39,5 | 6,4 | 13,7 |
| Other p. | 0,0 | 0,6 | 0,0 | 0,0 | 0,0 | 2,1 | 0,3 |
| Sum | 100,0 | 100,0 | 100,0 | 100,0 | 100,0 | 100,0 | 100,0 |
| N | 282 | 159 | 122 | 27 | 43 | 47 | 680 |
| **Denmark 1990s** | | | | | | | |
| | Workers | Routine non-man. | Lower-level service cl. | Higher-level service cl. | Employers | Farmers | All voters |
| Left soc. | 11,8 | 14,2 | 17,5 | 16,6 | 7,9 | 0,7 | 13,9 |
| Soc. democrats | 53,5 | 35,6 | 29,4 | 18,4 | 16,8 | 5,4 | 34,8 |
| Centrist p. | 6,2 | 10,1 | 12,8 | 11,8 | 7,9 | 4,7 | 9,6 |
| Agrarian Lib. | 13,6 | 20,3 | 22,1 | 27,2 | 32,5 | 72,5 | 22,3 |
| Conservative p. | 6,1 | 12,3 | 14,1 | 22,9 | 25,0 | 9,4 | 12,8 |
| Progress p. | 8,4 | 7,1 | 3,8 | 2,8 | 9,3 | 7,4 | 6,3 |
| Other p. | 0,3 | 0,5 | 0,3 | 0,3 | 0,7 | 0,0 | 0,3 |
| Sum | 100,0 | 100,0 | 100,0 | 100,0 | 100,0 | 100,0 | 100,0 |
| N | 1174 | 1043 | 1253 | 397 | 280 | 149 | 4296 |

| Norway 1969 | | | | | | | |
|---|---|---|---|---|---|---|---|
| | Workers | Routine non-man. | Lower-level service cl. | Higher-level service cl. | Employers | Farmers | All voters |
| Left soc. | 4,4 | 4,3 | 4,6 | 0,0 | 1,6 | 1,0 | 3,4 |
| Soc. democrats | 68,8 | 48,6 | 27,6 | 33,8 | 25,0 | 17,3 | 48,5 |
| Centrist p. | 20,2 | 28,6 | 35,6 | 21,5 | 29,7 | 71,4 | 30,3 |
| Conservative p. | 5,2 | 18,6 | 32,2 | 43,1 | 43,8 | 10,2 | 17,0 |
| Other p. | 1,4 | 0,0 | 0,0 | 1,5 | 0,0 | 0,0 | 0,7 |
| Sum | 100,0 | 100,0 | 100,0 | 100,0 | 100,0 | 100,0 | 100,0 |
| N | 362 | 140 | 87 | 65 | 64 | 98 | 816 |

### 1990s

| | Workers | Routine non-man. | Lower-level service cl. | Higher-level service cl. | Employers | Farmers | All voters |
|---|---|---|---|---|---|---|---|
| Left soc. | 5,1 | 6,7 | 12,7 | 8,7 | 4,4 | 3,5 | 7,8 |
| Soc. democrats | 51,4 | 41,6 | 34,2 | 31,9 | 31,1 | 13,2 | 38,0 |
| Centrist p. | 25,8 | 29,9 | 24,3 | 21,8 | 28,5 | 77,8 | 28,5 |
| Conservative p. | 5,4 | 13,1 | 20,9 | 30,0 | 21,9 | 2,8 | 16,4 |
| Progress p. | 9,9 | 7,2 | 6,6 | 7,2 | 12,7 | 2,1 | 7,8 |
| Other p. | 2,3 | 1,4 | 1,3 | 0,8 | 1,3 | 0,7 | 1,5 |
| Sum | 100,0 | 100,0 | 100,0 | 100,0 | 100,0 | 100,0 | 100,0 |
| N | 644 | 639 | 748 | 473 | 228 | 144 | 2876 |

### Sweden 1970s

| | Workers | Routine non-man. | Lower-level service cl. | Higher-level service cl. | Employers | Farmers | All voters |
|---|---|---|---|---|---|---|---|
| Left soc. | 5,1 | 4,0 | 6,8 | 3,2 | 3,7 | 1,3 | 4,7 |
| Soc. democrats | 66,6 | 48,0 | 34,2 | 22,4 | 19,0 | 7,3 | 46,1 |
| Centrist p. | 23,3 | 32,8 | 36,1 | 35,9 | 35,5 | 71,4 | 32,3 |
| Conservative p. | 4,7 | 14,8 | 22,7 | 38,4 | 41,9 | 20,1 | 16,7 |
| Other p. | 0,2 | 0,4 | 0,1 | | | | 0,2 |
| Sum | 100,0 | 100,0 | 100,0 | 100,0 | 100,0 | 100,0 | 100,0 |
| N | 1741 | 1065 | 866 | 401 | 327 | 234 | 4634 |

### 1990s

| | Workers | Routine non-man. | Lower-level service cl. | Higher-level service cl. | Employers | Farmers | All voters |
|---|---|---|---|---|---|---|---|
| Left soc. | 7,5 | 9,4 | 7,4 | 4,3 | 3,3 | 1,9 | 7,0 |
| Soc. democrats | 58,0 | 42,8 | 38,1 | 28,3 | 17,9 | 3,1 | 40,7 |
| Centrist p. | 15,4 | 21,6 | 23,5 | 25,2 | 25,8 | 64,8 | 22,4 |
| Conservative p. | 10,8 | 17,7 | 23,1 | 33,8 | 43,7 | 21,6 | 21,6 |
| Environmental p. | 3,2 | 4,1 | 5,2 | 5,4 | 3,1 | 5,6 | 4,2 |
| New Democracy | 3,6 | 2,9 | 2,2 | 2,7 | 5,0 | 2,5 | 3,1 |
| Other p. | 1,5 | 1,5 | 0,5 | 0,3 | 1,1 | 0,6 | 1,0 |
| Sum | 100,0 | 100,0 | 100,0 | 100,0 | 100,0 | 100,0 | 100,0 |
| N | 1632 | 1427 | 1479 | 745 | 542 | 162 | 5987 |

The data from the 1990s are based on a cumulative file comprising all election surveys in the decade.

There has been a fairly large change in the size of the various social classes from the early 1970s to the late 1990s according to the election surveys. The three "old" classes have all together declined from about 55 per cent to 35 per cent. Workers comprised about 40 per cent of the population in the early 1970s and 25 per cent in the late 1990s; self-employed in the primary industries comprised 5–9 per cent in the early 1970s and only 2–4 per cent in the late 1990s. The proportion of employers remains fairly stable over time at 7–9 per cent. The non-manual groups (the service class and the routine non-manuals) have increased correspondingly from about 45 per cent to 65 per cent, the service class from 20 per cent to 40 per cent, while the routine non-manual group is fairly stable at 20–25 per cent.

Let us now examine how these non-manual strata voted in the early 1970s and how it changed to the 1990s.

Table 4.1 shows the relationship between social class and party choice in the 1970s and 1990s. For Denmark and Norway we show the relationship in the election survey before the 1973 earthquake elections in these countries. For Sweden, which had a more stable pattern for the 1970s, we have collapsed the data from two election surveys. Furthermore, the data from the 1990s are based on data from all election surveys in all three countries. We have collapsed the various centrist non-socialist parties[19] and also the various left socialist (and communist) forces. For Denmark, the Conservatives and the Agrarian Liberals are shown separately. Our aim here is to compare the three groups of non-manual workers with each other and with the employers.

In *Denmark* Table 4.1 shows that all the non-socialist party groups clearly gain most support from the higher-level service class in 1971. This is most pronounced for the Conservatives, less so for the Agrarian Liberals. The Social Democrats gain most support from workers, declining rapidly as we move up the hierarchy to the higher-level non-manual strata. The same applies, though to a much smaller extent, to the left socialists.

Comparing the early 1970s and the 1990s, we find the following changes: The left socialists gain strongest support among the two tiers of the service class and smallest support among workers in the 1990s. Support increases among the service class but remains stable among workers. We basically find the same pattern for the Social Democrats and the three groups of non-socialist parties as in the early 1970s, though the differences between the various employee classes have become smaller. This change is most pronounced for the Social Democrats and the Conservatives. The Agrarian Liberals gain more support than the Conservatives among the service class, but the increase from the early 1970s is fairly similar for all employee classes. The radical rightist parties (Progress Party and Danish People's Party) gain most support from workers and the two groups of employers, a pattern that remains basically unchanged since the emergence of the Radical Right in 1973.

In Norway, there are fairly small differences between the employee classes regarding support for the left socialists in 1969. Support for the Labour Party declines steeply as we move from workers to the service class, but is nevertheless considerable also among salaried occupations. The centrist parties have a surprisingly weak class profile among the employee classes while support for the Conservative Party rises steeply from workers to the higher level service class.

The changes that reached fruition in the 1990s can be summed up as follows. Left socialist support is highest among the service class, particularly among lower level service class workers. Worker and routine non-manual group support for the Labour Party declined, though it remained fairly stable among the service class. Support for the centrist parties is even less class based than in the late 1960s. Support for the Conservatives remains strongest among the (higher echelons of the) service class, but has nevertheless declined considerably in these strata. Support for the Radical Right is strongest among employers and workers and least strong among farmers.

Sweden imitates the two other countries in the 1970s, and the changes over time are also similar. A main difference is that the left socialists do not gain strongest support from the service class as in Denmark and Norway. In the 1980s, Sweden again largely duplicates the pattern of Denmark and Norway, but in the elections of 1994 and 1998, differences emerge with the left socialists enjoying their best election results in the period. It appears as if many workers defected from the social democrats to support the left socialists. On the other hand, the new Green Party found the service class most inclined to back it, and seemed to capture some of the new radicalism of this class.

In sum, Rokkan's model continues to provide a fruitful framework for analysing social classes and party choice, although some of its basic assumptions can be questioned. The assumption that most voters belong to the major classes of the poles and vote for their core party is less valid today than in the immediate post-war years, and the importance of the electoral struggle close to the F-pole has become less significant (as indeed Rokkan predicted it would). The model's focus on the increased importance of the service class and the political struggle along the L-B front is a fruitful point of departure for analysing political struggles and strategies related to social class, as the analysis above has illustrated.

TOTAL CLASS VOTING: THE ALFORD INDEX

The conventional way of measuring for class voting is by the Alford index. It is based on a much simpler model of class voting than the Rokkan modell, and has two dichotomised variables:

–   Party choice is dichotomized into socialist and non-socialist parties
–   The class variable is dichotomized into workers versus all other social classes

Class voting according to the Alford index is simply the proportion of workers who vote for the socialist parties minus the proportion of the other social classes who do the same. If, for example, 80 per cent of the workers and 40 per cent of the other social classes support the socialist parties, class voting would be 40 pp. according to the Alford index.

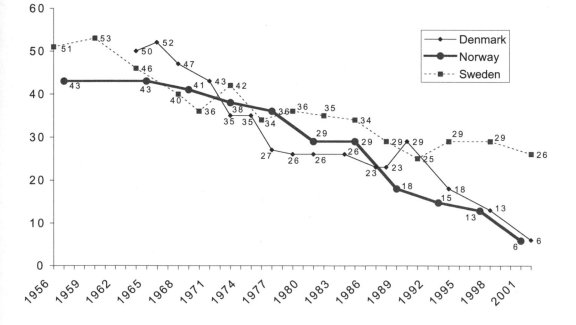

Figure 4.2 *Trends in class voting according to the Alford index in Denmark, Norway and Sweden, 1956-2002*

Figure 4.2 shows how class voting as defined by the Alford index declined fairly dramatically in the three countries and sums up many of the various tendencies shown in greater detail above. In sum, class voting was somewhat smaller in Norway in the 1950s and early 1960s than in Denmark and Sweden, fairly similar around 1970, but since the early 1980s it has been largest in Sweden. There is a sharp decline in class voting in Denmark and Norway from the mid 1980s, almost disappearing completely in the first election after 2000. By contrast, class voting shows a persistent pattern at 25–29 per cent in Sweden after the mid 1980s.

## New Structural Cleavages

### SECTOR EMPLOYMENT

There are two types of reasons why sector employment has developed into a considerable cleavage in the Nordic countries, and both are coupled to general and specific factors related to the Nordic welfare model (Knutsen 2001).

The varying extent to which own economic interests are linked to political decisions provides the most noticeable way of distinguishing employees in the public and the private sector. The public employee has a clear interest in substantial public budgets, a well-developed welfare state and market restrictions. A large public sector means more jobs, better career prospects and higher economic rewards. Many public sector employees have to deal with social problems in their work, something which is likely to create attitudes which favour social reforms and more public initiatives. Furthermore, the ethics of welfare occupations, coupled with professional norms about what is best for clients, often lead to focusing on a lack of resources and demands for stronger public intervention, fuelling a stronger public sector ideology as the result. Large numbers of middle-class public employees are recruited from educational institutions and educational backgrounds characterised by the values of a public sector ideology (professional training, the social sciences, etc.).

One could argue that the social democratic welfare state, with its much larger public sector than other advanced western European countries, generates its own political conflicts over the size of public budgets, and structural conflicts between public and private employees. It may be that sector is particularly important as a political cleavage in the Scandinavian countries.

The main pattern of sector employment influence on party choice is as follows. Public employees tend to support the socialist parties, especially the left socialist parties, more than private sector employees. Private sector employees, on the other hand, are more likely to support the Conservative and radical rightist parties than public sector workers. The impact of sector employment increases over time and is generally strongest in Denmark and weakest in Sweden. The sector cleavage increasingly follows the left–right division of parties.

Based on all electoral surveys for the various decades, we can sum up the details as follows.

In *Denmark*, sector differences in support for the socialist parties rise from 1 to 16 pp. between the 1970s and the 1990s; in *Norway* the increase is much smaller, from 7 to 8 pp. In Sweden, public employees tended to support the non-socialist parties in the 1970s (5 pp.), the reverse being the case in the 1990s (3 pp.). The likelihood that private employees support the rightist parties[20] increases from 6 to 18 pp. in Denmark, and 6 to 12 pp. in Norway. In *Sweden*, private sector workers were more likely to support the socialist parties in the 1970s (4 pp.), as against 7 pp. for the non-socialists in the 1990s.

In both Denmark and Norway the impact of sector employment on socialist/non-socialist voting in the 1990s approached that of social class. For example, class voting (according to the Alford index), was 20 pp. while sector differences for the socialist and rightist party groups were 16–18 pp. in Denmark in the 1990s. Similar figures for Norway are 14 and 8–12 pp.

The impact of sector is particularly important within the service class. It is in support for the rightist parties that we find the strongest sector differences in the service class, accompanied by large differences in support for the left socialist parties. The impact of sector increases within all classes but is particularly pronounced within the service class. The impact of sector within the service class can be illustrated by some of the data from the 1990s: In Denmark 28 per cent of the service class in the public sector supported the left socialists compared with 7 per cent in the private sector. Fifty-six per cent in the private sector and 26 per cent in the public sector support the rightist parties. In Norway the corresponding figures are 5 per cent and 17 per cent for the left socialists, and 44 per cent and 21 per cent for the rightist parties respectively. The Swedish figures are considerably smaller, but follow the same general direction.

Comparative research confirms that the considerable impact of sector is unique for the Nordic countries. The Nordic welfare state model creates an important new party cleavage (Knutsen forthcoming).

GENDER

Until the end of the 1960s, the political orientation of women was more conservative than men's. Comparative studies show that women were more in-

clined to vote for religious and conservative parties and less inclined to vote
for socialist parties than men. Differences tended to follow what could be
termed women's "traditional" values, i.e., the private concerns of religion,
home and family responsibilities. A further factor is that women have tended
to stand outside the trade unions and working-class culture, and have therefore had less reason to act collectively or in solidarity than men.

Twenty years ago, women in many western countries were more conservative than their male counterparts; today they are more radical. Researchers
speak in terms of a transformation from a traditional to a modern gender gap.

Gender has been weakly correlated with party choice compared with the traditional social cleavages, and the transition from traditional to modern gender
gap has followed slightly different paths in Denmark, Norway and Sweden.

In *Denmark*, there was hardly any sign of a traditional gender gap in the
1960s and early 1970s. What gender differences there were in voting behaviour
remained small and unsystematic (Borre and Andersen 1997: 182–184). By the
1977 general election, a modern gender gap had appeared where women tended to support the socialist parties and men the rightist parties. Nevertheless,
in the late 1970s and all through the 1980s this gender gap remained largely
insignificant (2–4 pp.). In the 1990s and in 2001 it has widened to 6–10 pp.

*Norway* does evince a traditional gender gap in the 1950s and 1960s. Women
tended then to support the Christian People's Party far more than men, who
supported the socialist parties. That said, this traditional gender gap was fairly
narrow, at about 5 pp. Women's support for the Christian People's Party has
been a fairly persistent trend over time, but the gender balance in support for
the socialist and rightist parties has changed in the wake of the transition to a
modern gender gap, and the transformed worldviews that fuelled it. The most
important change concerns support for the rightist parties. Since the 1970s,
men have consistently supported the rightist parties more than women; this
gender gap widens furthermore from 3 pp. in the 1970s to 6–8 pp. in the 1980s
and 1990s, peaking at 12 pp. in 2001. Women tend to support the socialist parties more than men, but this tendency is smaller and emerges later than the
former. It was first evident in 1985 and remained at 3–5 pp. until 2001, when it
reached 8 pp.

In *Sweden* gender differences in voting behaviour have been small. In the
1950s, 60s and 70s a small traditional gender gap can be detected. Women
tended to support the centrist parties (the Liberal Party in particular) while
men supported the socialist parties (Holmberg and Oscarsson 2004: 155–156).
Women's support for the centrist parties continues in the 1980s and 90s, and is

increasingly associated with the Christian Democrats. From the late 1970s men tend to support the rightist parties also in Sweden, as reflected in the 4–7 and 7–8 pps. of the 1980s and 90s respectively. There is no gender gap of significance in socialist support in Sweden in the 1980s and 90s; what gender gap there is stays mainly within the non-socialist camp.

In sum, the traditional gender gap was significant in Norway; less so in Sweden, and not at all in Denmark. The modern gender gap is found in all three countries in the 1980s and 1990s, but varies somewhat in strength.

In the Nordic countries the modern gender gap has been associated with the comparatively high level of female employment, especially in the public sector. Work outside the home gives women the experiential ammunition to question traditional gender roles. The fact that women are almost fully integrated into the labour market affects the way they vote more than any other factor, such as religious or traditional family values. Women's structural position in the public sector and in the lower non-manual strata may explain their leftist vote, though only the first of these appears to be have a significant effect. The public sector employs 55–60 per cent of all working women, compared with 30–35 per cent of all working men (Knutsen 2001: 317). A large slice of the modern gender gap is explained by the different sector location (Knutsen 2001: 338–344).

In addition to these explanations, political attitudes and generational replacement are important. Women are affiliating themselves with economic leftist and green values and political attitudes more than men. Such political values and attitudes straddle modern conflict lines and explain why women vote for leftist and green parties. The modern gender gap is also most pronounced among the post-war cohorts of voters (Oskarson 1995).

In sum, sector employment has become an important social cleavage in the Nordic countries, approaching the impact of social class in Denmark and Norway. The modern gender gap varies in strength and form in the three countries, and gender is considerably less important than sector employment as a social cleavage around 2000. Both sector employment and gender are important cleavages within the non-manual strata and the service class in particular.

## Value Based Conflicts/Cleavages

### POLITICAL VALUE ORIENTATIONS
Parallel to the discussion of structural dealignment or realignment, the impact of new political issues and value orientations for explaining party choice

has attracted considerable scholarly attention among political scientists. To grasp the role of value orientations, we would do well to remember that important value orientations underlay the conflict structure of industrial society. Christian values focus on the importance of Christian moral guidelines and principles in schools, society and politics. Economic left–right values refer in particular to the role of government in extending economic equality in society versus the need for economic incentives and efficiency. Such value orientations incorporate value conflicts related to control, power, and the degree of distribution of resources in the production sphere, and include workers' control and state regulation of the economy versus private enterprise, private property and the market economy; economic and social equality versus the need for differentiated rewards for stimulating effort (Knutsen 1995).

The moral value dimension and economic left–right value axis are often referred to as "Old Politics" inasmuch as they capture the essence of the lines of conflict of industrial society. In contrast, "New Politics" refers to value conflicts emerging from post-industrial society. More specifically, new politics-related value dimensions involve conflicts over a more modern set of issues related to, for instance, environmental quality, alternative life styles, social and political participation, minority rights and social equality.

There are, however, different ways of conceptualising the new politics value dimensions. According to Ronald Inglehart, value conflicts related to *materialist/post-materialist value orientations* reflect the new politics conflict dimension. Inglehart argues that "new" post-materialist values are deeply rooted and stand in opposition to more traditional materialist values. He identifies a "silent revolution", a gradual change along the materialist/post-materialist value dimension. The spread of post-materialist values is explained by generational replacement, the growth of the service class and the spread of higher education (Inglehart 1977: 1990).

Another way of conceptualising "New Politics" is by *environmental versus economic growth values*. Today, this conflict is firmly rooted in the public mind, and in many western European countries conflicts over environmental values seem to be the most manifest expression of the "New Politics" conflict. A clear manifestation of this is the emergence of green parties that have gained considerable electoral support in many western democracies.

Furthermore, Scott Flanagan has in a series of articles emphasised *libertarian/ authoritarian value orientations* as the central New Politics dimension. Authoritarian value orientation "designates a broader cluster of values, which, along with concerns for security and order, includes respect for authority, discipline and

dutifulness, patriotism and intolerance for minorities, conformity to customs" (Flanagan 1987: 1305). The libertarian/authoritarian value orientations
are also the central components in Herbert Kitschelt's (1994, 1995) important
work on changes in the party systems of Western democracies, in particular
the emergence of the Radical Right.

NEW POLITICS IN THE PARTY SYSTEMS IN THE NORDIC COUNTRIES
New politics have championed a new set of issues related to environmental
quality. Campaigns and protests have been launched against nuclear energy,
the construction of hydroelectric dams, the building of roads and highways,
degradation of fertile agricultural soil by expansion of cities and construction
of airports, and threats to human health through the spreading of fertilizers
and pesticides in farming. Certain aspects of the centralized bureaucratic welfare state and the hegemony of professional expertise in public policy and society have also come under fire. Post-materialist values have also revived issues
that remained dormant in the 1950s and early 60s. Disarmament, codeter-
mination in the workplace and social equality are three of them, reinterpreted
in terms of the new value perspective (Knutsen 1990). Since the mid 1980s immigration has loomed large in political debates, in particular in Denmark and
Norway.

The impact of New Politics has altered party polarisation, generally pitting
the New Left against the New Right. How is this reflected in the party systems
of the Nordic countries? Which parties articulate post-materialist, libertarian
or green values and which the authoritarian and growth values (Knutsen
1990)?

The left socialist parties in Denmark and Norway adopted green and libertarian issues in the 1960s and 70s, transforming themselves into New Left/New
Politics parties. Centrist parties, i.e., the liberal parties in the main, also pursued green issues in these countries. The Progress parties, which originally
placed themselves on the extreme right of the economic left–right dimension,
changed course in the mid 1980s, adopted New Right garments and a liking
for immigration issues and authoritarian and anti-green orientations.

The nuclear energy question in Sweden cut across the left–right spectrum.
The Agrarian Party and the Communist Left Party were against the programme; the other non-socialist parties (the Conservatives and the Liberals)
and the Social Democrats supported it. In the 1981 national referendum, the
anti-nuclear campaign lost. The failure of an established, anti-nuclear party,
the Agrarian Party, to effect any substantial change in Swedish nuclear energy

policy while part of the Government, was a major factor behind the establishment of the new Green Party in 1981. This party competes with the Left Party for the green and left-libertarian vote.

### THE IMPACT OF VALUES ON PARTY CHOICE

In a comprehensive analysis of the impact of Old and New Politics orientations on party choice, Knutsen and Kumlin (2003) use the two dimensions of Old Political orientations (economic left–right and Christian/secular values) and the two dimensions of New Politics orientations (ecology/growth and libertarian/authoritarian values) to examine trends in the strength of Old and New Politics and how voters for various parties are located on the various orientations.

In *Denmark* economic left–right values explain much of the party choice during the 1970s and 1980s. The impact of these values declines after the early 1980s. New politics orientations and libertarian/authoritarian values in particular impact increasingly on party choice, particularly in the late 1990s, and are already neck-and-neck with economic left–right orientations. In Denmark the new orientations are partly adding to the explanatory power of the old, and partly replacing the impact of the old. The variance which value orientations explains in the party choice variable grows from about 25 per cent in the 1970s to 40 per cent in the late 1990s.[21]

The Old Politics value orientations are most strongly correlated with party choice in the *Norwegian* electorate. The impact of economic left–right orientations declines steeply from the early 1980s to the late 1990s, but they remain the most closely correlated value orientations with party choice. The two New Politics orientations are also of significant importance, though their impact has remained unchanged since the early 1980s in absolute terms. Relatively, however, they have evidently gained in importance because the impact of the old politics orientations has been declining in recent decades. The impact of value orientations on party choice is large, though fluctuating in Norway, rising from about 30 per cent in the late 1960s to nearly 60 per cent in the early 1980s, and then dropping slowly to 43 per cent in the late 1990s due to the declining impact of Old Politics.

Economic left–right orientations figure prominently in explanations of party choice in *Sweden*. The impact of ecology/growth values nearly equal that of the economic left–right orientations around 1990, but later subsides relative to the economic left–right orientations. The impact of Christian values and libertarian/authoritarian values also declines somewhat after the 1991 election. The explanatory power of value orientations is 52 per cent in party choice around 1980, rising to 55 per cent in 1991, then tapering off to 48 per cent in 1998.

In sum, value orientations possess significant explanatory power when it comes to party choice. They have a much larger impact than social structure variables in all three countries. Apart from the Danish pattern in the late 1990s and 2001 (Borre 2003), the Old Politics orientations and the economic left–right values are still the most important, but New Politics orientations also play an important role in determining the vote.

## Conclusion

The voting behaviour of the Nordic voters has been largely determined by functional-economic cleavages – also in a wider comparative setting. Their significance has diminished due to changes in the size of the social classes located at the poles in Rokkan's model, and to electoral dealignment. Class politics and political strategies have increasingly centred on gaining the votes of the various strata within the non-manual groups. Sector employment followed by gender have generated new, significant social cleavages, in particular within the non-manual strata.

The influence of social class on party choice has also undergone changes, and is probably most clearly at work in the altered class make-up in support for the Radical Right, the socialist left and green forces. The Radical Right is usurping increasing support from workers, while the socialist left is winning support among the service class. This is a new type of "class voting", and is not captured by conventional indictors of class voting.

Value orientations have become increasingly important for voters' party choice, although it has not been a linear progression. Old Politics values and, in particular, economic left–right values, remain very influential. Only in Denmark have New Politics orientations become equally important for determining the vote. The large and persistent impact of economic left–right orientations helps explain the fact that the old class parties still gain most of the votes at elections. These orientations are the value equivalent of the structural labour market cleavage. The strong and fairly stable impact of these "class" values explains in part why the old parties continue to dominate despite wide-ranging class dealignment.

# Chapter 5: Civic Society in Transition

*Per Selle and Tommy Tranvik*

Scandinavian politics have been characterized by high levels of institutional centralization and state friendliness (Kuhnle and Selle 1992). It is, for instance, the state – rather than markets, religious institutions or local community associations – that has been the paramount agent of social and economic reform, most notably the development of comprehensive welfare schemes and the system of corporative economic planning (where the state is the most important participant). It is therefore tempting, especially, perhaps, for political scientists of Anglo-American origin, to conclude that, in the Scandinavian countries, there is too much trust in, and too much dependence upon, the state bureaucracy, while, at the same time, too few checks and balances limiting the scope of state power. Even if it is hard to brush off these (and similar) criticisms of "the Scandinavian polity" as misguided, they tend nevertheless to be informed by a relatively simplistic view of democracy, the so-called protective model (Held 1996).

According to this model, institutional centralization and state friendliness are at odds with the notion of democracy because democracy works only when power is decentralized, when citizens are legally protected from being interfered with by the "tentacles of the state" and when everyone is free to carry out his or her own life plans as they see fit. The challenge of democracy, as viewed through the lenses of the protective model, is therefore to constrain the exercise of state power. In Scandinavia, however, the democratic challenge is perceived rather differently. Institutional centralization is not a problem, it has been reasoned, so long as there are ways ordinary citizens can influence the exercise of state power. State friendliness, it is further argued, is the clearest manifestation of the democratization of centralized state power: citizens view the state in a benign light because they are thoroughly plugged into – through ideological mass movements – the running of the state (Wollebæk and Selle

2002). It is this social contract – high levels of institutional centralization balanced by high levels of citizen control – that is now being eroded (Tranvik and Selle 2003, 2004).

What the transformations are all about, we propose, is the attempt to design so-called flexible forms of organization. Flexible organizations can be described in terms of three key features. First, these organizations have a flat hierarchical structure, which means more direct contact between the top and bottom of the hierarchies. Second, they operate with shorter time frames, meaning that flat organizations are meant to work faster and (hopefully) better than before. The third feature is increasing centralization of power, that is, leaders are granted more authority in the running of the organization's activities. The result is not only centralization within organizations or institutions, but also across scale levels, i.e. geographic centralization.

Since we have much better data on Norway than the other Scandinavian countries, this is mainly an article about Norway. However, we use the term "Scandinavian" when we address more common features; in general we believe that much of what is going on in Norway is also to be found in the other Scandinavian countries. First, we review the size, composition and revenue structure of the contemporary voluntary sector, comparing Norway with the rest of Scandinavia and other EU countries. We proceed to give a short and oversimplified presentation of the traditional organizational features of Norwegian civic (and political) participation (ca. 1880–1980), before discussing the new forms of civic participation (ca. 1980 to the present), focusing on the likely democratic consequences of these changes. In the conclusion we comment on the political and social consequences of the decline we have traced in the democratic infrastructure and ask whether Norwegian and Scandinavian associational exceptionalism is increasingly something of the past.

## Size, Composition and Revenue Structure[22]

In a comparative perspective the contemporary Norwegian voluntary sector is relatively small, viewed in employment and economic terms. Including religion, the Norwegian voluntary sector had operating expenditures amounting to 3.7 per cent of the country's gross domestic product. The paid workforce behind these expenditures equals 3.9 per cent of all nonagricultural employees in the country. In comparison, the EU countries[23] had an average of 7 per cent, ranging from Finland with 3.1 per cent to the Netherlands with 12.7 per cent.

Even if the number of paid jobs is small in a European perspective, the Norwegian voluntary sector disposes considerable resources in terms of volunteer inputs. Indeed, as much as half the Norwegian population reports to contribute of their time to voluntary organizations over one year. This translates into 6.8 per cent of total nonagricultural employment in the country, compared to an average of just 4.2 per cent in the EU countries. This brings the total of volunteer and paid employment in Norway up to 10.7 per cent of total employment, which is close to Sweden with 12.1 per cent and EU average of 11.2 per cent, ranging from Austria with 5.9 per cent to the Netherlands with 19.4 per cent.

Norway's employment rate is higher than most other European countries' due to high rates of female employment. Measuring the size of the voluntary sector as a percentage of total employment disguises the fact that Norwegians are very active in voluntary organizations. An alternative would be to use volunteer employment in relation to population as a measure. This shows that volunteering in Norway equals 26 fulltime employees per 1,000 inhabitants, whereas the EU average is 20, ranging from Austria with just 5 to UK and the Netherlands with 28 fulltime employees per 1,000 inhabitants. Measured in this way, the volunteering of the Norwegian population in voluntary organizations is among the largest in the world.

In addition to volunteering extensively, Norwegians share an even higher propensity to join organizations as members. The total number of memberships in Norway is estimated to 8.4 million, which equals almost two per inhabitant. Thirty-six per cent of memberships are in cultural and recreational organizations. Professional associations (21 %), development and housing (13 %), health (12 %) and civic and advocacy activities (6 %) and religion (4 %) comprise the bulk of the remaining memberships. According to the Survey on Giving and Volunteering (1998), 73 per cent of the population were members of an organization, and 43 per cent held two or more memberships (Wollebæk et al 2000). In comparative surveys, Norway ranks among the countries with the highest proportion of members in the population (Dekker and van den Broek 1998).

Although the majority of these members are passive, volunteering is inextricably linked to the status as a member. Many do not volunteer, but very few volunteers are not members. The membership institutionalizes the relationship between the organization and the volunteer, provides her with democratic rights and strengthens the affective bonds to the association (Wollebæk et al. 2000, 175–176). The extensive number of memberships means, firstly, that the pool of resources from which organizations can draw is larger in Norway than in most other countries. Many members drift in and out of more or less active roles, and express willingness to take part actively when needed (Wollebæk et al. 2000: 84). Thus, extensive membership contributes to explaining high levels of volunteering. Second, the importance of the membership at least partially explains the relatively minor extent of private donations in Norway. The membership fees paid by passive members are very important for the organizations, in some respects they are a functional equivalent of the monetary private donations found in countries with a weaker membership tradition (e.g. the US).

When volunteers are added to paid work, it is not only the scale of the sector that changes. What we see is a dramatic shift towards culture and recreation, rising from 12 to 37 per cent, making it by far the largest category. As a matter of fact, more than half of all volunteering in the sector takes place here. It indicates something of the regard in which sports and cultural organizations are held in the Norwegian population. The categories development, religion, and environment, and advocacy also gain their share. However, welfare services and professional organizations have insignificant shares of volunteering.

Of all the work done in the Norwegian not-for-profit sector, 64 per cent is voluntary work. This is one of the highest rates of all the countries in the CNP project, only second to Sweden with 78 per cent (Western European average is 42 per cent, with Finland at 53 per cent). In culture and recreation, environment, community development, and civic and advocacy, more than 80 per cent of the work is done by volunteers.

The Norwegian voluntary sector is more economically self-sustained than the EU average. As much as 56 per cent of the revenue comes from fees and charges, of which sales and membership dues each account for around 21 per cent of the total. In Sweden and Finland, the revenues from fees and charges are 60 and 57 per cent, compared to just 38 per cent in the other EU countries. Private donations in Norway are 9 per cent of total revenue. The average of the EU countries is 7 per cent, ranging from Germany and the Netherlands with 3 per cent, to the UK with 11. Sweden and Finland have 12 and 7 per cent respectively. This means that private donations in Norway are on a level between top and average of the EU-countries.

Furthermore, only 35 per cent of the revenue of the voluntary sector in Norway comes from the public sector, compared to 55 per cent in the EU countries. In Sweden and Finland, the corresponding figures are 29 and 36 per cent. The other EU countries range from Ireland with 75 to the UK with 45 per cent. This means that the share of public funding in all Nordic countries is lower than in all of the selected EU countries. In fact, it is even lower than in the liberal UK. This is not in accordance with the conventional image of the voluntary sectors in the social democratic Nordic countries as highly dependent on the public sector.

To explain the low level of revenue from public sources, we have to take a look at the differences in revenue structure across the subfields of the voluntary sector. We find that public sector income is dominant in welfare services: health, social services, and education. Private donations are negligible in these subfields, whereas fees and charges constitute 14 per cent in health, 32 in social services, and 46 per cent in education. In the latter category, higher, adult, and continuing education, and research activities are rather self-sustained subfields with between 50 and 65 per cent of revenues from fees and charges, whereas primary and secondary education is more reliant on public funding.

The differences in revenue structure across the subfields can explain some characteristic features. In welfare services, public sector is a dominant source of income in Norway as it is in the EU countries (Helander and Sivesind 2001). Public sector has the main responsibility for funding and supervision of essential services not only in Scandinavia, but also in other European welfare countries. The low level of public income of the Norwegian voluntary sector is fundamentally related to the welfare services' smaller share, in comparison with the EU countries. In other words, the make-up and role of the voluntary sector in Norway and Scandinavia differ from those of most EU countries.

If we look at membership subcategories organization fees and charges dominate in most cases. In professional and development organizations membership dues are the largest sources of revenue. In environment, culture and recreation, and civic and advocacy, sales income represents a larger part of the fees and charges than membership dues. International and religious organizations, where donations reach sizable proportions, are the only subcategories with more or less balanced rates of income from earnings, donations and government.

This distribution of income results from the way Norwegians participate in membership organizations. First, donating is one major way to help religious and international organizations. Second, in the remaining membership organizations, the incidence of membership dues and, in many cases, passive membership is relatively high. Third, substantial income is generated by sales in environment, culture and recreation sectors, and the civic and advocacy sector.

To paint a more detailed picture of the exceptionalism of the Norwegian and Scandinavian voluntary sector and understand why it differs from the rest of Europe (and the US), we need to put it in its historical context. How did the sector acquire its specific structure and how and why did the changes come about? What are the social and democratic consequences of these changes?

## Associational Exceptionalism 1880–1980[24]

### THE INTEGRATIVE ORGANIZATIONAL MODEL

Contrary to most other Western European countries, Norway and the rest of Scandinavia for a long time did not develop a two-tiered civil society, i.e. one set of organizations on the local level, a different set on the national level, and few (if any) institutionalized channels for inter-level communication. The first exceptional feature of historical Scandinavian associationalism, therefore, is strong vertical (local-to-national) integration. Even if there always were some local associations with little apparent interest in joining regional and national organizations, and some national associations that lacked a dense network of regional and local chapters, it was the exception, not the rule. The arrangement gave local and regional chapters a large measure of autonomy despite being nominally subordinate to a central office. Hence, hierarchical subordination in combination with organizational decentralization were the structural characteristics that made Scandinavian associationalism in general, and Norway's in particular, different from what we find on the continent (and, to some extent, in North America). And since these vertically structured associations were membership based, democratically governed and ideologically motivated, they were concerned with the welfare of society rather than with promoting narrow, special-interest issues. Consequently, the historically significant associations – the peasant movement, the labour movement, the prohibition movement, the Christian laymen's movement, the movement for New Norwegian, social and humanitarian movements, and, somewhat later, the sports movement – reached out and touched people wherever they lived, turning passive subjects into full-blown citizens.

The second exceptional feature of Scandinavian associationalism – a feature that is probably more pronounced in Norway than in, for instance, Sweden and Denmark – is horizontal integration: as civil society organizations became an integral part of the state machinery the members of these organizations exercised a fair amount of indirect control over central government decision-making (Kuhnle and Selle 1992, Tranvik and Selle 2003). Tight horizontal integration – what is referred to as corporative pluralism (Rokkan 1966) – must, in the Norwegian case, be explained by a rather weak state, an even weaker market, and no landed gentry. The decisive social and political mobilization proc-

esses that shaped the political system, arose during the period of nation building and democratisation in the second half of the nineteenth century.

The resulting Norwegian hierarchical order features three key aspects that
sit uncomfortably with the structure of the flexible organization. First, the
time frame was one of historical continuity; Norwegian-ness rests essentially
in the idea of the periphery's popular traditionalism rather than the centre's
avant-garde, elitist culture. Second, the ideological legitimacy of the periphery
led to a relatively wide distribution of powers; in Norway, the geographical
area around the capital was never the centre of dominant political, cultural or
economic powers that it was in, for example, Sweden and Denmark. And
third, in a mountainous country where the peripheries look with suspicion on
the centre, and where human habitation is few and far between, the nurturing
of intermediaries was crucial to maintain political unity. All this had direct
consequences for the structure of civil society.

A traditionally weak state created a vacancy for partners for the nation planners in Oslo to build a modern industrial state, able to fend for itself in a competitive international environment. What state there was, was just not strong
enough to embark on such an ambitious enterprise by itself: it lacked the necessary economic resources and manpower. But there were not that many very
suitable partners around. The lack of a landed aristocracy precluded nation
building based on agrarian militarism, the Eastern European route (which, incidentally, sets Norwegian and Swedish nation-building processes apart). And
the small, capital-starved domestic market more or less ruled out the Western
European route, i.e., nation building based on urban trade and commerce
(Denmark followed the Western European road to a greater extent than any of
the other Scandinavian countries). For Norway, therefore, the most realistic av-
enue was for the state establishment to join forces with the emerging mass
movements that commanded the loyalty of an ever-increasing number of citizens. According to the marriage agreement, the two parties committed themselves to institutional centralization, as the state establishment wanted, in exchange for citizen control over the centralization process, as the mass
movements were looking for. The marriage, however, was not without its fric-
tions and skirmishes. Dissension reached an all-time high in the struggle over
parliamentarism in the early 1880s. The state establishment was forced to give
in, and a loose alliance of periphery groups – the spearheads of Norwegian associational life – gained power. And by putting one hand on the state machinery's
wheel, and a foot on the pedals, horizontal integration spelled state friendliness
– the conviction that the centralized state could not do much of significance

without the explicit support of "our" organizations. This conviction was underpinned by organizational autonomy, i.e. that neither the state nor the market would interfere with how the associations conducted their internal affairs.

So, to summarize thus far, historical Norwegian associationalism was characterized by vertical integration across scale levels (from the local via the regional to the national level) and by horizontal integration at all levels (civic organizations influenced decisions made by local, regional and national authorities). An important consequence of this horizontal integration – or co-optation as some have it (Dryzek et al, 2003) – is the failure of the Norwegian voluntary sector to develop a collective identity as a moral force outside, and partly in opposition to the state, constituting a self-understanding as a sector in its own right. Because of the close connections and collaboration with a segmented state,[25] the voluntary field itself was piecemeal, lacking effective interorganizational or cross-sectoral contacts and facilities (Sivesind et al 2002). Another important consequence of state–voluntary sector collaboration is the absence in Norway of powerful sub-political groups autonomous of the state since the institutionalization of the welfare state (Grendstad et al, 2004; Dryzak et al 2003).

This system worked because the popular movements espoused an ideological outlook that encouraged patience and optimism: associational engagement was a political investment that, if it did not pay off immediately, would bear fruits if the members (and their elected leaders) stayed around long enough and campaigned hard enough. In the end, public authorities would be forced to pay attention to their rightful concerns – a feeling strengthened by the associations' relative autonomy in relation to the state and the market. Vertical and horizontal integration, moreover, foreclosed widespread political marginalization – all social groups of importance and from all corners of the country had a chance to make their voices heard.

THE GROWTH OF LEISURE ORGANIZATIONS AND THE DECLINE OF IDEOLOGICAL SOCIAL MOVEMENTS

The organizational landscape that took shape around 1900, which represented the core of Norwegian associationalism, remained largely in place to about 1980. In particular, the gradual emergence of a national social policy from the inter-war period, the reconstruction work after the Second World War and Keynesian economic planning from the end of the war till the early 1980s, contributed to the close horizontal integration between the state and the voluntary sector. Stability and continuity notwithstanding, new trends also emerged over the latter part of this period. Here we are talking about the leisure associationalism that expanded and matured during the 1960s and the 1970s. Leisure associationalism is important because it gives a foretaste of the profound structural changes that were yet to come.

The growth of leisure associationalism was obviously conditioned by the rise of a leisure class with (a) plenty of spare time on their hands and (b) more money in their wallets than was needed to feed a hungry family. In the leisure society, therefore, "time off" – waking-hours not occupied by work – becomes a social category of its own. And during "time off", we pay scant attention to Protestant ethics: indulgence or meaningful recreation being usually the spirit of leisure. But, to begin with, filling the void of "time off" – engaging in organizations founded on singing, music or sports or exploring the attractions of various hobby clubs – was viewed as an integral part of public life: a good citizen devoted some of his or her leisure time to these new types of organizations. Especially organizations for children – financed and regulated by the state – were supposed to serve as mechanisms for socialization and national integration. At the same time, women started joining traditionally male-dominated organizations, turning their backs on the social and humanitarian movements (Wollebæk and Selle 2004). As leisure associationalism proliferated – particularly with organizations for children and adolescents and the new patterns of female engagement – civil society became much more dense and more differentiated, even in quite small communities. What seems characteristic of leisure civicness, then, is greater organizational fragmentation and less autonomy in relation to their general environments and less influence towards the state. Furthermore, the leisure organizations had few ties to the popular mass-movements that, by this time, showed clear signs of old age: Religious organizations, for instance, or the prohibition movement, had stagnated and were heading for a full-scale membership crisis, accompanied by a sharp drop in organized activities (Wollebæk and Selle 2003).

These, and a number of other ideology-based mass movements, were out of touch in the new leisure society, where civic participation reached closer than ever to people's homes. The leisure zone, we could say, was also a politics free and public duty free zone (politics, like work, is associated with the public sphere, while leisure is generally connected with our private lives). Increasingly, organized activities had to provide a sense of individual fulfilment, or satisfy special interests (as the special purpose hobby clubs did), while the long-termism of ideologically motivated engagement gradually went out of fashion. The history of public spirited associationalism was, in other words, in the process of being usurped by the hyped up individualistic spirit of late twentieth-century society. This, in fairly simplified and condensed terms, seems to have been the state of the Norwegian civic sphere as modern-day globalization entered the stage.

Current developments in the voluntary sector (and within local government) must be seen in light of current globalization and accompanying rise of the neo-liberal New Public Management ideology (Christensen and Lægreid 2001, see also Chapter 2 in this volume). Because this ideology is changing the quality of the relationship of the state to other sectors, we see more clearly the difference between the "old" system of state–sector cooperation, based on close integration and mutual trust, and the new "contract culture" with its focus on competition, time-limited contracts, legal control and accountability (Eikaas and Selle 2002). How has the voluntary sector responded to these sweeping structural changes?

## 1980s-: The Decline of the Democratic Infrastructure

### DISLOCATED CIVICNESS
Originally, and in spite of the formal hierarchical-bureaucratic structure of the traditional mass movements, the local was the most important level. It was here that most of the organizational activity took place and it was here that the mobilization potential was found. Local groups enjoyed autonomy within the bureaucratic system of which they were part, though it goes without saying that autonomy was greater in some movements than in others. It was exactly because of this system Norway and to a certain extent the rest of Scandinavia developed geographically and socially an integrating society of organizations. Elsewhere in Europe, organizational society was often split in two with some organizations existing only locally, others only nationally. In Norway, such a division would have been virtually unthinkable: after all, how could there be political influence without the organization's roots being firmly planted in the native soil from which, according to Romantic notions, the nation grew, remote rural communities deep in the mountain valleys and fjords and along the North Sea coast?

It was this combination of ideological orientation and hierarchical integration that crosscut the centre-periphery cleavage and produced, vitally, the hallmarks of optimism and patience mentioned above. For the organizations, optimism meant a belief that organizational participation and involvement could change society for the better, while patience meant a conviction that efforts for social change would ultimately bear fruit in spite of periodical failure,

which was to be expected. The historic mass movements provided stable channels of communication with the political centre for provincial local communities, and thus gave form and content to Norwegian democracy.

It is precisely this democratic infrastructure that is currently facing increasing pressure from new, flexible organizational forms. It started around the
mid 1960s with a sudden rise in the numbers of locally based organizations,
especially in the field of culture and recreation. Many of these had neither national nor political objectives to speak of. Gradually, therefore, the integrated
local–national organizations that had stamped society were under threat from
the dual model; i.e. one organization society at the local level and another and
very different one at the national level. At the same time, a process of localized
centralization impacted on associational life. Small communities lost many of
their functions and institutions (e.g. school, post office, local store), and im-
proved communication infrastructures facilitated better and faster contact between small communities and municipal centres. Thus, organizational identity became less tied to the rural community (Wollebæk and Selle 2002).

Despite these developments, the historical organizations did not disappear.
In 1980, the vast majority of local organizations were still part of bigger, dem-
ocratic-hierarchical structures. But their hegemony was being eroded, slowly
at first, but increasingly rapidly during the 1990s. Among the newest organizations, i.e. from the 1990s, only a minority had connections with overarching
national networks (Wollebæk and Selle 2002). The result is to undermine the
role of voluntary associations as identity-creating institutions, with participation becoming more random and short-term. Increasingly, volunteering takes
place outside the membership institution, as the ties between volunteer and
organization are severed.

The changes were, on the one hand, structural and functional, in the sense
that new objectives could more rationally be achieved by new means. But
these were accompanied by a cognitive shift: views of how to organize became
increasingly differentiated – several competing ways of structuring associations were made available to organizational entrepreneurs.

Smaller and faster-moving associations that are not overtly political or
rooted in traditional social solidarities, are producing a form of civil society
that reflects the features of flexibility. First, as organizational hierarchies are
flattened out, new associations lose the capacity to integrate across the centre-
periphery division. Because, the channels of communication or influence between national and local levels are either absent or extremely weak, more and
more people are less and less part of the process by which the state exercises

power: organizational society is increasingly unable to bring the needs and wishes of ordinary citizens out of the local community into the national arena. At the same time, it becomes difficult to gain popular acceptance for decisions made centrally, because support for, or opposition to, public policies are usually ad hoc, media-driven and fragmented.

Second, a shorter time frame means that organizational activity must be tailored to the members' particular needs or interests. This coincides with the decline of ideology: the belief that voluntary involvement can bring about social change is losing out to the idea that the individual must get some personal fulfilment and satisfaction from his or her participation. If participation is not sufficiently suited to individual needs, the members rapidly drop out. Ideological optimism and patience are thus not resources that the flexible organizational society fosters.

Third, the shortened time frame seems to lead to increased centralization of power and professionalization. As members avoid administrative work, help must be hired in to keep up the level of activity, which means that organizations are more dependent on public or private sponsors to finance the hiring of outside expertise. But dependence on sponsors leads to a less autonomous organization, as external funding is often tied to conditions regarding how the funds are to be spent. This, in turn, means that a flexible civil society is less able to function as a political and ideological counterpart to the state and the market. And, of course, professionalization and more external monitoring concentrate power at the centre: ordinary members have less say in what the organization does, the leadership more. That said, leadership influence is also largely a result of the weak identification of the members with their organization.

Fewer hierarchical layers and organizational divisions, shorter time frames for membership and participation, and greater centralization of power and professionalization tell us something about changes in the relationship between centre and periphery in Norwegian politics (changes we think are more extensive in Norway than elsewhere in Scandinavia). If the traditional organizational society assumed the form it did as a result of the large part played by the periphery in the nation-building project, then it is also likely that flexible associationalism's break with traditional organizational structures is indicative of a decline in the periphery's political clout. And when the cultural balance between centre and periphery is shifting in favour of the former, organizations can be scaled back and made more flexible: after all, in this situation they do not need to build up large-scale democratic-bureaucratic structures to mobilize support or gain popular legitimacy. The political influence and legitimacy of flexible organizations are, in other words, not dependent on their presence in the periphery, but become more dependent on the quality of full or part-time staffers, and their ability to stage events that titillate the curiosity of the mass media. Let us take a closer look into this important transformation of our democratic infrastructure.

## THE NEW ORGANIZATIONAL TYPE

The changes civil society has undergone over the last 20 years represent the definitive break with the traditional mass–movement approach to popular action. Broad-based memberships, local/national integration and organizational democracy are not things Norwegians typically opt for – the mass movement has lost most of its attraction as a cognitive model of reference. Instead, we have seen the rise of a new organizational type whose overall logic is the rapid satisfaction of immediately felt needs and wishes, i.e. an extreme type of member-focused associationalism. The strong focus on members/supporters and the satisfaction of their needs and wishes seems to be a result of the sharply reduced time horizon compared to the mass–movements of old. Rather than ideologically inspired optimism and patience, qualities that tended to foster loyalty and give a voice to the people, these organizations dance to a much faster tune: if personal satisfaction or sense of individual fulfilment is delayed, members' sense of loyalty to the association will be jeopardised, and they will either withdraw from voluntary work altogether or turn to organizations that are better at giving the members what they want – exit over loyalty and voice. This is clearly evident in the increased turnover rates of organizations and individual membership (Wollebæk and Selle 2002). A final note, the shortening of the time horizon has great implications for the relationship between members and leaders; vertical integration across scale-levels; and the horizontal integration across sectors (the civic sphere, the state and the market).

For civic participation to be experienced as personally fulfilling, there must be a direct relationship between members and leaders. It is, after all, the decisions of the leadership – what to do or not to do – that determine an organization's ability to satisfy the needs and wishes of its members, and, therefore, the short and long-term success of the organization. For this to happen, there must be as few levels of bureaucracy as possible between the leadership and the rank and file: when time is of the essence, intermediaries must go. Consequently, power and resources that once were held, and decisions that were once made, by intermediate officials tend to migrate towards the top leadership. Centralization of control is also aided by the marginal involvement of members in administrative work. As personal fulfilment becomes one of the most important reasons for civic engagement, action is more telling than planning. It is the excitement of civic role enactment, and not the dullness of making things happen, that seems to be perceived as the real value of voluntary participation. Members, therefore, tend to withdraw from administrative planning processes, and are happy to leave this kind of work to full or part-time staffers (Wollebæk et al 2000, Wollebæk and Selle 2002). This means that flatter hierarchies lead to centralization of control through the professionalization of administrative work, as confirmed by the increased frequency of board meetings and decreased frequency of membership meetings within the organizational society (Wollebæk and Selle 2002).

The new organizational types are particularly numerous at the local – or community – level. They do not, however, represent local community solidarities, cultures or identities, but community-independent leisure, hobby and other close-to-home interests. Since many of the real-timers are locally oriented, they do not usually join forces for the local good. It is apparent in the fall in collaboration among voluntary organizations over the last 20 years (Wollebæk and Selle 2002). Nor do they attempt to join or form regional and national umbrella organizations. On the national level, the best example is the increasing number of social or health-related self-help associations. Here we also find a new type of hybrid organization – national associations that encourage the spinning-off of specialised, professionalized and other more or less autonomous sub-units. Increasingly, national-level organizations choose not to be membership based and democratically governed, because, according to their spokespersons, this would divert resources from campaigning or lobbying to "endless internal debates about goals, methods and strategies". The environmental movement has been particularly prone to developments like this (Grendstad et. al 2004). What seems to emerge, then, is that the vertically integrated system of interest representation is gradually coming apart. While the hierarchical and bureaucratic mass movements proved successful in linking local concerns to national decision-making (and in convincing members to accept the outcome), the growth of the new associations signals the bifurcation of civil society with one type of association operating on the local level, and the other type at the national level, with few (if any) reliable and permanent systems that enable cross-level communication. Over time, bifurcation may well increase the institutional and cognitive distance of ordinary citizens to central state powers, causing greater political alienation and instability than Norwegians have been used to.

A bifurcated civil society also means a considerably more fragmented sphere of voluntary action than before.[26] As noted earlier, the rise of leisure associationalism during the 1960s, started the first wave of organizational differentiation: the proliferation, although rather tentative, of relatively small special-interest organizations. This trend has gained momentum over the last 20 years or so. These organizations, it seems, have heeded the call of neo-liberal globalization – it is better to be nimble and fast-moving than bureaucratic and slow. Unfortunately, however, speed and flexibility come at a price: loss of autonomy. The historic mass movements may have been bureaucratic and slow, but they did not let themselves get caught up in encroaching external dependencies, most notably, corporate or state sponsorships.[27] Sure, many mass movements received financial support from the state, but as long as they enjoyed wide-ranging popular backing and it was part of the political culture never to interfere in internal organizational processes, their autonomy was never in question. Tight horizontal integration between mass movements and state institutions did not prove to be a significant threat to their autonomy either. Rather than the state taking over the mass movements, it was the mass-movements that (in some policy areas, at least) "took over" the state.[28] For the new organizational type, on the other hand, a different story is unfolding.

Particularly at the national level the new type of association is small in terms of popular support (including the new social movements), while, at the same time, being large in terms of the resources needed to keep them afloat (relative to the number of members). These organizations are not financially viable without external backing,[29] as they are quite simply unable to raise enough money themselves to pay for higher levels of centralization and professionalization. (Of course, organizations who do not have members at all, rely entirely on external sources.) Instead, they either turn to corporate sponsors or local/state authorities (or both) in search of financial aid. It creates a new type of horizontal integration, but now without much autonomy, and is further encouraged by a government increasingly disenchanted with unconditional support and increasingly enamoured of project support. The point is that external funding comes with judicially binding rules and regulations – stipulating, for instance, what the money can be used for or how activities should be organized – and new administrative procedures for documenting and reporting that the money was spent as agreed: there is less trust, more control, in other words. There are close ties here with the implementation of

NPM principles and increased use of "contracting"; some of the new organizations are increasingly becoming a service-producing branch of the state, since they tend to get funding for carrying out specific public service-related tasks or responsibilities, often in cooperation with public institutions and/or market actors. This is so even in the cases where the organizations also play an important part in defining such projects. Contrary to the traditional mass movement, therefore, these new organizations are about to be "taken over" by the state rather than seeking to influence state policies, i.e. less autonomy and more co-optation, or they become increasingly irrelevant to the state system.

Hence, a rapidly expanding part of the voluntary sector – which was supposed to be an arena where concerns were given voice and representations made, independent of the state and the market – is unsustainable without generous handouts from businesses or the state budget. In a democratic perspective, it is probably particularly worrying in unitary states, because there are usually fewer centres of alternative influence available to the citizens than in federal systems. And the absence of strong sub-political groups only reinforces the problem.

## Conclusion

The Scandinavian voluntary sector is small in terms of the numbers of people it employs, but it is large when volunteering is considered, in particular in relation to the size of the population. Volunteering can often substitute for paid employment in voluntary organizations. The fact that the voluntary sector in Norway and the rest of Scandinavia is small in terms of paid employment is therefore not just a reflection of a large public sector. It is also a consequence of the strength of the social movement and culture of participation, which also goes a long way to explain the high levels of volunteering. This means that the Scandinavian voluntary sector is different from elsewhere in Europe, not small. There is thus little evidence to support the idea that extensive welfare states will have small not-for-profit sectors. The hypothesis that a large public sector is crowding out the voluntary sector has a more limited area of validity than commonly assumed.

However, profound change is under way. What we see is a turning away from the large-scale ideological mass movements, and a greater interest in smaller, flexible and non-ideological organizations that are better at catering for individual needs and wishes, but poorer at plugging members into the central decision-making institutions. These changes have profound consequences for how our democracy works, making insights from the protective model of democracy more relevant even in the Scandinavian context.

Altogether these new trends challenge the traditional order of the Scandinavian voluntary sector. Even if old organizational forms remain, the new forms do challenge and break with historical roots in so far as they often produce new and less hierarchical organizational forms. These new types of organizations often have centralized leadership, but no specific ideology or political programme; they explore market-oriented and private management inspired strategies; they shift attention towards new forms of welfare provision; they introduce contracts both towards public authorities and with regard to their volunteers; and they gradually undermine the notion of voluntarism and the distinction between paid and voluntary work. The weakening of the role of the traditional social movements and the growth of organizations which are not membership based and democratically built indicate that we may now be in the midst of a transformation of the voluntary sector, gradually eroding some of the historically important characteristics of society. What we see is no less than a decline in the democratic infrastructure (Tranvik and Selle 2003).

Citizens are connected to society at large in a different way than before. In a democratic perspective, the possibility citizens enjoy to use organizations as one means among others of democratic influence is weakened when institutional ties are absent. The upshot is not necessarily less volunteering and participation, but a weakening of institutions of tremendous importance for democracy and social integration and cohesion. The accumulated effect of these developments may be that the centre–periphery relations, so important to the structure of Norwegian democracy, are undergoing profound changes. From being relations of popular influence and participation, they may now have become a channel for centralized commandeering.

It is interesting to note that a large Harvard-based research project has found that many of the changes in civil society organization that we have given a short presentation of here, are also noted in the United States (see, for instance, Skocpol 2003; Skocpol, Ganz and Munson 2000). This may indicate that there is more at play here than the usual mantra of Scandinavian exceptionalism.

# Chapter 6: Patterns of Corporatist Intermediation

Trond Nordby[30]

*The Nordic Model* as a concept expresses post-war social organization. One central aspect is centralized forms of wage determination accomplished by unitary organizations of labour and capital – with macroeconomic stability, effective labour allocation and joint distribution of wages as an outcome (Høgsnes and Longva 2001). Referring to this specific social organization, the Norwegian sociologist *Lars Mjøset*, argues that a Nordic model never existed, even if "it may gain strength in the future" (Mjøset 1992:652). According to Mjøset it is more appropriate to talk about a *Scandinavian Model.* On the other hand, Sweden, Denmark and Norway do not exhibit exactly the same patterns either. As pointed out by the Swedish scholar *Nils Elvander* (Elvander 2002), different political regulations and deregulations have come and gone over time in each of them.

Similar conclusions on Scandinavian conformity can be drawn regarding the extensive cooperation between labour, business and the state at the *administrative level.* In spite of some organizational variations on how government authorities intervene, governments have encouraged organizations to participate actively in policy-making processes for the purpose of reaping the benefit of the organizations' expertise in their respective areas and get them to share responsibility for decisions taken. The organizations, on their part, have been concerned to exert as much influence as possible.

In addition to the points on *wage determination* and *cooperation at an administrative level* one should bring into the analysis how state authorities influence the *internal affairs* of organizations. If the state successfully affects the organizations' internal affairs, one may speak of a type of *state colonization.*

In instances where the state does not intervene, the organizations acquire a more *autonomous position.* Bringing this perspective into the analysis raises the question whether the already mentioned areas of collaboration tend to reinforce the state's capacity to govern or widen the opportunities organizations have to press their case on the government, and mould state politics as a result. I confine myself to a discussion of the general topography from a historical perspective, that is, from 1945 to the present. The principal question is *who governs whom*.

## An Institutional Approach

My approach is influenced by the area of political science known as *neo-corporatism* – which derives from a model developed by *Philippe C. Schmitter* in the early 1970s (Schmitter 1974).[31] He raised the question, by way of his article's title, whether the twentieth century was *"Still the Century of Corporatism?"* For the period after World War II he pointed to a definite type of democratic corporatism. He built his analysis on two main categories: *societal corporatism* and *pluralism*, each of which marked the outer points of a scale along which he placed western democracies. As examples, Austria and Norway were located near the societal corporatist pole, USA near the pluralistic. Schmitter put forward a third category, *state corporatism*, which, in the first instance, was reserved for fascist dictatorships. This category is less relevant for democratic states; hence I prefer to use the label *corporatism* when speaking of societal corporatism.

According to the model a corporatist system contains one organization for each sector of society, or, alternatively, several organizations hierarchically ordered in relation to one another. The state exerts control by means of various certification and financing arrangements. In return, the organizations acquire a monopoly on bargaining with public authorities. The organizations are, for their part, led from the top, and a relatively autonomous leadership communicates to the members the decisions that emerge from bargaining with the state. In Schmitter's terminology, they act as *corporatist intermediaries*, and membership is compulsory for producers in the sector in question.

Corporatism is primarily related to state intervention in wage bargaining and the production of goods and services. The wage level has macroeconomic consequences, and partners can go to strike or lockout. The producer organizations possess – in contrast to consumer organizations – information needed by the authorities, and can refuse to cooperate. Hence there is more scope for bargaining than under state–corporatist arrangements – where the state is assumed to have virtually complete control. The organizations are also free throughout to participate or to decline to do so, or, in the event, to opt out altogether.

Corporatist operations are governed by procedural regulations. To the extent that state authorities establish the institutions, formulate their mandates and encircle their activity with laws, they have ample opportunity to control outcomes. Simultaneously, corporatist arrangements mark themselves out in the very distinctive way they promote *consensus*: for negotiators the objective is normally compromise. In other contexts the participants discuss their way to an agreed statement, they issue an agreed recommendation, pass an agreed resolution etc. In a real sense, guidelines are inherent in these arrangements, guidelines which pull in the direction of coordination and agreement.

In the case of looser contacts, like consultations without specially set up institutions, hearings and lobbyism, those who express opinions are in a far freer position. Statements can be issued singly, without it being necessary for organizations to argue for them vis-à-vis other parties or representatives of the state. In other words, they act like pressure groups, without being held responsible for the final decisions. Consequently, the final decisions are less binding on those who involve themselves, which is why such contacts are called *pluralistic*.

Furthermore, and in accordance with Schmitter's model, a pluralistic system could have *several organizations* competing against one another within one and the same sector. Members are then free to break out and join a new organization. The leadership is therefore kept under control from below. Organizations are relatively autonomous in relation to the state, they have their own resources, and the state is not entitled to encroach on their internal business – apart from in a judicial capacity in legal disputes.

While this model cannot be transferred unconditionally to Scandinavia, it does provide the best basis for understanding historical changes in state control through corporatist arrangements. Moreover, in empirical research there can be no talk of making a simple classification. Instead, the main categories have to be utilised as ideal types; i.e. fleshed out with concrete content – in a manner which shows the most important types of congruence and deviation. Connected to the concept of a Scandinavian model I argue that elements of corporatism and pluralism always have been woven together, in all three countries, and that pluralistic sectors over the last thirty years have been under expansion.

In my studies the concept is applied firstly to what I have termed *bargaining corporatism* (Nordby 1994, Nordby1999). The implicated parties bargain in institutions established for the purpose; that is to say, institutions for the settlement of pay and conditions of employment. In the second place, we are dealing with *corporatism linked to the administration* (Nordby 1994; Nordby 1999), whose anchor is in the form of state committees which draw participants from sector organizations.[32] Members are appointed either by the cabinet or a particular ministry. Moreover, the same authorities formulate their mandates and decide their terms of action.

At this stage I would like to add some precision to my initial question: How far can we safely go in saying that political systems in Scandinavia are corporatist and/or pluralist as defined above? My basic assumption is that connections organized in a corporatist manner promote state control, i.e. the state governs by means of organized interest groups. Alternatively decisions taken by state authorities are, more or less, taken under pressure.

## Varieties of Corporatism and Pluralism

Scholars in the field of comparative political science have argued that corporatism is most widespread in countries where *social democratic reformist* parties occupied a strong position (Rothstein 1992:39). To successfully explain Scandinavian macroeconomic stability, we need to understand that social democratic parties grew up together with the trade unions. Although unions were autonomous from an early stage, connections with the parties remained close. Among other things, union representatives were elected to the party secretariats and vice versa. From the 1930s on, these parties created alliances with the peasantry as well, and they permitted Keynesian full-employment policies and comprehensive welfare programmes (Esping-Andersen 1985: 88). This got them the votes they needed to remain in government for long periods. All in all, the social democratic party became more powerful in Norway and Sweden than in Denmark.

The Scandinavian social democratic parties all wanted to see centralised planning in place, but they never developed comprehensive programmes for it, as the liberalists of the nineteenth century had done. This lack of defined aims confirms Karl Polanyi's general statement to the effect that "laissez faire was planned; planning was not" (Polanyi 1971:141). Within the framework of fairly diffuse ideologies, corporatist arrangements were introduced by Scandinavian social democrats to implement ad hoc solutions and attain limited objectives. Despite this lack of rigour, the societal effects were remarkable.

### WAGE DETERMINATION
*Nils Elvander* introduced the notion of *"labour market regime"* to describe the role of the *state* in wage settlements (Elvander 2002). There were basic similarities

among the Scandinavian states as far as political and economic systems were concerned, he writes, though he goes on to add that "the differences in labour market institutions ... are in some cases substantial" (Elvander 2002:119). First of all, each of the Scandinavian countries were quick to install mediation services in close contact with the labour market parties.

These states have either assisted (by "conciliation") or played a more intrusive role (by "mediation") in proposing settlement terms (Stokke 2002:135). Norway introduced a separate mediation institution by an Act of Parliament in 1916. Later this bargaining system was redefined and came under stricter regulation under the Labour Disputes Act (1927) and Public Sector Labour Disputes Act (1958). Sweden had, as the first country in Scandinavia, a national mediation service Act as early as 1906. In practice, mediation was essentially voluntary, and for decades, this system underwent only minor changes. After lengthy discussion in the 1980s and 90s, however, mediation came under Mediation Institute, founded in 2000. Denmark put a separate mediation institution in place in 1910. After many and wide-ranging modifications, the Conciliation in Industrial Disputes Act – with amendments – passed into law in 1934 (Stokke 2002:137).

Norway in particular has seen *direct* state intervention as a significant factor. State representatives act as arbitrators, and parliament frequently intervenes as soon as strikes or lockouts threaten essential services. In Sweden, stability has been upheld by strong *union structures* and a "relatively advanced social partner responsibility for bargaining outcomes and conflict resolution ... although sometimes against the background of threats of state intervention" (Elvander 2002:117). In contrast to Norway and Sweden, Danish state interventionism and union structures have tended to occupy a more moderate position. These differences had striking effects. After World War II, strike action in Sweden and Norway fell to very low levels (Korpi 1983:163). Even if the scale and frequency of strikes in Denmark were not comparable, the numbers of days lost to strikes or lockouts were lower than in United Kingdom – at least prior to the 1970s (Korpi 1983:163).

The *Norwegian* system of wage settlement has been described as extremely centralized. In addition to the arbitrating role of the state authorities, they have involved themselves as one of the parties of a *tripartite system*. The government has offered subsidies to keep down prices on agricultural products, and the existence of a *National Wage Board* is quite unique (Elvander 2002:120). For many years since 1945, the political authorities also aspired to keep settlements under a pre-agreed level in real economic terms. Liaison bodies, where the state, business and labour could lay out and discuss terms in advance of official negotiations, were established as well. At these pre-negotiation negotiations, efforts would be made to set a real economic framework for transfers and income settlements. In the period of reconstruction after World War II, the government appointed an *Economic Coordinating Council*, which lasted until 1952. Ten years later, in 1962, a similarly tasked board, named the *Liaison Committee*, was appointed. Finally, state authorities also made offers on an open basis of confidence. Final decisions have normally been taken by ballot among the members. Therefore, to a certain degree, we could characterize the Norwegian system as decentralized as well.

Norwegian income settlements fluctuated between *centralised versus local bargaining* and *bargaining versus compulsory arbitration*. State control of the settlements was strongest in the 1970s – first with the so-called *combined settlements* (1975–77), next with the *freeze on wages* (a 16-month period from 1978 by law). The non-socialist government which came to power after the 1981 elections, dissociated itself, on ideological grounds, from state intervention. The Conservative (H), centre-right government, under premier *Kåre Willoch*, could not be sure of the *Norwegian Confederation of Trade Unions* (LO) loyalty. Hence the stage was set for the state's withdrawal from that particular stage. The Government decentralised bargaining at the same time. Since the end of the 1980s, on the other hand, the state again played a more active role in bargaining. From 1992 to 2000, all parties accepted what was expressively named the *Solidarity Alternative*. This alternative was based on macro-economic considerations i.e., wage levels among countries competing in the same markets as Norway. In practice, the system had been in function since 1987, when *Gro Harlem Brundtland* became prime minister, a point that persuaded union leaders to agree to moderate wage demands.

At the organizational level all Scandinavian countries, in different ways, also deviate from Schmitter's ideal type of corporatism. During the immediate post-war period, the *Norwegian Confederation of Trade Unions* (LO) monopolized bargaining on behalf of the workers. A few decades on, though, from the late 1970s, competing unions and confederations like the *Federation of Norwegian Professional Associations* (AF) and the *Confederation of Vocational Unions* (YS) appeared. In private sectors, decentralized forms of bargaining at a local and individual level made final adjustments to wages to fit market conditions (*wage drift*). The result of all this has been one of widespread decentralization. Sweden went down a similar path, at least since 1992, when the centralized coordination of settlements was stopped. The system was replaced by industry-level wage settlements. The Danish system is still largely *based* on wage drift, though labour and capital do come together in pre-bargaining sessions to set settlement ceilings.

All in all, well-run collective bargaining systems still feature predominantly in Scandinavia. Although the Norwegian LO has ceased to oversee these duties on behalf of workers, Scandinavian management and labour – in a broadly comparative perspective – are well organized. As Torgeir Aarvaag Stokke observes, they are obliged "to notify both each other and the mediation institution" as well (Stokke 2002:157). Despite wider differences, especially concerning the state's role, the impression of a strongly corporatist structure to the Norwegian settlement arrangement remains solidly in place.

### CORPORATISM AT THE ADMINISTRATIVE LEVEL

At an administrative level, cooperation between state and organizations has assumed several different forms, ranging from the more or less *specialized institution to informal contacts*. The specialized institutions consist of great numbers of state committees – both permanent and temporary, and special-purpose bodies. Members of *state committees* are generally public servants, experts, business and labour representatives or representatives of other types of organizations, and ordinary citizens. In other words, representatives of public and private sector interests.

These committees are external to government departments, but not of government as such. Public authorities appoint members, formulate mandates and regulate activities by laws. As a consequence, the state has ample opportunity to influence outcomes. In practice, this kind of committee exercises delegated decision-making authority, and as such may take part in the supervision of state institutions or deal with complaints. They can also be assigned judicial powers within a delimited area. They provide advice for government – when, that is, they are asked to do so. Such counselling may be on a lasting basis within a defined area, or it may be temporary, and wedded to a specific purpose. The *temporary* committees could be termed corporatist, as contact among members is not institutionalised in the same way as for the permanent committees. Finally, there are bodies appointed for the purpose of bargaining, as is the case in Norway with the *Technical Reporting Committee on the Income Settlement*, which establishes a real economic framework for income settlements before wage bargaining proper gets off the mark.

One useful feature of this type of institution is that they render the outcomes more predictable. In the last resort, though, it is up to the authorities to go along with advice rendered, or not. Working under such circumstances, interest groups as well will be accountable for decisions formally taken by public authorities. In general, they inhabit a grey area, between the government on the one side and the community at large on the other. Government representatives take a break from their everyday jobs in the bureaucracy to participate in shaping proposals and demands which they may meet again at a later stage – as ministry employees. There are no systematic guidelines governing the composition of these committees either, which is reason to see them as institutional orphans.

Similarities between Denmark and Norway are striking. In Denmark, the corporatist system at the administrative level of government culminated in the 1960s (Munk Christiansen and Nørgaard 2003:89), in Norway, it happened a decade later, in the 1970s (Nordby 1999). In 1972 Denmark, as the first of the Scandinavian countries, joined the European Union. From then on, the committees got lots of new functions – mainly to facilitate the implementation of European decisions. Seen in the broader perspective, however, these differences are of minor importance.

The Swedes have organized their ministry system rather differently. Government offices primarily have advisory duties in political questions, and have fewer employees than those of the other Scandinavian countries. The responsibilities of the permanent committees in Sweden tend therefore to be much more executive than in Denmark and Norway. For a few decades after World War II, Swedish committees were filled with a large number of representatives of interest groups – as indeed they were in the two other countries. In 1991 the *Swedish Employers' Confederation* (SAF) decided, unexpectedly, to back out from all committee work, citing time wastage and a sense of being "hostage" in committees which, in the last resort, are ruled by state authorities. The following year, the government itself took over all appointments, and from then on members of all committees have met on an individual basis. The portion of members coming from the interest organizations declined, although *Confederation of Swedish Enterprises,*[33] nevertheless, consented to send a few representatives.

At a structural level, there have been few major differences between Scandinavian countries. Due to the stability of members and the fact that institutionalization spawns a special type of culture, the outcomes of their deliberations tend to be relatively predictable. Sitting on what are labelled as *permanent committees*, industry comes together to find a common approach to the problems. No formal voting takes place, and they aim normally to achieve compromise solutions (*consensus*).

While the number of functioning committees has fallen over the last thirty years, sectoral interests have stepped up their efforts to influence discussions and the voting of MPs, either by lobbying themselves or hiring professional agencies to do it for them. Historically, the consequences are striking. Corporatist structures are on the decline, and only a few representatives of interest organizations remain as hostages to the government on these state-controlled bodies.

EXPANDING PLURALISTIC SECTORS

Those who are involved in lobbyism prefer to keep their activities out of the public eye, and it is difficult to estimate the scope or extent of the informal contacts professional lobbying involves. Studies do indicate, however, that lobbyism has risen sharply during the last decades in Sweden (Hermansson et al. 1999), Denmark (Munk Christiansen and Nørgaard 2003) and Norway (Rommetvedt 2002). It should also be added that interest groups tend to initiate contact with MPs mostly when minority governments are in power.

In cases of *lobbyism*, and *consultations* as well, people or organizations who express their opinions and try to influence decisions by arguments are independent, particularly of political institutions. The parties involved issue their statements in writing; there are no special-purpose channels set up to do it for them. Consequently, statements can be issued unilaterally, without prior agreement with other bodies, organizations or representatives of the state. Of course, it happens that the government or parliament amend their proposals after consultation responses have been submitted, but the final decision is not binding on those who have expressed an opinion – as is the case when partners meet in corporatist institutions.

## Conclusion

This study was based on a model developed by Philippe C. Schmitter, who pointed out differences between various corporatist arrangements in terms of types of action and institutional design. In engaging with this model, on the basis of empirical findings, I came to certain conclusions on Scandinavian wage determination and corporatism at an administrative level. It cannot be denied that the three nations have evolved differently to some degree. But seen in a broad comparative perspective, there are striking similarities. Throughout the post-war period, state authorities constituted a core of authority. And in contrast to pluralistic systems, as the USA's, corporatist structures dominated entirely.

At present, however, pluralism is gaining the upper hand, and institutions controlled by the state are being sidelined by forms of contact which give the organizations concerned a relatively free hand to express and pursue their concerns. As a result, state authorities have lost much of their societal control. At least, this is true of the mounting levels of lobbying on behalf of corporatist structures at an administrative level. All things considered, corporatist structures are not as dominating as they were, and the hold state authorities, parliaments and Governments once had is slipping from their grasp.

# Chapter 7: Parliamentary Nominations and Political Representation – Group Representation or Party Mandates?

*Hanne Marthe Narud*

What does Nordic representative democracy look like? Who are the people's representatives? "Political representation" is about the relationship between the governors and the governed, between representatives and voters. It concerns the question of elite responsiveness and how well the elected represent the interests of the "absent others". The process of nominations is about how the political representatives are selected, and the criteria by which we pick those who shall govern. Nominations are thus the instruments that parties use to link the interests and preferences of the party to various parts of the electorate. Consequently, by putting forward those eligible for people's choice in the upcoming election, the party nominations form a crucial part of the process of representation. The problems involved in these processes are of fundamental importance for understanding how democratic government works.

Political developments in the Nordic area have been marked by great diffusion in the area of ideas. The most outstanding example is the joint welfare policies – most commonly known as the "Nordic welfare state model" (cf. Chapter 12, this volume). The Nordic countries also share several relevant political characteristics, i.e. the party systems and patterns of voter alignments (cf. chapters 3 and 4 above). Yet we are faced with five different countries, each concerned with its own integrity and special character. They differ with regard to geographical location and territorial size. Their foreign policy orientations have traditionally differed as well, owing to variations in strategic position and economic resources (cf. chapters 13 and 14 below). Overall, economic developments, social pressures on the welfare state, and rapid changes in the international environment have presented new challenges to the Nordic representative systems in general, and to their elected representatives in particular. The main concern of this chapter is then to discuss the impact of the above factors on patterns of representation in the Nordic countries. Is there a "Nordic Model" of political representation? Or do nation-specific representation patterns prevail?

In the first part I discuss the *concept* of representation, and give a brief overview of the various theoretical approaches to the phenomenon. In so doing, a distinction is made between "background representation" and "opinion representation" and the various combination possibilities thereof. We then move on to discussing the so-called "Mandate-Independence Controversy", which formed the basis for the normative discussions three centuries ago. The next part approaches the concept of "attached interests", gives an overview of the process of nominations in the Nordic countries and discusses the consequences for the social and demographic composition of the Nordic legislatures. The final part examines the level of mass and elite opinion agreement in light of the party mandate model of representation. The chapter concludes by presenting a general map of representation patterns in the Nordic countries.

## The Concept of Representation

What does the term "representation" actually mean? To illuminate this question, we can lean on the classical contribution by Hanna Pitkin (1967:144). Representation, she states, simply means "the making present of something which is nevertheless not literally present". In every society, demands for efficiency and competence lead to a system of division of labour and specialization. Unlike the ancient city-state of Athens, where direct rule by the citizens defined democracy, today's decision-makers need to delegate authority from a general level to more specialized bodies. Pitkin, after an exhaustive analysis of the multiple uses of the term, summarizes her view thus: "representing means acting in the interest of the represented, in a manner *responsive* to them". However, she adds that "the representative must act *independently*; his action must involve discretion and judgment; he must be the one who acts" (p. 209). Representation must not be merely "taking care of things".

Hence, according to Pitkin, political representation involves at least two key characteristics; "responsiveness" on the one hand, and "independence" on the other. Yet these are two seemingly incompatible objectives. How can you secure independent representation and at the same time be responsive to the demands and needs of your constituents? Before addressing this question, let me offer a typology where different forms of representation can be combined by making a distinction between "persons" and "opinions" (Hernes and Martinussen, 1980:76 (Table 7.1).

Table 7.1  Combinations of theories of representation: Opinions and persons

| | | Representative of Opinions | |
|---|---|---|---|
| | | Yes | No |
| Representative of Persons | Yes | Ideal democracy | Background representation |
| | No | Advocate representation | Caretaker representation |

Source: Hernes and Martinussen, 1980

In the *ideal-democracy model*, representatives share the social characteristics as well as the opinions of those who have elected them. They are "models in miniature" of those they represent. Policy decisions are thus made "by people – from the people – for the people" (Hernes and Martinussen, 1980:76). The basic idea is that parliament should make the decisions that people themselves would have made had they been able to decide themselves. The best guarantee for this actually happening is a national assembly that mirrors the range of social and demographic groups found in society. This model is similar to the so-called theory of "demographic representation" – which rests on the underlying premise that only first-hand experience (one's own background) is related to political interest and, hence, to political attitudes and behaviour (see e.g., Norris and Lovenduski, 1993).

By contrast, the term *background representation* refers to a situation in which MPs are socially representative of their voters, but have adopted values and opinions different from their constituents'. In the third type of model, which Hernes and Martinussen (1980) call *advocate representation*, those who share the opinions of a specific group are not necessarily themselves a part of that group. They represent, that is, the opinions of a group from which they deviate socially. Finally, the *caretaker* form of representation resembles the classical ideas from the "delegate model" – or what we may refer to as the "independent theory" of representation. According to this model, elected representatives may deviate from their voters both socially and in terms of opinion. They make decisions on behalf of the electorate, but they are not tied to the opinions of their constituents.

The framework displayed in Table 7 1 is a typology for the classification of political representation in the Nordic countries. The interesting question, though, is which of them provide the closest fit with the Nordic democracies. Before answering, it would be useful to revisit the "classical" debate on political representation.

## The Mandate-Independence Controversy

The philosophers of the Age of Enlightenment, such as Burke, Mill and Rousseau, were absorbed by the normative question: What is "good" representation? Should the elected representative take instructions or mandates from his constituency and do what his constituents want? Or should he be free to act as he sees fit in pursuit of their welfare? This is the essential dilemma in what is commonly known as the *Mandate-Independence Controversy* of political representation (see e.g. Eulau et al. 1959; Pitkin 1967).

In the *first* view we may look at the representative as an ambassador – a *delegate* – who is tied by the directions given to him by his constituents. In its extreme version, we could say he has the role of a postman – to deliver the mail entrusted to him – in this case, the interests of his constituents. Historically, such a view of representation dates back several hundred years, to the old European monarchies. It is a legacy of the feudalism of the thirteenth and fourteenth centuries, where rights and powers depended on the ownership of land. The early elected assemblies were formed by the representatives of the different regions of the country who would defend local interests vis-à-vis the king. Their assignments were combined with the right to recall, that is, when dissatisfied with their representative, the constituency could call him back and send another.

By contrast, in the *second* view, most often referred to as the liberal form of representation, the representative has the role of an *independent* "expert" – a "trustee", well qualified to take decisions on objective grounds and in the interest of the entire nation. Here, the representative resembles a judge – not the messenger of the first view. The leading advocate of this representation ideology was Edmund Burke. "Guidance and directions" are to be given by the ruling group of a "natural aristocracy", he argued, a genuine elite, whose superiority lies in judgment, wisdom and virtue derived from experience. Accordingly, a representative is *not* to consult the wishes of his constituents; government is *not* to be conducted according to anyone's desires. The political representatives shall discover and enact what is best for the nation, because *"the mass of the people are incapable of governing themselves ... they were not made to think or act without guidance and direction"* (Burke cited in Pitkin 1967:169).

For Burke, political representation has nothing to do with obeying popular wishes. Right decisions are to come from parliamentary deliberation; representation means the enactment of the *national good* by a select elite. Hence, Burke rejects individual interests or the selfish wishes of parts of the nation (constituencies). He states this view most explicitly in his famous speech to the electors of Bristol (Pitkin 1967:171):

> [B]ut Parliament is a deliberative assembly of one nation, with one interest, that is the whole – where no local prejudices ought to guide, but the general good, resulting from the general reason of the whole. You choose a member, indeed, but when you have chosen him he is not a member of Bristol, but he is a member of parliament.

Contemporary views of political representation do not give much weight to unattached and impersonal interests. Neither would it be legitimate to endorse a "natural aristocracy" of elected elites. One of the most widely recognized theories of representative democracy today, in the Nordic countries and elsewhere, holds that elected representatives should "mirror" those they represent, not just in social, economic and demographic terms, but also – and more importantly – in terms of values, beliefs and opinions (the "ideal democracy" denomination of Table 7.1). To put it bluntly, in present society political representation can be defined as the representation of "attached interests", focusing more on background representation.

## Representing "Attached Interests"

The intriguing question is how do we secure, if not ideal, at least "good" representatives in terms of background, interests and attitudes. Here we need to take account of the most important component of modern parliamentary systems, the *political party*. In contrast to the theories discussed above, the focus of which was the direct link between the representative and his constituents, the party represents an *indirect link* between the ordinary citizen and the elected. In parliamentary systems, like the Nordic ones, the political party selects candidates for public office, attempts to form the opinion of the citizens, and carries out policy decisions through the representative chain of governance. Interest aggregation as well as articulation takes place through the political party, and the "contract" linking the political elites to the voters is the party programme (party manifesto). Consequently, the elected representative has a *party mandate*, and the extent to which he/she can fulfil the programmatic commitments stated there defines what is "good" or "bad" representation.

In the subsequent pages, I will pay attention to the following questions: How well do the parties perform as the "people's" representatives"? What is the impact of the party nominations on the social and demographic composition of the elected bodies? And to what extent are the elected elites "representative" of their voters in terms of background and opinions?

## Nominations

Nominations are the first step – and provide the primary screening devices – in the process of representation. Forming a crucial part of the electoral process, they are mechanisms both for electing delegates to parliament and for holding them accountable (see e.g. Fearon 1999). In many European countries, including the Nordics, the nomination system is shaped by legal, electoral and party systems which constitute the broad context in which individual candidates are recruited. These contexts may be referred to as the "opportunity structure" of potential candidates (Norris and Lovenduski 1995; Norris, 1997; Schlesinger 1994). In terms of social and demographic representativeness, it is often argued that multi-member proportional systems promote a better balance of different interests than first-past-the-post systems with primary elections. In the first type, the selectors employ criteria like age, gender, social status, race, religion, group affiliation and locality, aiming for a ticket which "balances" certain ascribed characteristics, and then use achievement criteria to pick the individuals (Gallagher and Marsh, 1988; Narud et al. 2002). Open primaries, on the other hand, which we find for instance in the US, promote candidate-centred politics, in which personal qualities, and not so much group affiliation, are important criteria for selection. The Nordic countries are all multi-member proportional systems, but they differ in the extent to which they have included the electorate in the selection process. Among the Nordic countries, we find the most inclusive nomination process among some of the Icelandic parties, which have adopted the primary system of nominations.

Denmark, Finland, Iceland and Sweden have incorporated different forms of preference voting. Norway, on the other hand, has maintained the closed list system under which the selection of candidates has been restricted to the local party branches.[34] However, the general criteria applied for balancing the list are strikingly similar across countries.

## Selection Criteria

When discussing the screening mechanisms applied by the political parties, we may begin by distinguishing between two stages in the recruitment process (Seligman 1967). The first stage provides the *certification* of candidates, i.e. a process of social screening and political channelling which results in eligibility for candidacy. At this stage, the aspirants' personal abilities are evaluated, e.g. their professional and political competence (see e.g. Norris and Lovenduski, 1995; Valen, 1988). The next stage consists in the *selection*, the actual decision on who is going to represent the party in the election.

The number of office-seeking aspirants tends to be higher than the available "openings". Many aspirants are eliminated during the parties' first preselection screening, and the collective profile of the population will change along the way. The characteristics of the successful candidates differ from those of the unsuccessful ones, but empirically it is not easy to pinpoint exactly how. In the Nordic countries, various types of "group representation" criteria are applied as screening mechanisms in the selection process (Johansson, 1999; Narud et al. 2002). The four most prominent ones, which we find also in a variety of other nations, are the following (Narud et al. 2002; Ranney, 1981):

1   Incumbency is by far the most widely prized – or criticized – characteristic of selected candidates. The fact that incumbent candidates have legislative experience makes them of value to the party as professionals. Not only are they likely to make better candidates than non-incumbents, they are also known to the voters and to the selectorates, a fact that may constitute an electoral advantage to the party (Ranney, 1981:98–102). Ambitious aspirants may see this differently.

2   Most parties in most countries favour candidates with strong local connections (Gallagher and Marsh, 1988; Kjær and Pedersen, 2004; Narud et al. 2002). Even though the Constitution of the US and a handful of parties elsewhere have local residence requirements, it is not common that parties have formal

rules concerning the residence of the candidate. It is, however, a widespread norm in many parties to favour local candidates.

3 Many parties nurture visible affiliation with key interest groups. To select candidates with membership background in e.g. labour unions, ecclesiastical organizations etc. is quite common in many countries. Balancing the list with organized interests may give the party electoral as well as economic advantages.

4 The balancing of particular factional interests is also an important criterion, at least for some parties. Factional affiliation, if organized, may be seen as a subcategory of interest group affiliation, but most commonly they are of a more informal nature. By balancing the lists in terms of gender, age, occupation, etc., the parties attempt to satisfy intra-party factional demands. In addition, list balancing is expected to satisfy certain segments of the electorate.

Assuming that the composition of the list has a direct effect on the preferences of the voters, the parties are inclined to choose candidates who appeal to various subsets of the electorate. Since the electoral bases of the competing parties vary, the character of group representation also tends to vary from one party to another. Yet some tendencies seem to prevail in all the Nordic parties. Most general is the demand for geographical representation. This demand is of particular importance in Norway, Finland and Iceland. Each constituency in these three sparsely populated countries tends to cover a sizable area. Hence, parties select candidates from all over the territory. In fact – and it seems to be the normal pattern, at least in Finland and Norway – each constituency is divided into territorial subunits that compete for nominations within the respective parties. Nominating more than one candidate from a given local community to a safe spot on the same list almost never happens (Kuitunen, 2002; Valen et al., 2002).

The concern for *geographical background* is reflected in a demand that prospective candidates should be linked to the constituency in which they are nominated, either by family ties or by residence of some duration. The attachment of candidates to the constituency is a well-established norm in three of the countries, Finland, Iceland and Norway, but it is not required by law. Geographical affiliation seems to be less of a requirement in nominations in Denmark, which is the most densely populated and the smallest country in terms of territory (Pedersen 2002; Pedersen et al. 2004).

Another major mechanism for selection is *gender*. Until around 1970, women were one of several competing groups to be represented with a couple of candidates on each list. In most cases they were not located in a safe spot, though quite a few female candidates were granted a pivotal place on the list, obviously in order to appeal to the large number of female voters. The number of female candidates has increased considerably both in absolute and in relative terms over the last three decades as equality of representation for men and women has become a general demand in most parties. Some explain it with reference to the fairly egalitarian political culture in the Nordic countries. Others point to institutional and structural factors, such as multimember PR systems, women's notable proportion of the labour force and a strong and active women's movement (see e.g. Matland 1993; Skjeie 1997). However, the passion for gender equality is not evenly distributed among the parties: Right wing parties – conservatives and populists – are less passionate than the left-wing and centre parties who are more likely to espouse some form of quota system to ensure women's representation (Wägnerud 2000).

Most list candidates are in the *age* bracket of 35–55 years. There has always been a demand for increased representation of the younger voters. Of course, youth organizations support this demand, which provides a continuous renewal of parliamentary representation. The interesting question is if a similar demand will arise concerning the older cohorts – given the fact that the number of senior citizens will increase dramatically in the years to come.

In their search for candidates, political parties pay considerable attention to *occupational background*. For one thing, the parliamentary caucus of the respective parties requires some candidates with specific skills. But equally important is the appeal to occupational groups in which given parties may expect to maintain or increase their vote, e.g. organized labour, farmers, fisheries or particular middle-class occupations. Thus, each electoral list in these countries covers a wide range of occupational positions. In this respect, Nordic parties deviate from a general pattern in most countries of nominating professionals, and most notably lawyers (Putnam 1976). Nonetheless, the nominated candidates belong to the upper strata of their respective occupational groups.

As stated initially, balancing the list performs the important function of linking the parties' interests to various sub-groups of the electorate. Group representation contributes to the parties' *electoral profile* and aims at giving the party a specific appeal to certain categories of voters and interest organizations. Hence, an interesting question is in which way the screening of candidates affects the actual composition of parliament. Let us have a closer look at the social and demographic outlook of the elected candidates.

We can use Table 7.1 as a point of reference (p. 110). It should immediately be noted that reality in no way replicates the "ideal" type of democracy described in the first cell. An inter-Nordic comparative study reveals that the Nordic parliamentarians do not by any means "mirror in miniature" the populations that voted for them (Esaiasson 2000; Narud and Valen, 2000). Rather, despite strong demands for the inclusion of various social and demographic groups during nominations, the socio-economic status of parliamentarians in the Nordic region is well above that of voters on average, as measured in terms of income, occupational background and education. Consequently, people with a middle-class background (in educational and occupational terms) are over-represented, while the lower strata are correspondingly under-represented. The public sector, furthermore, is over-represented at the expense of the private sector. As far as demographic variables are concerned, men are clearly over-represented, as are the middle-aged. Hence, as is the case with other parliaments of the Western world, the Nordic democracies fit well into the "iron law" of social bias (see e.g. Narud 2003; Norris 1997; Putnam 1976).

The Nordic legislatures have featured mounting levels of higher education over the years, a developmental pattern common to virtually all other European legislatures (see e.g. Best and Cotta 2000). Women have also increased their share of public office – despite continued male dominance in the national assemblies. One reason surely has to do with the nomination procedures of the parties and the female "quota" systems adopted by several parties a couple of decades ago. In addition, more women participate in elections and politics than before; hence, the "pool" of possible candidates has increased considerably.

Does group representation have any impact on the opinion patterns of the elected representatives? In other words, does background matter? Or does the "party mandate" overshadow the group affiliation of the MPs? These are the final questions to be addressed in this chapter.

## A Party or a Group Mandate?

I want to approach the question of opinion patterns by looking at the basic requirements of what is termed the party-mandate model. It may seem a paradox that Burke was the first to realize the instrumental significance of political parties in the establishment of modern government. In extension, he might see ideology as an important basis for party representation (Thomassen 1994). However, he would probably not enjoy being regarded as a progenitor of the party model in the form it took a couple of centuries later. The *party–mandate model* was developed in accordance with the idea that the competition for votes forms the basis on which the legitimacy of the parties is founded. In this model, three basic conditions need to be met (see, e.g. Thomassen 1994; Matthews and Valen 1999).

1. Parties must present different alternatives to the voters (formulated in their party manifestos);
2. Party discipline must be such that it enables the parties to implement their policy programme;
3. Voters must vote rationally, that is, for the party whose programme is closest to their own policy preferences.
   This requirement means that
   a) Voters must have policy preferences;
   b) Voters must be able to distinguish between parties.

In empirical research, the most common way of measuring the "fitness" of this model has been to analyze the level of mass and elite opinion-agreement. The more consistently the opinions of the elected representatives match those of the voters, the more "responsive" the political party. In effect, this interpretation of the party mandate derives from a *bottom-up* understanding of opinion-agreement. It reflects a populist view of representation, in which the political leaders are sensitive to public sentiments and adapt to voters' attitudes and opinions. An alternative understanding of the party mandate is incorporated in *the Responsible Party Model*, which allows for a *top-down* approach to opinion-formation. Parties compete for voters' support on the basis of programmes, opinion formation takes place from above, and the defining features of the representative link are leadership and accountability (Esaiasson and Holmberg 1996).

The important point here is that the party mandate is the dominant form of representation in modern parliaments of today. The party is decisive for the representatives' *definition of their roles* as well as their representational *focus*, that is, which interests they should represent (Esaiasson 2000). Party discipline in parliamentary votes is also very high. Consequently, in a party-dominated context like the Nordic legislatures, the representatives are expected to put the interest of the party first. The emphasis on group representation during the nominations, however, opens up for other – and alternative – role definitions. Hence Esaiasson (2000:58) points out that, together with the interest of the party and the Burkean principle of independence, three types of interests enjoy a substantial number of champions in the Nordic parliaments: a) promoting constituency interests; b) helping private citizens; and c) endorsing women, youth and other socio-economically disadvantaged groups. So the pertinent question concerns the impact of group affiliation on the representatives' attitudes and opinions. Do persons from different regions, for example, hold different attitudes on certain issues? Do men articulate different concerns from those of women? Or does party loyalty "structure" the opinions of the elected representatives irrespective of group attachment? In the following I examine these questions, limiting the discussion to the impact of geography and gender, the two most prominent group demands during the party nominations.

## The Impact of Geography on Opinions

Let us first link the territorially defined interests to the "Mandate-Independence Controversy" that was accounted for earlier. In Burke's view, i.e. the liberal theory of representation, there is no legitimate interest save that of the public – the nation as a whole. The elected representative must be left "free of instructions", to cite Pitkin (1967:147). By contrast, the idea of geographical representation rests on the assumption that the representative holds a restricted mandate. The style and focus of the elected MPs are linked to the interests of their constituency (Eulau et al. 1959; Wahlke et al. 1962).

A number of studies have demonstrated that territorially defined interests have an impact upon the elected representatives' views of their task as well as their behaviour in parliament. Consequently, "[t]he relatively strong support for constituency representation shows that old traditions live in the Nordic parliaments, irrespective of election systems or cohesive national parties" (Esaiasson 2000:61). Furthermore, cooperation in parliament across party lines is rather common – particularly on localization and other local and regional issues. These patterns are most widespread in Finland and Norway, probably due to the relatively sharper cleavage between centre and periphery in these two countries (Jensen 2000). An interesting question is whether variations in policy opinions exist between specified regions of given countries.

In relying on the basic arguments from the theory of nation-building (e.g. Rokkan 1970), Valen, Narud and Hardarsson (2000) analyze variations in the structure of opinions *within* the Nordic countries, arranging the various regions in a centre–periphery perspective. In so doing, they make a distinction between two types of conflicts, *functional* conflicts, one the one hand, in which several nation-wide interests are involved; and *territorial* conflicts, on the other, in which areas or regions with opposed interests confront one another. In terms of political representation, functional conflicts are expressed in the competition among political parties, most commonly along the left–right dimension. The normal pattern is that each party takes a collective stand on issues related to functional conflicts, and that individual MPs are expected to support the party line. Geographical representation, on the other hand, presumes that representatives are alert to issues of relevance to their own constituency. Consequently, as far as territorial conflicts are concerned, they are likely to display split loyalties between party and geography. What should we expect in terms of inter-Nordic variation and similarity?

First, irrespective of country, one should expect that on issues related to territorial conflicts congruence between voters and representatives is likely to be higher in the periphery than in the centre (Valen et al. 2000:108). The "rationale" behind this thesis has to do with the process of nation-building, as first formulated by Stein Rokkan (cf. Chapter 1 above). This process starts at the centre and the subsequent penetration and mobilization of peripheral parts of the territory is likely to create feelings of protest and regional identification, feelings directed against the centre (Rokkan 1970). As a result, the population of the periphery tends to be highly aware of its own territorial interests and policy issues, and the pressure on MPs to conform to constituency interests is presumably stronger in the periphery than in the centre.

Second, assuming that the tradition of territorial representation is related to historical, geographical and institutional circumstances in each individual country, one should expect patterns of political representation to exhibit substantial variations *between* the Nordic nations as well. It would be reasonable to expect considerable variations between centre and periphery in Iceland, Finland and Norway, which are fairly "new" nation-states. In the old nation-states of Denmark and Sweden, in contrast, integration of the national territory has been proceeding for centuries, so we would expect only minor territorial variations within these countries.

The two hypotheses are summarized in Table 7.2.

Table 7.2 *Expected congruence between voters and representatives by region*

|  |  | Type of region | |
|---|---|---|---|
|  |  | Centre | Periphery |
| Type of conflict | Functional | National average | National average |
|  | Territorial | National average | High issue-congruence |

Source: Valen, Narud and Hardarson, 2000: 111

As the table makes clear, the extent to which representatives express the opinions of their electorates is conditioned first by the *type of policy issues* considered, and second the *type of pressures* (conditioned by region) to which representatives are exposed (Valen et al. 2000: 111). Functional issues, which are articulated through competition among nationwide political parties, call for MPs – irrespective of regional background – to show loyalty with their party. Territorial issues, on the other hand, are less affected by partisan affiliations, since regional interests are at stake.[35]

By dividing each country into different regions, the *effect of regional differences* on elite perceptions and priorities may easily be tested. One approach is to present political leaders with a list of major tasks and ask them to rank them in importance to them as MPs. Another is to explore patterns of differences between voters and leaders in regard to various sets of policy views. Let us consider these two options, and look at some findings from empirical analyses.

## Major Tasks

In relation to the MP's role definition, a distinction can be made between different types of tasks.[36] Parliamentarians must (1) try to help individual voters who have contacted them; (2) champion the interests/opinions of their own constituency/region; and (3) advocate the policies of their party. In light of the distinction between a territorial mandate vs. a party mandate, one would expect the first two of these items to reflect regional variations, and the third to be unaffected by region. How does Nordic reality fit this probability?

First of all, in all of the countries and throughout each national territory, MPs consider it highly important to advocate the policies of their party. The pattern is different for the other two tasks: trying to help individual voters on the one hand, and promoting the expressed interests of the constituency on the other. In all of the countries, representatives pay closer attention to these interests in peripheral than in central regions. On the issue "advocating the interest of own region", the difference is most pronounced in Iceland and Sweden (Valen et al. 2000). We find similar tendencies when respondents are asked about cooperation across party lines on such questions as where to build roads, locate agencies, etc., as well as on other questions related to the respondent's constituency or region. MPs from the periphery are more inclined than those from the centre to respond affirmatively (Jensen 2000). Hence, the analyses suggest that representatives from peripheral parts of the territory are more alert to problems of a regional character than are representatives from central constituencies.

## Policy Views

Consistent with the distinction between functional and territorial questions, we can use different sets of issues to tap variations within each of the Nordic countries. Left–right position is generally seen as a measurement of functional issues, and here, empirical analysis indicates that the differences between regions are tiny (Valen et al. 2000:119). On specific policy issues, however, the patterns vary a bit between the countries. Concerning Denmark, Iceland and Sweden, congruence between voters and leaders on functional issues (e.g. "reduce the public sector" or "increase taxes on higher incomes") reflects a national average in all regions. This pattern is also found in the Norwegian electorate, but not among the leaders. Hence, among the Norwegian MPs centre–periphery differences are clearly evident. A possible explanation for the deviating pattern in Norway may be found in the historically deep-rooted concern for decentralization in Norwegian politics. The EU debate in the 1990s only strengthened this tradition, during which the saliency of the centre–periphery controversy increased markedly. This highly divisive issue may have affected party competition in different ways from one region to another.

Concerning regional issues (e.g. "increased support for rural districts" or "increased allocation for the construction of roads and tunnels in the outlying districts"), empirical analysis gives only weak support to the expectation that mass and elite opinion congruence is stronger in the periphery than at the centre. The results indicate that regional variations on the voter level, as well as on the elite level, are stronger in Iceland and Norway than in Denmark and Sweden. Overall, opinion congruence between voters and leaders tends to be higher for territorial than for functional issues. In addition, as expected, MPs from peripheral areas are more inclined than their colleagues from the centre to express concern for the interests of their constituency and region. Finally, the thesis that centre–periphery variations are more pronounced in the "new" nations Norway and Iceland than in the "old" nation-states Sweden and Denmark receives general support. As to the latter, the peripheral regions differ somewhat from the rest of the territory, but the relatively small differences in these countries do not seem to affect mass–elite linkages.

## The Impact of Gender on Opinions

As was argued initially, the "rationale" for social representation derives from demands for "equity" and "legitimacy". The most common argument is that background and experience are important for the "representativeness" of MPs' priorities, attitudes and behaviour. As we have seen, a strong ideological support for the idea of social representation, and an active part in the role of women themselves, are important factors in the high level of female representation in the Nordic societies. There are important differences between the political parties, however, in their view of the proposed means for increasing the number of women elected. Generally, the parties of the left tend to prefer affirmative action (quota systems) more than their conservative counterparts (cf. Chapter 9). On the question of quotas, the impact of gender on MPs' attitudes is rather modest compared to that of party affiliation (Wägnerud 2000:140). Quite the opposite is true when it comes to legislative behaviour. Female representatives report regular contact with women's organizations and other activities with a bearing on gender equality (Wägnerud 2000:142). In light of these findings, we might ask whether women's policy attitudes differ from those held by their male colleagues. Do male MPs articulate different concerns than female MPs?

The answer to this question is unequivocally "yes". On left–right issues, as well as "new politics" issues, men and women differ significantly. Women are more "leftist" than men, and they are more favourable towards "new politics" (i.e., towards introducing a six-hour working day, banning driving in city centres, and adopting systems of female quotas for higher positions). Furthermore, they are much more sceptical about pornography and gene manipulation than men are, and they are less in favour of reducing the number of refugees (Narud

and Valen, 2000:93). Other background characteristics matter as well; sector, occupation, education and age affect the MPs' policy views. Sector generates very
similar opinion patterns as gender. That is, legislators recruited from the public sector express pretty much the same views as women, while MPs from the
private sector express views similar to men's. Observe, however, that the two variables are probably intercorrelated (i.e. the public sector is dominated by women and the private sector by men) (Narud and Valen, 2000:106).

Does the impact of group affiliation disappear when party is controlled for?
In a number of cases gender differences between members of the Nordic legislatures remain significant after controlling for party. This is the case on both
"left–right" issues and "new politics" issues, as well as on the questions of pornography, refugees and gene manipulation. But also other background characteristics show significant effects. Consequently, the effects of sector and occupation remain significant on a number of issues, while the remaining two
background indicators, education and age, have very few significant effects on
any of the issues. Occupation, finally, has a significant effect on attitudes towards pornography, but gender is by far the most important variable here,
even after party is controlled for (Narud and Valen 2000:95).

What is the impact of gender on the level of issue agreement between leaders and voters? Here, comparisons can be made separately for female and for
male voters and for female and male MPs. In terms of the issue positions tak-
en, we would expect female MPs to be closer to female than to male voters, and
male MPs to be closer to male than to female voters. As far as average differences are concerned, empirical evidence show that male elites consistently represent the views of male voters better than those of female voters (Narud and
Valen 2000:101). The corresponding tendencies are evident for female MPs in
Iceland and Sweden, but not for those in Denmark and Norway. On practical-
ly all questions, the tendency is consistent for male representatives; for female
representatives it is more blurred. The most striking discrepancy between female MPs and voters appears in Sweden concerning the question of EU membership. On this issue, male MPs are also out of tune with male voters, although to a slightly lesser extent. The same tendency is evident in the case of
Norwegian female MPs; on the question of EU membership, they actually represent the views of male voters better than those of female voters. Inter-group
comparisons reveal that male MPs are consistently better representatives than
female MPs of the opinions of male voters. The converse tendency is also true:
female MPs represent the views of female voters better than male MPs do.
That said, the observed patterns are issue-specific.

## Patterns of Representation

The purpose of this chapter was to compare the patterns of representation in the Nordic countries. Do the elected representatives have "free" or "instructed" mandates? Are they representatives of persons or opinions? As the discussion shows, there is no clear-cut or straightforward answer to this question. Whereas the liberal philosophers of the Age of Enlightenment believed in free mandates and unattached interests, the ideas of modern democracies encompass some sort of attached interests in which the political party and various social and demographic groups are involved. How do you ensure that the interests of the "absent others" – the ordinary citizens – are represented in policy, service or symbolic ways? One answer lies in the nomination procedures of the political parties, by the development of proper screening mechanisms for candidate selection. Much effort is put in balancing group demands during the party nominations. The most important ones that we have discussed in this chapter concern gender and geography, but other types of affiliations are important too. The end product is a list representative of multiple interests. Despite this fact, we have seen that the Nordic parliaments are no "mirror images" of the population from which they are drawn. There, as elsewhere, the "iron law of social bias" is valid. The question is – does it matter "who" governs?

An answer is presented in Table 7.3, which offers a summary of the "patterns of representation" in the Nordic democracies.

Table 7.3  Patterns of representation. Background and attitudes of Nordic MPs

| Background | Representativeness | Significant attitude differences after party affiliation is controlled for | | | | | |
|---|---|---|---|---|---|---|---|
| | | left–right | new politics | porno-graphy | refugees | gene manipu-lation | support to agriculture |
| Gender | Women under-represented | yes | yes | yes | yes | yes | no |
| Sector | public sector over-represented | yes | yes | yes | no | no | no |
| Occupation | higher status over-represented | yes | yes | yes | no | yes | no |
| Education | higher education over-represented | no | no | no | yes | no | no |
| Age | Young voters under-represented | no | no | no | no | yes | yes |

Should we relate these dimensions to the types of representation ideologies presented in Table 7.1, the findings suggest that the Nordic democracies are split between "advocate" representation and "caretaker" representation. We may argue that women (who are systematically under-represented) are subjected to "caretaker representation" to a greater extent than are men, both because they are fewer in parliament, and because female MPs are less in line with female voters. In general, groups who are over-represented in parliament enjoy a favourable position in the policy-making process, provided there is opinion agreement between representatives and their voters.

The Nordic experience demonstrates that background indeed matters for the conduct and opinions of representatives. Although the party mandate dominates the representation focus of Nordic parliamentarians, interesting territorial variations are evident. The observed differences between Denmark and Sweden on the one hand, and Iceland and Norway on the other, are consistent with the central assumption of nation-building theory. The process of territorial integration takes a long time. In well-integrated nation-states, the process has been going on for centuries, and protest attitudes in distant parts of the territory are rare. In "new" states, on the other hand, the centre–periphery contrast constitutes an important cleavage in national politics. However, the similarities between the Nordic countries are more striking than the differences. In all countries, the impact of gender is substantial and other background characteristics matter as well. Hence, we may conclude that the "Nordic model" includes a range of representation types where opinion patterns are conditioned on the types of issues at hand and the group base of the MPs.

# Chapter 8: Parliamentary Government

*Bjørn Erik Rasch*

The parliamentary system of government is one in which the members of parliament determine the formation of the cabinet and where any majority of the same members at virtually any time may vote the government ministers out of office. Thus, legislative majorities have control over the government. Still, majority governments are not always formed. Indeed, nearly one third of all governments in Western Europe since World War II have lacked majority support in their respective national assemblies (Strøm 1990; Rasch 2004:119). No region has experienced minority governments more frequently than Scandinavia. In sharp contrast to Finland and Iceland, the Scandinavian countries Denmark, Sweden and Norway have had minority governments for more than two-thirds of the time since the end of the Second World War. In the Danish case, minority governments have been in office for more than four-fifths of the time.

The purpose of this chapter is to discuss legislative-executive relations in the Nordic region and, in particular, to shed some light on the distinctly Scandinavian form of parliamentarism. Why do minority governments occur so frequently in Scandinavia, while broad majority coalitions seem to be the norm in the two other – apparently quite similar – countries in the region?

## Background

The Nordic countries have a long parliamentary history. Iceland's *Althingi* can even trace its roots as a consultative assembly as far back as 930, before it was abolished in 1800. All the Nordic countries were democratized during the first quarter of the twentieth century, as universal suffrage for parliamentary elections was introduced in this period. All of the countries have had a parliamentary system of government for many decades: Denmark from 1901, Finland

and Sweden from 1917, and the two other countries from before independence. The first parliamentary cabinet was formed in Norway in 1884 and in Iceland in 1904.

All of the Nordic parliaments are elected as unicameral bodies, but the Norwegian *Storting* partly functions in a bicameral manner. After each election, Norwegian legislators divide themselves into two – the *Odelsting* and the *Lagting* – which handle non-financial legislation.[37] Iceland had a similar quasi-bicameral system until 1991. Denmark and Sweden abolished their upper houses in 1953 and 1971 respectively.

Table 8.1    Nordic parliaments and electoral systems

| Parliament | Cameral structure and size (seats) | Electoral formulae (per cent adjustment seats) | District magnitude[3] | Deviation from proportionality[5] (Loosemore-Hanby index) |
|---|---|---|---|---|
| Folketinget (Denmark) | Unicameral (since 1953) 175+4 seats | Modified Sainte-Laguë and LR-Hare (23% adj. seats) | M = 7.3 | D = 3.3 |
| Stortinget (Norway) | Partly Bicameral 165 seats[1] | Modified Sainte-Laguë (5% adj. seats)[2] | M = 8.3[4] | D = 6.1 |
| Riksdagen (Sweden) | Unicameral (since 1971) 349 seats | Modified Sainte-Laguë (11% adj. seats) | M = 11.1 | D = 2.6 |
| Eduskunta (Finland) | Unicameral 200 seats | D'Hondt (No adj. seats) | M = 13.2 | D = 5.1 |
| Althing (Iceland) | Unicameral (since 1991) 63 seats | LR Hare and D'Hondt (21% adj. seats) | M = 6.1 | D = 4.0 |

[1]  The Norwegian parliament will have 169 seats from the 2005 election.
[2]  The Norwegian parliament will have 19 adjustment seats (11%) from the 2005 election (one for each electoral district).
[3]  Source: Lijphart (1994). M is calculated by taking the total number of seats minus adjustment seats, divided by the number of districts or constituencies.
[4]  M = 7.9 from the 2005 Storting election.
[5]  Source: Lijphart (1994), except for Norway. D is the total percentage by which over-represented parties are overrepresented (or underrepresented parties underrepresented).

Proportional representation also has a long history in the Nordic region (Grofman and Lijphart 2002). The first instance was Finland in 1906, when the unicameral, partly autonomous *Eduskunta* was established. By 1920, PR had replaced elections in single-member districts in every country but Iceland,
which, from 1923 to 1959, combined first-past-the post and PR in various
ways. Some aspects of the current electoral systems are shown in Table 8.1. We
note that the Nordic parliaments use quite similar list systems of representation. Only the Finnish PR system exhibits some deviating features. Although
Finland has no adjustment seats, deviation from perfect proportionality is not
remarkable in a European perspective. Part of the reason is that the average
multi-member district is quite large (i.e., has high "district magnitude"). Finland also is the only country which uses an open list system, which means that
the voters vote for party candidates rather than (pre-determined) party lists.

With respect to proportionality, Sweden and Denmark perform well. The
highest level of disproportionality is found in Norway, mainly due to an electoral system with few adjustment seats and relatively small constituencies. A
new electoral law was adopted in 2003, and the number of adjustment seats
will be more than doubled in the upcoming 2005 general election.

The size of the Nordic legislatures mainly reflects population figures. Sweden, however, has a much larger parliament than its population would lead
one to expect. This can be seen as a legacy of the bicameral era. The single
chamber got almost as many seats as the former first and second chambers
combined (von Sydow 1991; Stjernquist 1996).[38]

## Nordic Governments

In a parliamentary democracy, the executive is supported, or at least *tolerated*,
by the parliament. Table 8.2 shows Nordic governments by type and country
since parliamentarism was introduced (or since independence in the case of
Iceland). To ensure a unique parliamentary basis for each government, we
consider a change of government has occurred if (i) the partisan composition
of the cabinet changes; (ii) a new prime minister takes office; or (iii) general
elections are held (whether or not the same government remains in power). A
few short-lived national crisis coalitions in Norway and Denmark are excluded, as are some caretaker administrations in Finland. The table is based on two
dimensions. First, we distinguish between majority and minority governments. Second, governments are coalitions of parliamentary parties or one-
party cabinets. This yields four types of governments. Danish and Swedish

governments before unicameralism are seen as accountable to the popularly elected lower chamber only.[39] Norwegian governments (and Icelandic governments before 1991) are accountable to the entire legislative assembly.

Table 8.2 Governments in Nordic countries[1]

| Type of Government | Norway 1884–2004 | Denmark 1901–2004 | Sweden 1917–2004 | Finland 1917–2004 | Iceland 1944–2004 |
|---|---|---|---|---|---|
| Majority One-Party | 21% (14) | 0% (0) | 37% (39) | 0% (0) | 0% (0) |
| Majority Coalition | 15% (10) | 29% (36) | 27% (28) | 65% (41) | 88% (22) |
| Minority One-Party | 49% (32) | 48% (61) | 30% (31) | 13% (8) | 12% (3) |
| Minority Coalition | 15% (10) | 23% (29) | 6% (6) | 22% (14) | 0% (0) |
| Total number of governments | N=66 | N=126 | N=104 | N=63 | N=25 |
| Share of time governed by minority cabinets after 1945[2] | 56% | 83% | 73% | 22% | 3% |

[1]   The latest governments included in the table are Bondevik 2001 in Norway, Fogh Rasmussen 2001 in Denmark, Persson 2002 in Sweden, Oddson 2003 in Iceland and Vanhanen 2003 in Finland.

[2]   Source for the percentages: See Rasch (2004:118).

If we look at their entire parliamentary history, Denmark and Norway have had more minority governments than majority governments (71 and 64 per cent, respectively). Most of the minority governments in both countries have not been coalitions, but single-party cabinets. Iceland, on the other hand, has a history of majority coalitions; minority governments have been few and short-lived. Patterns in Finland and Sweden after 1917 are quite similar. Almost two-thirds of the governments have had majority support from the legislature. Finland, however, had most of its minority governments before the Second World War, while in Sweden it is the other way round. Majority coalitions have been the norm in Finland since the 1940s. In Sweden, single-party minority governments have emerged as the norm in recent decades, just as in the Danish and Norwegian cases.

The table shows a remarkable variation in terms of government stability. On average, cabinets have been more durable in Iceland and Norway than in Denmark and Sweden. Finnish governments fall somewhere in the middle; since the early 1980s Finland has moved towards stable majority governments (Raunio 2004). If we only consider the period after 1945, Finland and Denmark have had a substantially higher number of governments than the other Nordic countries.

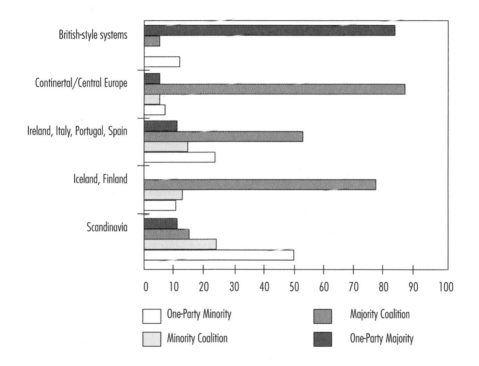

*Figure 8.1  Governments in parliamentary countries after 1945 (source: Rasch 2004: 119). Scandinavia includes Denmark, Norway and Sweden. British-style countries include Great Britain, Canada and New Zealand. Continental Europe includes France, Germany, Luxembourg, Belgium, the Netherlands and Austria.*

The Scandinavian form of parliamentarism has two distinctive features. First, and most important, is the prevalence of minority governments. Second, one-party governments occur frequently, which may mean that political parties are reluctant to form coalitions (Strøm 1986; Sannerstedt 1996). These features become apparent in Figure 8.1, which shows cabinet types in a selection of 18 countries (almost all of them Western European). The British-style democracies are dominated by one-party majority governments. Iceland and Finland have the same governmental experience as the Continent, and, to some extent, Southern Europe. What is remarkable about Scandinavia, is the high number of minority governments (74 per cent) and one-party administrations (61 per cent).

## Why Minority Governments in Scandinavia?

The literature dealing with minority governments is relatively sparse (but see Strøm 1984, 1986 and 1990). There is no general agreement on why minority governments form, and why they – in some political systems – clearly are viable and stable cabinet solutions. It is no easy task to explain why minority governments currently dominate in Scandinavia, while majority governments prevail in Finland and Iceland. In many respects, the polities of the Nordic countries are similar and some of the differences clearly have no influence on government formation. One approach could be to try and locate causal factors that are shared by the Scandinavian countries, but not by the entire Nordic region. As mentioned earlier, it also is worth noting that some of the countries over time have slid from minority to majority governments (Finland) or vice versa (Sweden). Also, Norway has had majority parliamentarism over substantial spans of time, e.g. from 1945 to 1961. If the constitutional framework has remained relatively stable over time in all countries, it might be hard to trace the occurrence of minority governments back to differences in constitutional details. Instead, the most likely explanation for the Nordic patterns of government formation seems to be the party system.

Traditionally, minority governments also have been explained as a consequence of party fragmentation and polarization. In an early discussion, Janson (1928) pointed to the gradual development of a multi-party legislature and a reluctance to enter coalitions as the main background for the formation of Swedish minority governments in the 1920s. Some authors suggest that minority cabinets tend to be formed in unstable and highly conflictual political systems, emerging when everything else has failed. In general, these claims have not been substantiated. Herman and Pope (1973) demonstrated that minority governments were more common than previously assumed (36 per cent in their cross-national data). They also suggested a variety of reasons for this phenomenon. First, a substantial part of the minority governments they studied were caretaker administrations. These governments typically came to power as a result of some sort of crisis, and were deliberately established for only a short period of time. Second, some minority governments took office because one or more coalition partners withdrew from majority governments. Third, a few minority governments came to office because elections that usually provided one party with a legislative majority, surprisingly ended in an open minority situation (and, probably, a new election after a short while). Fourth, minority cabinets may be caused by the fact that the extreme parties on both sides of the political spectrum are simply "beyond the pale", and therefore out of the frame as credible, coalition partners for the more moderate parties. Fifth, and probably the most interesting explanation in our context, some minority cabinets were formed in situations in which one of the parties was only a few seats short of a legislative majority. Often, the dominant party has formed a one-party minority government, and in most of the cases with formal support from one of the smaller parties.

Before we take a closer look at the relevance of the party system in understanding Nordic government formation, we will consider the impact of some institutional factors.

### NEGATIVE PARLIAMENTARISM

In countries with a majoritarian electoral system, the process of government formation is relatively simple – at least as long as one party receives a majority of the seats. In multi-party systems, the formation processes may be complicated and lengthy, involving several actors in intense negotiations that can drag on for weeks or even months. Typically, a complex set of formal and informal rules regulates government formation. Finland, in particular from 2000, and Sweden have substantive constitutional provisions, while the other Nordic constitutions – most notably the Norwegian one – hardly provide for any specific constraints on formation (and resignation) processes. That is not to say, however, that relatively transparent practices and expectations have not evolved over time.

Parliamentary rules, be they formal or not, may be *negative* or *positive*. The negative rule implies that the government has to be tolerated by the legislative majority,[40] but it does not need to achieve the active support of the majority. A vote of no confidence (or censure) is the instrument by which it is made apparent whether a cabinet is tolerated or not. In a system of positive parliamentarism, on the other hand, all prospective governments need to win a vote of investiture or confidence from the parliament before they can assume power. The government has to have active support from a majority of legislators.

Until recently, all the Nordic countries had negative formation practices. Finland introduced an investiture vote in the mid-1990s. Swedish prime ministers also need to survive an investiture vote, but the decision rule is rather weak. It says that a proposal for a prime minister is accepted as long as an absolute majority in the Riksdag does not reject it. Thus, majority backing is not required. This is equivalent to saying that the government must be tolerated by the majority.

Today, the head of state is not actively involved in government formation in any of the Nordic countries. The powers of the Finnish president have recently been reduced, and the country fully "parliamentarized". In the former system, which was semi-presidential in nature, "the president was the incontestable executive head of Finland" (Paloheimo 2003:222). The president often had a relatively free hand to select the prime minister, especially before the 1980s. Under the current constitutional framework, the parliament nominates the prime minister, and the only step the president is left with is to carry out the formal appointment. Thus, the president plays a role that is not very different from that of the monarch in Denmark and Norway. In Sweden, however, the new constitution of 1975 also stripped the king of his formal and symbolic duties related to government formation and resignation (Bergman 2004). Constitutionally, Iceland seems to have a rather strong head of state, directly elected by the people (Kristjánsson 2004). In practice, the country never has actually functioned as a truly semi-presidential system, and Icelandic presidents have been considerably weaker than the Finnish presidents used to be. With respect to government formation, the parliament and the parties undoubtedly have the upper hand.

Finland and Iceland have presidents, and have had dual executive power – at least on paper. Does this explain the overwhelming predominance of majority cabinets in the two countries? The answer is mainly negative. No one has demonstrated that majority governments primarily are the result of presidential influence, although strong presidents – such as Finland's Urho Kekkonen – may have been of help in finding viable governments (or blocking weak alternatives).[41] In fact, Finnish presidents strongly influenced government formation during the decades of largely minority governments. In a semi-presidential system, the executive branch tends to be stronger relative to the legislature than in a purely parliamentary system, and this may – as we discuss in the next section – be worth noting.

Strong Parliaments

Processes of government formation in minority situations may be complex. Several parties interact and each one of them tries to reach outcomes that are as good as possible given other players' preferences and actions. Party leaders and their more or less fractionalized party groups may be motivated by short as well as long-term goals; governmental office sometimes is an end in itself, but most politicians seek office as a means to affect policy decisions and legislation or to influence their electoral fortunes (Strøm 1990; Laver and Schofield 1990). Naturally, entering government and obtaining government portfolios is the only way to satisfy office-seeking motivations. Policy-seeking and vote-seeking parties, on the other hand, may find that they under some circumstances can achieve as much in opposition as in government. In general, parties will be more inclined to seek office if the net benefits of governing outweigh the net benefits of being in the opposition. Government participation almost always increases the policy influence of the party, but the extra influence normally comes at an electoral cost. Incumbent governments tend to lose support at the polls, which makes governing less attractive than it otherwise might have been. Governments in Western Europe have on average lost two-and-a half percentage points in post-WWII elections (Petersson et al. 2002). Losses have mounted decade by decade, peaking at more than six percentage points during elections in the 1990s. Again, in Western Europe, members of majority coalitions tend to lose more votes than parties in minority governments. Countries differ widely in the extent to which governments maintain their strength in the election that follows their term in office. Danish governments perform comparatively well, i.e., better than the European average (Müller and Strøm 2000:589). Norway is close to the average, while Finnish and Swedish governments have a poor record: three out of four governments have been punished by the voters.

Against this background we can hypothesize that the greater the potential influence of opposition groups in parliament, the less the benefits of governing and the less tempting governmental office becomes. Thus, we should expect minority governments to occur more frequently.[42]

If this is a relevant causal factor in the Nordic case, opposition groups should potentially be more influential in Scandinavian legislatures than they are in Finland and Iceland. Influence, of course, is hard to measure, and a comparative judgment based on extensive analyses of actual decision-making is not available.

Nordic parliaments can influence policy and legislation in a variety of ways. All of them have been regarded as "working parliaments", in contrast to the less influential "debating parliaments", which are also found in Europe (Arter 1999:211–217). Of particular significance for the character of the assembly are the decision rules and the internal structure, especially features of the committee system. Working parliaments have a specialized system of standing committees which broadly correspond to government ministries. They have rules of enactment and deliberation which give priority to committee recommendations, proposals and participation in the final stages of parliamentary decision making.

Committees can be organized to facilitate the dispersal of policy-making influence – also to opposition groups. Influential committees have "invested" in expertise, and use their specialized knowledge to control and revise, rather than just rubber stamp decisions from the government. In this light, potential influence is linked to such things as the occurrence of a relatively high number of (not too large) committees, constraints on the number of committee assignments per legislator (to allow MPs to gain expertise), the ability of committees to rewrite government bills and the proportional distribution of committee chairs. In the opinion of students of the Nordic committee systems, their performance in respect of these factors remains uncertain. Powell (2000:34) claims that committees in Scandinavian legislatures facilitate opposition influence to a larger degree than Finnish committees (Iceland is not included in his data set). Mattson and Strøm (1995) distinguish between the drafting authority (e.g. authority to initiate and rewrite bills and demand documents) and agenda control (e.g. control of timetable and right to summon witnesses) of standing committees, but Scandinavian committees do not come out consistently ahead of their Finnish and Icelandic counterparts. For instance, Finnish standing committees are among the strongest with respect to drafting authority, but are rather weak when agenda control is considered. Surprisingly, Mattson and Strøm's data indicate that Danish committees are among the weakest in Western Europe when it comes to the authority to initiate legislation and rewrite government bills. As we have seen, this is also the country with more minority governments than any other. Similarly, Döring (1995) does not consider the overall balance between the government and the standing committees with respect to setting the legislative agenda and passing legislation to vary significantly between the Nordic counties, but he notes that the institutional framework leaves Danish committees with a somewhat less central role than standing committees in the other countries.

In a broader perspective, Damgaard (1994) has noted that the Scandinavian parliaments stand out as strong and influential. Over time, he admits to observing a "decline of governments" or "resurgence of parliaments" rather than "decline of parliaments".[43] Kristjánsson (2004:159), on the other hand, notes that the Icelandic Althingi seems to possess formal means to assert itself as a principal institution, but the parliament has "steadily been losing power" to the executive. The semi-presidential character of the Finnish political system may, until recently, have generated a different legislative-executive balance than in the other Nordic countries. A slightly stronger executive branch also probably implies that the opposition will enjoy less policy-making influence. Damgaard (1990, 2000) also observes differences between Finnish and Scandinavian parliaments with respect to level of activity and involvement.

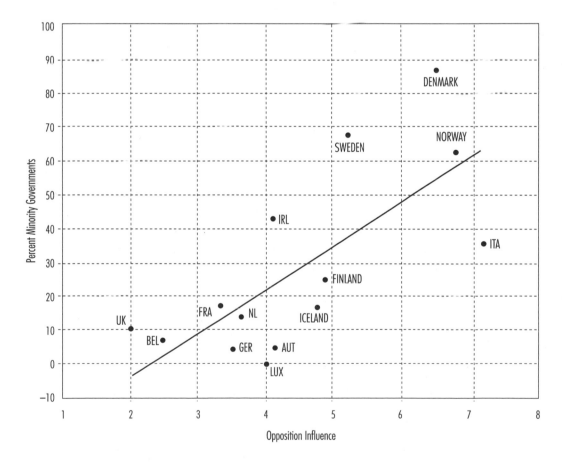

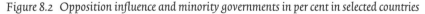

Figure 8.2  Opposition influence and minority governments in per cent in selected countries

Figure 8.2 illustrates a different approach (see Rasch 2004:80). Experts in selected countries were asked to evaluate the influence of opposition politicians
(Laver and Hunt 1992). On the basis of the their assessments, an index of opposition influence was constructed. As we can see from the figure, the experts
judge the opposition to be stronger in Denmark and Norway than in Finland
and Iceland. Sweden ends up in the middle, closer to the latter group. This
way of measuring influence is, however, highly disputable, and we would be
advised to take the correlation between opposition influence and frequency of
minority governments suggested by Figure 8.2 with a large pinch of salt.

DOMINANT AND CENTRAL PARTIES
All the Nordic countries have had multiparty systems since the 1920s at least.
There are important differences between them nonetheless in this respect,
along with substantial swings in the number and relative size of the parties
over time too. The number of seats in parliaments is the hard currency in coalition bargaining, obviously making the party system relevant in our context.
Not surprisingly, the party system variable seems to have resurfaced in recent
coalition research (e.g. Schofield 1993; Laver and Shepsle 2000; van Roozendaal
1992; Crombez 1996).

The Nordic party systems (except Iceland) are described by Heidar (Chapter
3 in this volume), and I will here concentrate on selected aspects only. As an indication of the overall level of party fragmentation after 1945, Figure 8.3 shows
the effective number of parties in each of the Nordic parliaments. This index is
calculated by one divided by the squares of the party seat proportions (Laakso
and Taagepera 1979). It gives the number of equally sized parties that reflects
the actual level of fractionalization in the parliament (i.e. the observed seat
shares). For most of the time covered here, the Finnish *Eduskunta* had the most
fragmented party system. From 1973 to the late 1980s, Danish elections resulted in an equally fragmented parliament. In recent years, Norway has reached
similar levels. Iceland had a fragmented legislature in the late 1980, but has
generally had a moderate (effective) number of parties. Sweden has, on average, had the lowest level of fragmentation.

It has been claimed that the predominance of majority coalitions in Finland can be explained by a fragmented party system (Mattila and Raunio
2002:266). This claim is at best only partly supported by the data in Figure 8.3.
More important than the overall level of fragmentation as measured by the effective number of parties, is the existence of one strong or dominant party in
the midst of the legislature. Even in a fragmented assembly without a majority

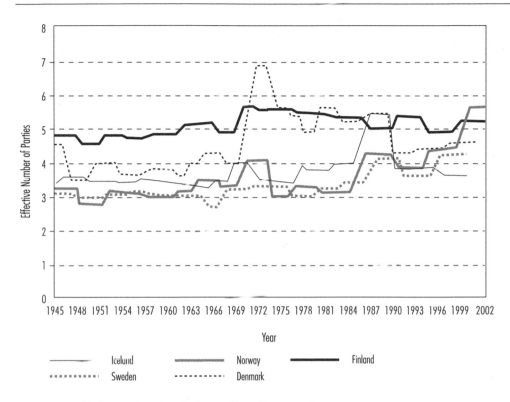

Figure 8.3  *Effective number of parties in Nordic parliaments after 1945*

party, if one party has a far larger share of the seats than any other party, it should have a strong bargaining position. In many minority situations, dominant parties will be able to negotiate their way into government offices as minority administrations. In fact, Crombez (1996) argues that as the largest party grows larger and more central, the more likely minority governments become. A number of cross-national studies support this hypothesis (e.g. Martin and Stevenson 2001; Volden and Carrubba 2004). Almost all minority governments in Schofield's (1993) data set were based on large, centrist parties. If we take a closer look at the Nordic party systems, the largest party in Finland after 1945 has, with few exceptions, been substantially smaller than the largest party in Scandinavian parliaments. The Scandinavian countries have all had a relatively centrist labour party as the dominant group. Iceland has also had a dominant party for most of the time. Here, however, the Conservatives have been the largest group in parliament. Data from party manifestos indicate that the Icelandic conservatives have tended to be less centrist on the left–right scale compared to the other Icelandic parties than the Scandinavian social democrats in their respective legislatures (Budge et al. 2001). Majority coalitions in Finland and Iceland and minority governments in Scandinavia, then, roughly seem to be in line with Crombez (1996) and others. If we look at the era of minority governments in Finland, the largest party was the Social Democratic Party; after some of the elections, it was the dominant force in the legislature (with over 30 per cent of the seats in most elections from 1919 to 1939).

## Concluding Remarks

This chapter has explored government formation in the parliamentary democracies of the Nordic region. We have observed that the Scandinavian countries have a long history of minority cabinets, while Finland and Iceland typically are governed by majority coalitions. In explaining the exceptional pattern of minority parliamentarism in Scandinavia, two factors were emphasized. First, the Scandinavian countries have strong parliaments, which means that parties in opposition have considerable decision-making clout. Participation in government is not necessary to gain influence, and, as a result, minority governments become more likely. Second, certain properties of the party system are important for government formation. Minority governments are more likely in systems with one centrally positioned, relatively large party. Such a pattern has been noted in the Scandinavian countries for decades, but is currently being eroded, at least in Denmark and Norway.

Why do majority coalitions typically govern in Finland and Iceland? In the Finnish case, a highly fragmented legislature without a dominant political force in the centre is an important part of the answer. The shift from minority governments to majority coalitions was probably also helped by a strong presidency in the early post-WWII era. In Iceland, a relatively weak legislature relative to the cabinet seems to be an essential part of the answer.

We have not raised the question of policy-making effectiveness. Minority governments are often associated with political instability and ineffective governance. Clearly, minority governments tend to be less stable than governments which are supported by a legislative majority. It has yet to be demonstrated that Scandinavian minority cabinets in general lack governing capacity (cf. Strøm 1990; Green-Pedersen 2001). If minority governments are centrally located and the opposition divided ideologically or in policy terms, the government has more than one way to build majorities behind its proposals. If, however, the opposition is easily united and can confront the cabinet en bloc, effective government virtually becomes impossible.

# Chapter 9: The Presence of Women in Parliamentary Politics

Nina C. Raaum

Comparative studies of gender and politics in the Nordic countries often emphasise the unity of the region, politically, culturally and socially. In respect of gender equality the Nordic region has also been considered a special instance of equality, both with regard to the relatively high proportion of women in politics and what have been called the women-friendly welfare policies. However, the most recent book on gender and politics in the Nordic countries, *Equal Democracies? Gender and politics in the Nordic countries*, emphasises both homogeneity and heterogeneity. The question mark of the title refers to two overriding questions: How equal are women and men in the Nordic countries and how homogeneous are the Nordic countries (Bergqvist, Borchorst, Christensen, Ramstedt-Silén, Raaum and Styrkársdóttir 1999)?

The extensive literature on women's political representation has developed two basic approaches (Lovenduski and Norris 2003). The first one focuses on *descriptive representation*, that is, on women representing or "standing as" women. This approach has concerned itself with mapping the proportion of women in elected bodies and to identify the reasons for the low, or in some cases, higher, levels of women's representation. How do different histories together with variations in contextual factors, institutional characteristics related to public policies, the election system, the role of party recruitment, and women's resources and motivation affect the political integration of women?

The second approach, *substantive representation*, asks whether, if elected, women make a difference, that is, whether they are "acting for" women as a group, assuming they have particular experiences and interest in the home, workplace and society beyond. As Lovenduski and Norris note, this issue has been of long standing theoretical interest but, in most countries, so far at least, so few women have been elected to most political bodies that it has been considered premature to explore what impact they may have had either on the substance of public policies or on political procedures. Even in the Nordic countries, where women have been relatively well represented over the last couple of decades, relatively modest empirical attention has been paid to their impact.

The success of women's struggle for political presence varies considerably across different political arenas and national contexts. Our aim, in this chapter, is to elucidate the political presence of women in Nordic parliamentary politics. In as much as we concentrate on the parliamentarian arena, we only shed light on one of many political arenas. In political science, not least in feminist scholarship, politics is a contested term with different meanings. Feminists have rightly argued that a narrow understanding of politics, for example related to formal political institutions such as we are focusing on here, excludes very important aspects of women's democratic citizenship (Siim 2000). Although we pay some attention to women's political activities and agencies outside the formal political system, for instance the significance of women's voluntary organisations and the women's movement, the intention is by no means to give a complete picture of all aspects concerning women's involvement in political life.

The chapter is structured around four institutional thresholds which every mobilising group must pass or overcome on their way up through the parliamentary system. These thresholds were originally identified by the Norwegian political scientist Stein Rokkan (1970, 1987), after conducting studies of political mobilisation among men. Although the model is also an appropriate point of departure in studies of women's mobilisation (Nagel 1995), the processes of mobilisation among Nordic men and women differ considerably. Thus, in order to explain gender differences both across and within Nordic countries, Rokkan's model certainly must be supplemented by feminist rethinking of citizenship.

Initially, let us briefly describe the different thresholds in relation to gender and give a hint of what passing a threshold may imply. In the next sections, we present data regarding the mobilisation of women in relation to the different thresholds, before we discuss how similar and dissimilar patterns of mobilisation across gender and nations may be explained.

## Passing Institutional Thresholds: The Significance of Critical Numbers

Based on historical analyses of processes of political mobilisation among male workers and peasants in seventeen West European countries, Rokkan identified *four thresholds*, namely legitimisation, incorporation, representation and executive power. According to Rokkan, each threshold represents an *institutional* barrier, but, in our view, the periods in between can also be comprehended as different phases of mobilisation. As chapter one gives a description of each of these institutional thresholds, we shall only *very* briefly comment on the gendered aspects of each of them.

The first threshold is *legitimisation*. At this stage women had to conquer public space for their values and interests (Nagel 2000). The so-called old women's movement or first wave feminism, which in the Nordic region was formally organised from 1870, faced several challenges in this initial phase. Women had to put the political gender opinion on the political agenda, they had to win allies among progressive men in the political elite(s), and they had – not least – to develop strategies and agencies to empower and involve women.

The next threshold is *incorporation*, i.e., introduction of universal suffrage and the right to stand for election. In relation to gender, this phase above all concerns the introduction of universal suffrage, though it also deals with the encouraging of female citizens to make use of their new political rights. In most countries, among men as well as among women, a couple of decades will most often pass before voter turnout among newly enfranchised groups equals that of formerly enfranchised ones. Although this is an important aspect of incorporation, we will not explore the details of these historical processes in this chapter.

The third threshold is political *representation* in parliament. Compared to the previous threshold, this one implies a more qualified political presence, that is, direct participation in decision-making processes. The political parties, as a link between voters and elected representatives, have had great impact on the recruitment of female legislators, as have certain properties of the election system and gender specific political arrangements (such as quotas, for example).

The fourth and final threshold is the step to *executive power*, that is, the achievement of cabinet and ministerial position. Following the introduction of a parliamentary system, the most important criterion of representation in executive bodies, as in legislative assemblies, is affiliation to political parties.

Gender as a criterion of representation is usually seen as a latecomer, often in relation to more or less formal gender quotas. However, as Nagel stresses, when gender does not mean women, but simply gender, it is evident that gender has been a criterion from the start. Following the introduction of representative democracy, men have historically assumed an exclusive right to political representation, and they kept this privilege for a long time (Nagel 2000:208).

When crossing one threshold, new pressures sooner or later will be generated and prompt changes to the next institutional barrier. Critics of the threshold perspective point to the model's alleged deterministic nature, arguing that it is ill adapted to explain the ambiguities and complexities in women's political mobilisation (see for example Christensen 1997; Skjeie and Siim 2000; Siim 1997). In our opinion this is not an adequate criticism.

First, Rokkan explicitly refers to the formal and institutionalised political system, founded on party politics. Of course, to give a complete portrayal of women's political activities, the picture of parliamentary politics must be supplemented by analyses of a much wider range of women's political activities and agencies. As Christensen and Raaum (1999) call attention to, the threshold perspective is certainly not particularly relevant in analyses of mobilisation processes which lie beyond, or on the fringes of, the formal political system, such as, for instance, the new social movements.

Second, Raaum and Christensen emphasise that the process of passing thresholds by no means is an automatic process. On the contrary, the underlying premise of the threshold perspective is that the time needed to break through institutional barriers will vary from country to country as well as between different groups of men and women. Different types of mobilisation patterns are generated across countries and gender precisely because mobilising groups encounter dissimilar contexts or opportunity structures, that is, different combinations of *structural, cultural* and *political* conditions. Rokkan did emphasise this, arguing that the actual point in time at which changes occur vary considerably from system to system: between nation-states and also between sub-national groups. The crux of the matter is that processes of democratisation are contextually determined. Combined with different types of strategies on the part of the political elite and the mobilising groups themselves, this contributes to a diversification of the processes of mobilisation.

Christensen and Raaum finally stress that a single theory or explanation cannot cover the complexity of women's political integration. Processes of political mobilisation are complex and diverse. In seeking out the general and the universal in mobilisation processes, we must also give room to differentiation and diversity. Siim (2000) argues in a similar way, that there is no universal story of citizenship, since gendered citizenships are embedded in national histories, social institutions and political cultures.

So, what does it mean to pass or overcome an institutional threshold? Clearly, it must mean that women constitute a certain amount or a so-called critical number of a political group, i.e. many enough to affect public policies as voters or representatives, whether specifically women's issues or other political issues. Surely, a few, even very few, women pioneers can play crucial political roles, but with regard to the broader mobilisation of women *as a group*, reaching that critical number must at least imply that women in politics do not appear as an extreme, minority group. Inspired by Rosabeth Moss Kanter (1977), who studied gender relations within industrial relations, many feminist researchers have stressed that rather than a steady evolution, there seems to be a critical *"tipping point"* that depends on *relative* numbers (Lovenduski and Norris 2003:88). As Lovenduski and Norris point out, Kanter's argument is that the size of a minority matters. *Uniform* groups consist of only men or only women. *Balanced* groups, on the other hand, contain 40–60 per cent of each sex. In between these alternatives, *skewed* groups contain a large imbalance of men and women, up to about 15 per cent of the minority group, while *tilted* groups contain about 15–40 per cent of the opposite sex.

Kanter suggested that once a group reaches a certain size, somewhere in the tilted group range, the group is large enough to assert itself and potentially be in a position to transform institutional cultures and policies. Some feminists have suggested that women should constitute a ratio of about 30 per cent to reach that critical number. Others have rightly claimed that Kanter treats gender as a symmetric category. Counting numbers, without taking into consideration the overall masculine and asymmetric gender relations in society at large, can give a wrong impression of the impact of relative numbers. This discussion, however, concerns a more theoretical and principal question which we will not address here.

Strictly speaking, if a balanced representation of gender implies that a group contains 40–60 per cent of each sex, overcoming a threshold should imply that women constitute at least 40 – or not very far from 40 – per cent of a group, for example among citizens that actually cast a vote or among elected representatives. Still, we should not overstate this norm of gender balance without considering the duration and stability of somewhat lower female ratios in the tilted group range. In our opinion, we cannot decide a priori what a critical or sufficient relative number amounts to. In practice, this question has to be scrutinised empirically in relation to each different case. For example, although the likelihood of gaining influence in parliament is probably strengthened with an increased number of women; we can not presume that their political influence will increase proportionally with increasing female ratios in parliaments. What's more, the effects of an increasing number of women in politics do not happen automatically but manifest themselves under certain conditions which are not only dependent on critical numbers, but the processes of mobilisation that are made possible by women's presence in traditionally masculine or male-dominated institutions (Lovenduski and Norris 2003:88).

Among both men and women, political representation was broadened to include citizens from the well-to-do classes and later the peasants and the working class (Nagel 2000). However, as we shall see, looking forward from the initial struggles for democratic citizenship, the parliamentarian mobilisation of women (as of men) followed rather different paths in the individual Nordic countries.

## Legitimisation and Incorporation

When the political mobilisation of ordinary citizens evolved in the later part of the 1800s, only Denmark and Sweden enjoyed independent status and had any experience of successful state-building. The three remaining countries in the Nordic region were dependent socially, culturally, and politically (see Chapter 1, this volume).

The different timing of the legitimisation of women's democratic citizenship can be measured by (1) the establishment of feminist organisations centred on the women's movement society and (2) the formation of separate suffrage organisations fighting for women's political rights (Nagel 1995). These events started in the 1870s (see table 1). Danish women were the first to found a feminist organisation, in 1871, concurrently with the formation of the first Nordic political parties by Danish men. The formation of a women's suffrage association in Denmark did not take place until 1889, nearly twenty years later. In Sweden, Norway and Finland feminist organisations were founded in 1884, also in these countries more or less concurrently with the founding of male-dominated political parties (see Chapter 3, this volume). As in Denmark, the formation of a Swedish society for women's suffrage came nearly twenty years after the foundation of the first feminist organisation, in 1903. Finnish women worked for the right to vote in women's organisations and the labour movement, but never founded a society specifically for the purpose of campaigning for women's suffrage (Raaum 1999).

The political mobilisation of women in Norway and Iceland followed a somewhat different pattern. Norway experienced a simultaneous emergence of organisations for women's liberation and suffrage, in 1884 and 1885 respectively (Nagel 1995, 2000). Actually, Norwegian women founded the first Nordic society for women's suffrage. In Iceland, as in Denmark and Sweden, the first women's association was also founded prior to the first society for women's suffrage. This took place, however, before Icelandic men started to organise political parties in the post-1916 period (Raaum 1999). The belated development of political parties in Iceland, as compared to the other Nordic countries, is related to comparatively late industrialisation of the country and the relatively narrow scope of the political conflicts or cleavages at the time (Rokkan 1970, 1987).

Table 9.1 Institutionalisation of democratic citizenship in the Nordic region, legitimisation (political organisations) and incorporation (the enactment of the right to vote in general elections)

| | Denmark | Finland | Iceland | Norway | Sweden |
|---|---|---|---|---|---|
| Legitimisation, founding of women's agencies: | | | | | |
| – Feminist associations | 1871 | 1884 | 1894 | 1884 | 1884 |
| – Suffrage societies | 1889 | never | 1907 | 1885 | 1903 |
| Incorporation, the right to vote in national elections: | | | | | |
| – women | 1915 | 1906 | 1915/1920 | 1913 | 1921 |
| – men | 1849 | 1906 | 1915 | 1898 | 1909 |

Source: Nina C. Raaum (1999), "Women in parliamentary politics: Historical lines of development", In Christina Bergqvist et al. (eds.): Equal Democracies? Gender and politics in the Nordic countries, Oslo: Scandinavian University Press, p. 32, cf. p. 297

A radical Finnish reform of the voting system in 1906 introduced universal suffrage simultaneously for men and women. Thereby, Finnish women became the first to cross the second institutional threshold of incorporation. After Finland, women in Norway and Denmark gained the right to vote more or less at the same time, in 1913 and 1915 respectively. Sweden and Iceland were the last Nordic countries to introduce universal suffrage.

International statistics put the date of the introduction of universal female suffrage in Iceland as 1915 (IPU 2004), when the franchise was extended to women and servants. However, instead of an age requirement of 25, which was the general condition, in 1915 the age limit for women and servants was set at 40. This age limit was adopted with the proviso that it would be lowered step-wise, year by year, over the next 15 years. The rationale for citing 1915 as the year of universal suffrage is that the general principle was adopted then (Hard-arson 2002). To be sure, the 15-year phasing in period also applied to male servants, but they were a much smaller group than the female servants. This meant that a considerable number of women would not be on equal footing with men until 1930. However, it is probably just as correct to say that Icelandic universal suffrage was introduced in 1920. Firstly, there was a lot of opposition to female suffrage in Iceland, and it is assumed that the special age requirement was put in place to forestall the popular Women's Lists, which had been entered in three local elections, the first one as early as 1908 (Styrkársdóttir 1999). Secondly, in 1918, the Danish and the Icelandic Government decided that Iceland should be an independent realm under the Danish king, and that citizenship in Iceland and Denmark should be dual. Because the Danish political elites could not accept the prospect of Danish women as second-rate citizens in Iceland, the Icelandic parliament was therefore obliged to give women and men equal rights in 1920 (Raaum 1999).

The Icelandic case is interesting also because the women's lists were a mixture of political party and social movement. Indeed, women's lists were put up in several of the Nordic countries in the beginning of the 1900s, as well as a good number of European countries, though mostly in local elections (Styrkársdóttir 1999). What distinguishes the Icelandic experience is the presence of women's lists ahead of the formation of political parties among men, and also their re-emergence (as the so called Women's Alliance) in the 1980s and their subsequent success. The Icelandic women's list is really a distinctive example of gender as a political cleavage and basis of party formation.

Following the foundation of the first Nordic feminist association in Denmark in 1870, one hundred years would pass before Nordic women reached a critical number in the Nordic parliaments and governments. The years around 1970 became a *turning point*. Without doubt, the most dramatic change in Nordic citizenship at the end of last century was the ensuing integration of women into legislative and executive powers. As compared to the first two thresholds, the gender gap was widening dramatically with regard to the political presence of women in parliaments and cabinets.

## Representation and Executive Power

Once Nordic women achieved the right to vote, they were relatively quickly elected to parliament, though their numbers grew very slowly before 1970 (see table 9.2). Still, Finland distinguished itself prior to the Second World War. During the period between the introduction of universal suffrage and the 1960s, Finnish women actually held roughly 10 per cent of the seats in parliament (MPs). Subsequent to the Second World War, Swedish women gained 10 per cent of the Riksdag seats in the general election of 1953, while Danish women passed the 10 per cent level, achieving 11 per cent of the MPs in 1966. In Norway, and especially in Iceland, progress was slow, and prior to 1970, the Nordic region never experienced any national assembly that was not an extremely gender-skewed group.

During the 1970s, every Nordic country, with the partial exception of Iceland, witnessed a fresh mobilisation of women. Up to the mid-Eighties the parliamentary mobilisation of Norwegian women was probably the most far-reaching in the whole of the Nordic region (Raaum 1999). In the course of two elections in the Seventies, women passed first the 10 per cent threshold, then the 20 per cent level. The proportion of women in the Norwegian national assembly, the Storting, increased from 9 per cent prior to 1973, to 24 per cent in 1977. This put Norway abreast of Finland, Denmark and Sweden. Later, during the 1980s, women in these countries all reached a relatively high level of parliamentary representation of at least 30 per cent.

Concerning women's representation in parliament, Sweden and Iceland have been the most dissimilar cases within the Nordic region. It was only after the 1983 election that Icelandic women could celebrate a record, from 5 per cent in the 1979 election to 15 per cent in 1983. This was a result of the ensuing mobilisation behind the Icelandic Women's List in 1982. In the shape of the Women's Alliance, the list won 6 per cent of the votes in 1983, and 10 per cent in 1987. Besides, and as important, the women's list brought considerable pressure to bear on the other Icelandic parties to recruit more women. Today, the main cause of the low representation of Icelandic women is probably to be found in the electoral procedures. The proportion of Icelandic women running for office is still far higher than the proportion of women among the elected representatives. In the rest of the Nordic countries today, only small differences prevail between the proportion of women among the candidates and the numbers elected to office.

Table 9.2 *The integration of women as MPs (members in parliament) in the Nordic region*

|  | Denmark | Finland | Iceland | Norway | Sweden |
|---|---|---|---|---|---|
| – First women elected to parliament | 1918 | 1907 | 1922 | 1922 | 1922 |
| – First election at which female representation in parliament reached: | | | | | |
| 10% | 1966 | 1907 | 1983 | 1973 | 1953 |
| 20% | 1979 | 1970 | 1987 | 1977 | 1973 |
| 30% | 1988 | 1983 | 1999 | 1985 | 1986 |
| 40% | never | never | never | never | 1994 |
| – At present, 2004, % female of MPs | 38.0 | 37.5 | 30.2 | 36.4 | 45.3 |

Sources: Interparliamentary Union, Women in National Parliaments (www.ipu.org/ wmn-e/world.htm), Raaum (1999): "Women in parliamentary politics", in Bergqvist et al. (eds.): *Equal Democracies? Gender and politics in the Nordic countries*, Oslo: Scandinavian University Press (p. 32, cf. p. 296)

As the 1990s approached, Sweden was leading the way, with Norway only slightly behind. In Sweden, women gained a 40.4 per cent share of the seats in the Riksdag in 1994, a result that eclipsed all previous records in the Nordic region. It was achieved as a result of women's mobilisation in response to the so-called "backlash election" of 1991, when the proportion of women in the Riksdag fell from 38 to 33 per cent. This provoked a strong response and wide public debate. Political parties and public authorities were met with insistent demands to incorporate more women, and in the following 1994 election, not only did women win 40 per cent of seats in parliament, they were appointed to 50 per cent of the cabinet posts.

Denmark was lagging somewhat behind Sweden and Norway. For most of the decade after the Danish 1988 election, the proportion of women in parliament stagnated at about 33 per cent. In 1998, women gained 37.4 per cent of the seats (Bergqvist et al. 1999:298). The situation in Finland after 1970 has been more akin to that in Denmark than in Norway and Sweden. At the 1991 elections, Finnish women gained 39 per cent of the seats in the Finnish parliament, but throughout the remainder of the Eighties and Nineties, the percentage of women has been closer to 30 than 40. Not till the election of 1999, when women achieved 37 per cent representation, were Finnish women again close to a gender-balanced representation.

At present, in 2004, the most dissimilar cases are still Sweden and Iceland, where women MPs are now 45.3 and 30.2 of all MPs respectively. In the 1999 election, Icelandic women for the first time passed the 30 per cent threshold, with 34.9 per cent. At the next election, in 2003, they only obtained 30.2 per cent, which is presently the poorest showing in the Nordic region (IPU 2004). The percentage of women in the Danish, Finnish and Norwegian parliaments is now approximately at the same level, about 37/38 per cent. Norway no longer holds pole position together with Sweden, as the country did up to the 1990s, during the governments of the first Nordic woman prime minister, Gro Harlem Brundtland.

With regard to women's access to the *executive* branch, Finland stands out as a special case prior to the Second World War. A female attained a ministership as early as 1926. In contrast to the short incumbency of Denmark's first female minister in 1924, she remained in place for a very long time indeed, twenty years all told (Raaum 1999). In Norway and Sweden, each country appointed their first woman minister after the Second World War, in 1945 and 1947 respectively. The Icelandic cabinets, on the other hand, continued to be undiluted male executives right up to 1970. Of the two Nordic non-monarchies, Iceland and Finland, it was nevertheless Iceland that appointed the first woman president in 1980. With regard to the effect of women pioneers, she may well have served as a role model, contributing to the increasing integration of Icelandic women which followed during the 1980s.

In Norway, overcoming the fourth threshold, accession to executive power, happened very quickly indeed. After the 1973 general election, women secured 20 per cent of the seats in the cabinet. In 1981, the first Nordic female prime minister, Gro Harlem Brundtland, was appointed. A few years later in 1986, Brundtland's so-called "Women's Government" made the headlines worldwide with eight women in the eighteen-minister Cabinet. Since then, the proportion of women in the Norwegian Government has never sunk below 42 per cent. In point of fact, a Norwegian coalition government appointed in 1997 had 47 per cent women, but Norway has never equalled the Swedish world record.

Subsequent to the 1992 backlash election, Swedish women were appointed to 50 per cent of the ministerial positions in the two following governments in 1994 and 1998. At present, in 2004, they actually have all of 55 per cent of the Swedish cabinet. Following the election in 1991, Finnish women gained 41 per cent of the minister posts. In Denmark the female ratio in the cabinet has never passed 40 per cent. In 1993, it passed the 30 per cent mark for the first time,

with women in 33 per cent of the posts. In the two following Danish governments, appointed in 1994 and 1998, 35 per cent of the ministers were women,
but at present they only amount to 28 per cent. Regarding women's access to
the executive level, Iceland is far behind the other Nordic countries. At
present, Icelandic women make up almost the same ratio of ministers as in
Denmark, but only passed the 20 per cent level in 1999. In the preceding
period, women only had approximately 10 per cent of the cabinet posts in all
governments back to 1983.

*Table 9.3  Nordic women in executive office*

|  | Denmark | Finland | Iceland | Norway | Sweden |
|---|---|---|---|---|---|
| First woman minister | 1924 | 1926 | 1970 | 1945 | 1947 |
| First woman prime minister | never | 2003 | never | 1981 | never |
| First cabinet where women had at least: | | | | | |
| 10% of all posts | 1953 | 1953 | 1903 | 1965 | 1966 |
| 20% of all posts | 1981 | 1987 | 1999 | 1973 | 1976 |
| 30% of all posts | 1993 | 1995 | never | 1986 | 1991 |
| 40% of all posts | never | 1991 | never | 1986 | 1994 |
| 50% of all posts | never | never | never | never | 1994 |
| At present, 2004, % of women | 28 | 42 | 25 | 42 | 55 |
| First woman president (elected in Finland and Iceland only) | – | 2000 | 1980 | – | – |

Sources: Christina Bergqvist et al. (eds.), (1999): *Equal Democracies? Gender and politics in the
Nordic countries*, Oslo: Scandinavian University Press, pp. 306–310.

The political parties have played a crucial role in parliamentary politics. As a
link between electors and elected they formed one of the cornerstones of the
system of parliamentary representation. Nevertheless, both in the past and
present, considerable ambivalence has characterised their handling of the integration of women and the issue of gender equality. In their studies of party
strategies to enhance the women's representation, Lovenduski and Norris
(1993) found three strategies: (1) rhetorics, i.e., upbeat statements are made on
the importance of increasing women's influence in the parties; (2) "affirmative

action" – the development of programmes to support and encourage women to assume power; and (3) positive discrimination whereby gender quotas are allocated.

Concerning the last and most progressive strategy, Christensen (1999) refers to two kinds of quotas. First, gender quotas designed for party democracies. These *party quotas* are internal quotas within the party organisations; typically a statute is adopted to secure a 40–60 per cent gender ratio. Second, to further the political integration of women in parliaments and cabinets, *candidate quotas* can be used in election, i.e. in relation to the system of representative democracy. We lack complete data on the strategies of the Nordic parties in order to enhance women's representation. It is clear, however, that there are large disparities both between the national parties and between countries.

Christensen shows that Norway's political parties have developed the most radical integration strategy for women in the past twenty years in the Nordic area, by applying both party and candidate quotas. The political parties in Denmark and Iceland are clearly marked with the weakest integration strategies for women. In Denmark the party quota system has primarily been exercised by the Socialist People's Party and Social Democratic Party. However, both parties abolished gender quotas at their congresses in 1996. Furthermore, candidate quotas have only been used to a very limited extent in Denmark, as in Iceland. Sweden and Finland are probably the countries where the women's sections historically have made the strongest impact. Several of the political parties in the two countries have implemented party quotas, while the use of candidate quotas is much more limited. Within the Swedish parties, opposition to the idea of formalising gender quotas has been considerable. Instead, Sweden has practiced a more informal principle of "mixed lists". The demand for gender-balanced lists was so intense after the backlash election of 1991, that several of the Swedish parties adopted the principle of "sandwiched" or "Every Other Seat a Woman's Seat" lists (Bergqvist et al. 1999; Stark 1997), which gave women 40 per cent of the MPs and 50 per cent of the cabinet posts in 1994.

Contrary to what is often claimed in the international literature, the Nordic region is not such an unequivocal example of the exercise of quotas (Christensen 1999). There have been, and still are, important inter-Nordic differences with respect to the integration of women in the parliamentary arena. The question is how to explain the similarities and differences.

## Women's Political Influence Before 1970. A Brief Discussion

Just as each Nordic country had their own particular histories of state and nation-building and mobilisation patterns among men, the political mobilisation of women was also diffcrent. Although less evident in Iceland, there was a high degree of correlation between the first parties formed by Nordic men and the establishment of the first Nordic women's rights and suffragette organisations. Another common feature, except for Finland, is that women gained the right to vote somewhat later than men. Sweden and Iceland were the two last countries to enact universal suffrage. While Sweden's history of class governance tended to stem the tide of radical reforms, the slower development in Iceland was related to the relatively late industrialisation of the country and – in Nordic terms – the narrow scope of the issues of national independence behind which the citizens mobilised (Rokkan 1970, 1987).

What is more, in the three *dependent* Nordic countries at the end of the 1800s, political discord over the national independence issue contributed to hastening the enfranchisement of women (Raaum 1999). In Norway, the relatively early and simultaneous emergence of organisations for women's liberation and suffrage most likely reflects the special politicisation of Norwegian society at the time, with the introduction of parliamentary politics as early as in 1884, a sweeping cultural resistance movement and national mobilisation in support of independence from Sweden. The 1905 referendum on the dissolution of the Swedish-Norwegian union certainly fuelled the political mobilisation of women. Women were protesting their lack of voting rights in the referendum, and organised a petition on the issue. Lists from this so called "women's referendum" revealed extensive involvement of women and became an effective argument in favour of universal suffrage (Nagel 1995:65).

The radical voting reform which Finland enacted in 1906 probably reflects Finland's particular political situation, with extensive mobilisation in favour of independence from the Soviet Union. This mobilisation was rooted in deep-seated conflicts of a social, cultural and political nature, and was decisive for the abrupt transition (Rokkan 1970). Actually, Finland is a special case, since Finnish women had about a 10 per cent share of the seats in parliament from 1906 to the 1960s. It is assumed that the radical reform of voting rights in 1906 in itself contributed to the special situation in Finland, but a relatively high participation in paid work and early party political organising among Finnish women may also have had an effect (Raaum 1999). In Iceland, as mentioned, it was external rather than internal pressure that tipped the balance. It was only after demands from the Danish authorities that universal suffrage was brought forward from 1930 to 1920 (Raaum 1999; Styrkársdóttir 1999). A part of the explanation was that the Danish political elites were unwilling to see Danish women treated as potentially second-rate citizens in Iceland.

Although women were very poorly represented in formal political bodies during the first part of the 1900s, they still played important political roles through voluntary organisations of civil society, or so-called third sector. In contrast to the situation on the Continent, in the USA and in Great Britain, voluntary organisations in traditionally more "state-dominated" and highly organised societies such as the Nordics have been member-based and democratic. Rather than following market ideas and remaining separate from the state, they urged the development of the welfare state, in close collaboration with the public authorities (Berven and Selle 2001; Klausen and Selle 1996; Raaum 1999, 2001; Selle 1998).

The scope and influence of the various types of voluntary organisation – ranging from narrowly religious to broad-based welfare organisations and the co-operative movement – have varied within the Nordic region. Unfortunately, research on women's involvement in these organisations primarily deals with Norway and Sweden. Yet judging from the rates of female membership, both exclusively female and female-dominated organisations have without doubt played a more decisive political role than has previously been assumed (Selle 1998).

At the local level in Norway, municipal authorities and voluntary organisations, many of them female dominated, collaborated on the first local government welfare schemes, which appeared alongside the emergence of the political parties and universal suffrage. As Seip (1991:26 ff.) shows, this was not an accidental correlation, but a *political* result.

During the expansion of the welfare state, especially the first three decades after the Second World War, several associations with mainly female membership and leadership worked actively with the public authorities, not least at the national level (Bjarnar 2001). They pioneered new schemes, uncovered needs and provided a social service as welfare workers. What's more, they built up many extremely professional social welfare institutions. During the building of the welfare state women's extensive experience and expertise were of vital importance for the authorities. Women's organisations were also able to present the women's side of the needs that the growing welfare state was intended to meet.

Finally, women's voluntary organisations contributed crucially to the political empowerment of women. They were community and identity-building institutions which gave more and more women the opportunity to unite behind political programmes (Bjarnar 2001), thereby integrating new groups of women into political life. Besides, not least of their achievements were the connections they forged with the political authorities. The significance of such empowerment was highlighted by Helga Hernes (1987) in her analysis of the potentially woman-friendly Scandinavian welfare states. She introduced the term "state feminism", to describe how this potential on the part of the state had become evident exactly because of the *interplay* between a broad mobilization of women "from below" and relatively woman-friendly policies "from above".

Before the 1970s, the voluntary organisations were particularly important for women, whose presence in other areas of the public and market sectors was weak. From the middle of the 1800s, Nordic men were mobilised by political parties (connected to the state), the trade union movement (connected to the market), and voluntary organisations (connected to civil society). For Nordic women, however, the voluntary organisations represented their most important political arena to the end of the 1960s (Raaum 1999, 2001).

Not till the emergence of the new women's movement at the end of the 1960s, did Nordic women gain access to parliamentary bodies.

## The Point of No Return: Explaining Similarities and Differences After 1970

Compared to the first two thresholds of legitimisation and incorporation, the gender gap was even wider when it came to a place in formal political decision-making. Nordic women had to wait at least until the 1970s to break into parliamentary politics, and they faced a double burden of legitimisation. As had men, they had to cross the legitimacy threshold prior to their incorporation as voters, but in addition, in order to achieve significant numbers in Nordic parliaments and cabinets, they had to overcome another barrier of legitimisation. Of course, it could be argued that women had not really passed the first threshold of legitimisation, as it, strictly speaking, concerned both the right to vote and stand for election. In our view, though, due to the very long time lag behind men, in addition to the lack of active and collective feminist groups after universal suffrage was introduced and to the 1960s (Nagel 1995), it is more accurate to speak of an additional legitimating threshold for women.

Several factors contributed to the parliamentarian integration of women subsequent to 1970. Certainly, a crucial condition was that women themselves

actually mobilised. As Christensen and Raaum (1999) stress, processes of mobilisation concern *activities* as well as *values*. Political actions derive from political opinions and values, just as new interests, values and identities are formed
and shaped through the processes of mobilisation. Changing the political values of large numbers of women, such as the demand for political presence, was
essential to the mobilisation of women. Women's agencies, through independent organising and their capacity to influence formal politics, have been
the key element in the transformation of women's democratic citizenship (Siim 2000:127).

A shared characteristic of the Nordic countries is that women were fairly
well represented in parliamentary politics much earlier than women in most
other western countries. Actually, it is unique for the Nordic region that second wave feminism was followed by an incorporation of women into the political elite during the 1970s and 1980s (Siim 2000). The interplay of several
structural, cultural and political factors produced a contextual framework
which prepared the way for this unique development.

Firstly, concerning socio-economic factors, the improving economic situation of the Nordic region following the Second World War affected women's
living conditions in several ways. Technological progress simplified women's
traditional tasks in the household and new methods of contraception allowed
far better birth control. The increasing urbanisation, and general radicalisation at the end of the 1960s challenged traditional gender norms (Blom 1992).
Last, but not least, the growing employment and education rates, especially
among women, helped end women's social isolation and create a socially homogeneous platform consistent with a common *identity* for women (Togeby
1994:56). Togeby argues that women's participation in the labour market, and
more indirectly their involvement in the educational system, is the main factor behind their political mobilisation subsequent to 1970.

For example, women's relatively belated political mobilisation in Norway
in the years before 1970, which gained pace considerably thereafter, is definitely related to the increasing education and employment opportunities for
women (Raaum 1999). In the post-war period Norway was one of Europe's
leading "housewife countries"; women's employment rates were comparatively low. It was not until the Seventies that women's participation in the labour
market increased to any significant extent. In 1970, only 23 per cent of Norwegian women worked outside the home. In contrast, 53 per cent of Swedish
women had paid jobs. The low level of employment among Norwegian wom-
en may initially have contributed to delaying their political mobilisation. In a

similar fashion, the extraordinarily powerful growth in Norwegian women's employment throughout the Seventies probably promoted their political integration during the years following 1970.

Nevertheless, one shortcoming of structural theories, particularly in their focus on the labour market, for instance, is that a significant integration of women in the labour market does not necessarily hand together with political mobilisation (Christensen and Raaum 1999). Many Western countries have witnessed an equally powerful growth in women's paid employment without it having any noticeable impact on their political mobilisation, certainly not in the area of parliamentary politics.

Secondly, *cultural* factors also affect the political integration of women. With regard to the impact of religion, Protestantism, the prevailing religion of the Nordic region, is often considered as more "women friendly" compared to religions that advocate very traditional roles for women, such as Catholicism, Orthodox Christianity and Islam (Blom 1992). Moreover the Nordic region is characterised by a relatively egalitarian or social democratic political culture, reflecting the rather homogeneous population and class structure. The ideal of equality, which may not have been espoused equally by all the Nordic countries, has probably nevertheless been conducive to the political integration of women (Bergqvist et al. 1999).

The social democratic culture is, thirdly, reflected in the more basic *political* factors such as the policies of the Nordic welfare states and the Nordic election and party system. The Scandinavian or Nordic welfare policy model forms a type of social democratic regime characterised by social safeguards for more or less all sections of the population. Although the character of the so-called women-friendly policies of the Scandinavian model is disputed, when compared with other welfare models, the Nordic model provides relatively good opportunity to combine parenthood with paid work and political involvement (Bergqvist et al. 1999). Besides, the institutionalisation of gender equality through legislation and other public schemes is far more extensive than in other types of welfare regime (Borchorst 1999).

The proportional electoral systems of the Nordic countries, aid the recruitment of women more than majority vote or single constituency electoral systems (Rule and Zimmermann 1994). Proportional representation was introduced much earlier than 1970, however, so that of itself is certainly not sufficient to secure a high number of women in parliamentary politics. On the other hand, the use of gender quotas, more or less officially by the political parties, has certainly been successful.

Although the processes of women's integration into Nordic parliaments and executives have much in common, the breakthrough of women into parliaments and executive office proceeded at different rates in the Nordic countries. These dissimilar developments also relate to structural, cultural and political factors. We should not exaggerate the differences between the Nordic countries, the concluding chapter of the book *Equal Democracies? Gender and politics in the Nordic countries* shows that rather than a single Nordic gender profile, we can actually identify *five different gender profiles* in accordance with the particular characteristics of each country (Borchorst, Christensen and Raaum 1999:286–289).

Following the Second World War, things happened very quickly indeed in Sweden. First, the Swedish SAP, at the time the Nordic countries' most powerful social democratic party, and the Swedish public sector were rapidly expanding. Sweden had remained neutral during the Second World War, so while the other Nordic countries were faced with lengthy reconstruction programmes, as well as foreign policy worries, after the war, the Swedish social democrats were in a better position to address at an early date the situation of women in society. This favourable situation contributed to the relatively early upswing in Swedish women's representation. The combination of the great expansion of welfare and childcare policies and the institutionalisation of women's issues also contributed in a positive direction, bringing Sweden into the front line with regard to the political representation of women (Raaum 1999).

Today, the *Swedish* gender profile is high on every parameter (Borchorst, Christensen and Raaum 1999). The great expansion of welfare and childcare policy and the high level of institutionalisation by means of legislative developments and government policies on welfare and gender equality issues, has left its mark. The level of women's representation in Sweden has always been among the highest of the Nordic countries. At present, Swedish women hold a world record in representation in parliamentary politics. This is probably due to several things, women's social and political citizenship, the integration of women into the labour market, supported by long periods of social democratic government and the institutionalisation of gender equality issues through the political parties and the state.

In Norway, the practice of gender quotas has without doubt boosted the number of women in parliament, although it should be noted that unofficial quota arrangements have had a similar effect. The *Norwegian* gender profile, like the Swedish, is based on a relatively high level of institutionalisation of gender equality (Borchorst, Christensen and Raaum 1999). Though the integration of women into politics and the workforce took place later than in most of the other Nordic countries, it was accomplished much faster. The issue of gender equality has figured on the political programmes of the political parties and most governments following 1970. Before the 1990s, though, Norway lagged far behind Sweden and Denmark in the quality and quantity of its childcare provisions. Today, not least due to the more offensive gender equality policies introduced by Gro Harlem Brundtland's "women's government", the differences in the area are significantly smaller. In the Nordic region, Norwegian political parties have developed the most effective strategies to integrate women. Part of the explanation is that the ideology of difference, i.e. the perception that women represent other values and interests than men, seems to be more generally accepted than in most Nordic countries, apart from Iceland. Another explanation is that group representation in Norway in comparison with most other Western countries has always been relatively strong (Skjeie and Teigen 1993).

The main reason why *Iceland* had and still has the poorest representation of women in parliament, is probably that its electoral system is combined with a system of direct primaries (as in the USA), a circumstance which impedes the integration of women (Rule and Zimmerman 1994; Matland 1998). The low level of female political representation in Iceland puts the country at the bottom of the gender profile class. Icelandic society has been characterised by a strong male-breadwinner model, which caused child care facilities to be expanded much later than in the rest of the Nordic region. The political mobilisation of Icelandic women took place predominantly through the parties and the Women's Alliance, which combines the attributes of a political party and social movement. Besides winning parliamentary seats for women, it motivated other parties to address gender issues and nominate more female candidates.

The somewhat slower developments in *Denmark* during the 1970s and 1980s reflect, among other things, the relatively low level of women's involvement in party political organisations, the absence of specifically feminist organisations, and the lack of equal status measures, such as quotas, in the Danish political parties (Christensen 1999). In Denmark, it appears as if the membership crisis in the political parties was accelerated and reinforced by the low level of women's support of the parties. In Norway, on the other hand, the crisis was allayed, or at least postponed, by the integration of women into the political parties. The Danish gender profile has also been characterised by a formidable expansion of the welfare state, particularly with regard to publicly funded childcare (Borchorst, Christensen and Raaum 1999). Nevertheless, the Danish gender profile is the most "bottom-up" of all the countries. Gender issues were formulated and articulated by the social movements, and the institutionalisation of gender equality never progressed as far as in Norway and Sweden. Compared to Sweden and Norway, the political parties have tended to take gender equality less into account in their policies. The Danish political culture, with its strong bias on consensus, has tended to prevent a radicalisation of gender equality policies and may explain why controversial matters such as sexual violence, sexual harassment, etc. have been almost absent from the political agenda.

Finland is a special case in the Nordic connection (Borchorst, Christensen and Raaum 1999). The country was under Swedish domination for many years, was conquered by Russia in 1809 and became independent only with the Russian Revolution of 1917. The number of women in the workforce began to rise as early as in the fifties, along with women's representation. However, labour market developments never matched Denmark's or Sweden's, and took place without a comprehensive expansion of the welfare state's childcare programme. Finland distinguished itself prior to the Second World War, for example, with regard to the steady 10 per cent women won in parliamentary elections. Later, the level of female representation in Finland has generally been closer to Denmark than Norway and Sweden. Finland was the final country to enact gender equality legislation. Political parties, which have played a relatively dominant role in Finnish political culture, largely welcomed a parliamentary discussion of conflicts along gender lines. Women in Finland were primarily mobilised by the political parties, and social movements played a relatively minor role in comparison with the other Nordic countries, especially Denmark.

## Summing Up: Equal Democracies?

Until now there has been a tendency to exaggerate how common the Nordic countries actually are. Concerning the first two thresholds of legitimisation and incorporation, the gender gap was relatively modest. Nevertheless, in respect of gender equality, the political mobilisation of Nordic women and men followed very different patterns right from the start. Looking back to the period from the end of the 1800s to the 1970s, the mobilisation of Nordic men into politics was accomplished by several political channels, related to the state, the market and civil society. Most Nordic women were only mobilised through voluntary associations in the civil sector. Certainly, women's voluntary organisations, through their collaboration with public authorities, played a more important political role in the building of the social democratic welfare state than has previously been assumed, but this collaboration was not facilitated by parliamentary political bodies.

Again, the gender gap was much wider and difficult to cross when it came to political representation in national legislatures and access to executive office, than the two preceding thresholds, at least in terms of when women entered parliamentary politics. Nordic women, like women in other regions of the world, faced a double burden of legitimisation, and they were never present in any critical number in parliamentary politics before the emergence of second wave feminism. Before the 1970s, all Nordic parliaments were extremely gender skewed assemblies.

The years around 1970 were a turning point. During the next decades the proportion of women in Nordic parliaments increased rapidly. Compared to other Western countries, the Nordic region is unique in having its second wave feminism followed by such broad incorporation of women in the political elites. The several reasons are related to structural, cultural and political conditions. However, in spite of many similarities, the inter-Nordic parliamentarian mobilisation of women differed widely.

At present, in 2004, Sweden and Iceland are the most dissimilar cases within the Nordic region. Strictly speaking, if a gender-balanced representation is taken to mean that women have at least a 40 per cent representation in parliament and cabinet, only Sweden has gender equality in the parliamentary arena. But Denmark, Finland and Norway are not far off gender balance. Women's parliamentary presence in these countries has, however, more or less stagnated since the late 1980s, and crossing the critical threshold does not necessarily mean uninterrupted further progress. In Iceland, women had to wait until 1999 before crossing the 30 per cent threshold of parliamentary representation, and they have never surpassed more than 25 per cent in cabinet, which in a Nordic context is a very poor representation.

Although we should not overstate the differences between the Nordic countries with respect to gender and parliamentary politics, it is nonetheless reasonable to conclude that each of the countries has its own particular gender profile which needs to be perceived in relation to the special characteristics of each Nordic country.

# Chapter 10: Local Government and Politics

*Lawrence E. Rose*

In the comparative literature regarding different systems of local government and politics, the Nordic countries are often seen as comprising a special if not unique category to which various labels are attached. A recent Swedish publication (Lidström 2003), for example, refers to these countries as the "Northern European" system of local government, a term used to distinguish them from other northern and middle European systems of local government with which they have frequently been grouped (cf. Bennett 1993; Hesse and Sharpe 1990/ 91; Norton 1991, 1994; Page 1991; Page and Goldsmith 1987). There are certainly good reasons for considering the Nordic countries as a special subtype, but to suggest that these countries constitute a uniform, homogeneous system of local government and politics would be a gross oversimplification. Significant differences are to be found. The intent of this chapter is therefore to highlight both the broad lines of similarity as well as some of the important nuances and differences which are apparent among the systems of local government and politics in these countries.

In what follows attention will be focused on only four of the Nordic countries – Denmark, Finland, Norway and Sweden – with special emphasis being given to the Scandinavian core (i.e. Denmark, Norway and Sweden). First, the historical background and contemporary legal status of local government and politics in these countries is briefly reviewed. Thereafter consideration is given to several critical features relating to the organization and operation of local government and politics in the post-World War II era. This is followed by a discussion of important recent developments. The chapter then concludes with consideration of how the patterns of similarities and differences may be understood and what implications recent developments may hold for the Nordic model of local government and politics.

## Historical Background and Current Legal Status of Local Government

The roots of local government in Denmark, Finland, Norway and Sweden are deeply planted in the soil of history. The principle of local self-government can be traced back to the time of tribal life and subsequently Viking times. But even after unification of the countries under monarchies ruling under the guise of absolute power, there is clear evidence of authority being shared. Thus, already in medieval times a system of mutual obligations and responsibilities emerged with the blessings of enlightened monarchs. Borough charters were issued and peasants exercised certain personal, economic and political rights through various popular assemblies. The countries were divided into a set of territorial districts and a system of local administration was maintained.

Contemporary democratic local government, however, dates from more recent times – in particular following in the wake of the Enlightenment period and the American and French revolutions. By the beginning of the nineteenth century, local committees had generally been established to administer aid to the poor, and parish councils, in much the same vein, were given responsibility for operating local schools, assisting the poor and maintaining roads. But it was not until 1837, when laws on the local executive (*Formannskapslovene*) were passed in Norway, that the principle of local self-government with popularly elected local councils was formally recognized and given legal status. These laws were largely the result of local groups – primarily farmers and businessmen – seeking greater freedom from representatives of the central bureaucracy and additional rights to make decisions on matters affecting the local community according to local prerogatives.

In Denmark popularly elected local councils were created to advise the ruling magistry in the same year (1837). But the principle of local government exercising a degree of local autonomy was first given constitutional recognition (rather than recognition by special legislation, as was the case in Norway) in 1849, when a clause explicitly acknowledging "the right of local authorities to manage their own affairs under the control of the state" was included in the constitution adopted at the time. In Sweden, the Local Government Ordinances Act passed in 1862 served as a similar legal watershed, creating 2,500 municipalities and self-governing provincial and city councils. Constitutional recognition of local government did not occur, however, until 1975, when a new Instrument of Government (*Regjeringsform*) was adopted.

Despite extensive discussion, especially following passage of a strong recommendation by the Council of Europe that the principle of democratic local self-government should be incorporated within the constitutional documents of all member countries, this has not yet transpired in Norway. But this difference is not of great significance. The most important stipulations and provisions relating to the nature and operation of local government in all of the Nordic countries are contained in separate legislative acts, not in the constitutions. These acts tend to provide local governments with broad formal authority under terms of what is described as a *negative delimitation* of power. That is, local authorities are granted the right to engage in all activities that are not explicitly denied them or for which responsibility is assigned to other bodies. Such provisions stand in marked contrast to the principle of *ultra vires* which has been followed in the United Kingdom and several other countries – a principle which only permits local authorities to engage in activities specifically permitted or assigned to them.

While the discretionary authority granted local governments in the Nordic countries is thus in theory very wide ranging, in practice it is restricted by a variety of other conditions, the most important of which are stipulations contained in supplementary legislative acts, directives or regulations issued by national authorities, and the availability of local financial resources. These constraints will be elucidated further in the following section.

## The Organization of Local Government and Politics

To understand the contemporary operation of local government and politics, it is necessary to consider the territorial structure of local government, the responsibilities assigned to and exercised by local government, local government finance, and the internal organization of local government, both political and administrative.

### TERRITORIAL STRUCTURE

The political-administrative systems in each of the four countries consist at present of three levels of government – national, regional (county) and local. A distinction can nonetheless be made between a "Scandinavian model" on the one hand and a "Finnish model" on the other. This is because the Finnish system does not have regional authorities comparable to the elected county-level governments found in Denmark, Norway and Sweden. Finland, however, does have a system of intermunicipal cooperation that in many respects is the functional equivalent of regional governments found in the other three countries.

The regional level is dealt with in greater detail in chapter 11 and will therefore not be discussed further here.

Another distinction that can be drawn concerns the number of municipalities found in each country and the distribution of these municipalities in terms of their population size. In this case the line of division runs between Finland and Norway on the one side and Denmark and Sweden on the other. At the turn of the millennium both Finland and Norway had closer to 450 municipalities, whereas for Denmark and Sweden the number was around 275. Not only are there more municipalities in Finland and Norway, they also tend to be substantially smaller than their counterparts in Denmark and Sweden (see Table 10.1).

Table 10.1   Characteristic of local government in four Nordic countries as of 2000

|  | Denmark | Finland | Norway | Sweden |
|---|---|---|---|---|
| Number of municipalities | 275 | 436 | 435 | 289 |
| Largest municipality | 495 699 | 551 123 | 507 500 | 743 703 |
| Smallest municipality | 2 293 | 235 | 256 | 2 746 |
| Average size | 19 382 | 11 384 | 10 295 | 30 662 |

Source: Adapted from Table 2.1 in Mønnesland (2001:23).

These conditions reflect the results of somewhat different processes and strategies relating to municipal amalgamation carried out within each of the countries during the post-war period (cf. Albæk et al. 1996). In all of the countries central authorities were concerned about achieving what at the time was considered a more functionally appropriate structure of local government. This implied reducing the number of municipalities – especially the elimination of many small municipalities – and creating units of local government that would have a sufficiently strong socio-economic base to support viable development and cope with the expectations placed on local governments as agents for realization of various social welfare reforms. Following investigations by public commissions and extensive political debates, amalgamation reforms were carried out in Denmark, Norway and Sweden in the late 1960s and early 70s. The most drastic reform was that carried out in Sweden where the number of municipalities was reduced from nearly 2,500 in 1951 (there had been little change in the structure of local government in Sweden since 1862) to 274 in 1974. This was a reduction of nearly 90 per cent, a reduction which far exceeded comparable reforms that occurred in many other countries during the same period (cf. Martins 1995:446; Strömberg and Engen 1996:241–242). In Denmark and Norway, by comparison, reforms eliminated roughly 80 and 40 per cent respectively of the municipalities existing previously.

An amalgamation reform was also prepared in Finland during the same period, but due to more strident opposition, it failed to muster necessary parliamentary support. However, a number of voluntary amalgamations did take place in the aftermath of these debates with the result being a reduction in the number of municipalities from roughly 550 to 475 in the decade from 1965 to 1975 (cf. Ståhlberg 1996:91–94).

These major amalgamation reforms did not serve to eliminate the structure of local government as an issue of concern and debate. The matter remained on the public agenda and has come to the forefront with some regularity in each of the countries in the years since. In Norway a public commission appointed to investigate the question anew submitted a report in 1992 (NOU 1992:15). Among other things, the report recommended that all municipalities should have a minimum of 5,000 inhabitants – a recommendation that would have eliminated more than half of all existing municipalities were it to have been adopted. This recommendation was watered down in the proposal subsequently submitted to parliament for consideration, but even this softened version was not acceptable to a parliamentary majority, which instead passed a resolution in 1995 specifying that no further amalgamations should be imposed against the wishes of a majority of residents in the municipalities affected.

Responsibilities of local government

One of the reasons why efforts to achieve territorial restructuring have not born much fruit is the fact that it is an issue closely linked to the question of how responsibilities are to be allocated among public authorities. Although local governments in the Nordic countries have, as already noted, long had broad authority to engage in a wide range of discretionary activities, today's reality is more characterized by a situation in which a large portion of local government activity is mandated and/or subject to control by national policy making. Indeed, despite long historical roots, local government in the Nordic countries as it is known and functions today is of a more recent vintage, to a large degree being shaped by developments in the last 50 years. Thus, following World War II, national governments in all of these countries adopted a series of policy decisions designed to create what were to become known as the Scandinavian welfare states. The results of these decisions gave rise to what without misrepresentation has been termed the *welfare municipality* (Grønlie 1991), or what alternatively could be called the *local* welfare state, since to a large degree local governments were used as agents for implementation of many national welfare programmes. Not only were local governments to have responsibility for building, maintaining and operating schools and outpatient medical facilities along with other more traditional local infrastructural services (water supply, sewage and refuse disposal, and electric power supply); they were also to be first-line providers of various social security services – care for pre-school children and the elderly, social assistance for the needy and so forth.

It is important to emphasize that local governments have not merely been passive recipients and implementers of national plans; historically they have also been active initiators in developing many social welfare practices. In the period from 1945 to the late 70s, however, the primary source of expansion in local government activity came from a concerted push by central authorities to develop a set of welfare programmes, programmes that would provide a safety net and adequate standard of living for all inhabitants (cf. Flora 1986). Particularly important in this regard, moreover, was the idea that the availability and quality of public goods and services provided by local authorities should be virtually the same throughout the country. Given geographic conditions found in these countries – especially in Finland, Norway and Sweden – this was an ambitious and costly goal.

Looking across the four countries, there are some variations in the allocation of specific tasks and responsibilities from one setting to another. Secondary education, for example, is the responsibility of municipalities in Sweden, whereas it falls to counties in Denmark and Norway. Such differences notwithstanding, it is nonetheless possible to say that local government in the four Nordic countries – either primary municipalities or counties (and in the case of Finland joint municipal boards) – in general attend to a broad and largely comparable spectrum of tasks. These range from mandatory obligations in the fields of education, primary health care, care for the young and elderly, and a number of other social welfare programmes to more discretionary activities such as providing recreational and other leisure time facilities.

This situation is clearly reflected in terms of public finance and employment. As is evident from information displayed in the bottom two rows of Table 10.2, local government in all four countries accounted for roughly 60 to 70 per cent of all public expenditure and investments at the turn of the millennium, and an even greater portion of all public sector employment. (Of all employment, both public and private, local government accounts for between one-fifth and one-fourth in the four countries.) In terms of expenditures as a per cent of gross national product (GNP), Denmark ranks noticeably higher than the other three countries, but this is largely due to a practice of channelling old-age pension payments via local government budgets, whereas in the other countries these payments are made through national authorities. Regardless of national differences, the important point is that the figures found in Table 10.2, when placed in a broader cross-national context, serve to place all of the Nordic countries among the top of the list in terms of local government responsibilities and activities.

Table 10.2  Indicators of local government activity in four Nordic countries, 1999

|  | Denmark | Finland | Norway | Sweden |
|---|---|---|---|---|
| Expenditures as a per cent of GNP | 31 | 15 | 18 | 23 |
| Per cent of all employment | 24 | 21 | 24 | 26 |
| Per cent of total public sector |  |  |  |  |
| – Consumption and investment | 75 | 56 | 61 | 69 |
| – Average employment | 79 | 76 | 78 | 82 |

Source: Adapted from Table 2.2 in Mønnesland (2001:24).

LOCAL GOVERNMENT FINANCE
A question that arises in this regard is how these activities are financed. How are resources generated to cover the expenses involved? As Table 10.3 makes clear, variations are again to be detected, but there are also some obvious similarities. Revenue from personal income and wealth taxes constitutes the single

most important source in all four countries. (This income is supplemented by business and property taxes in Denmark and Finland, whereas in Norway and Sweden these taxes do not, to date, represent revenue sources of any significance.) Intergovernmental transfers in the form of both block grants and earmarked grants are also quite important, especially in Norway, less so in Finland. Transfers of this sort have traditionally been an important condition for fiscal redistribution, providing local authorities with resources permitting them to fulfil fundamental policy expectations and responsibilities.

With respect to user fees and charges, on the other hand, a different pattern is to be observed: in recent years these sources of revenue are most significant in Finland, least important in Norway. When placed in a longer time frame, however, it can be noted that user fees and charges have increased in relative importance in both Finland and Norway. In the case of Finland this is explained by the fact that intergovernmental transfers from national to local authorities were substantially reduced in the mid-1990s, largely as a result of economic difficulties faced by the country. For Norway, by comparison, the development is due more to constraints placed on local governments in determining their own revenue.

Table 10.3  Sources of local government revenue in four Nordic countries, 1999. In per cent

|  | Denmark | Finland | Norway | Sweden |
|---|---|---|---|---|
| Taxes |  |  |  |  |
| – Personal income and wealth | 52 | 42 | 40 | 60 |
| - Business and property taxes | 8 | 12 | 1 | – |
| Intergovernmental transfers |  |  |  |  |
| – Block grants | 10 | 17 | 23 | 16 |
| – Earmarked grants | 8 | 2 | 17 | 5 |
| User fees and charges | 21 | 25 | 14 | 18 |
| Other sources | 1 | 3 | 5 | 1 |
| Sum | 100 | 100 | 100 | 100 |

Source: Adapted from Table 2.3 in Mønnesland (2001:25).

Norway represents something of a special case in this regard. Local governments in Denmark, Finland and Sweden all have a legal right to set their own tax rates. In Denmark this is subject to negotiations between national and local authorities, and in Sweden there have been a number of temporary caps set on local taxation during the past decade due to economic contractions, but in both countries the right for local authorities to set tax rates is in principle guaranteed, as it is in Finland. In Norway, on the other hand, national regulations stipulate a narrow band for minimum and maximum local tax rates, and with only rare exceptions all local authorities have consistently adopted the maximum rate. In essence, in other words, national authorities set the tax rates. Borrowing money to cover operating expenses, moreover, is not allowed, and local governments are prohibited from deficit spending. These conditions place local authorities in a proverbial straightjacket; the only option for local governments to influence their revenue base being through adjustments of local user fees and charges. Even so, in the face of nationally mandated programmes and inadequate financing, not all authorities have been able to make ends meet in recent years. As a consequence nearly 100 municipalities in Norway are currently on a "black list" and have been put under stringent economic control by national authorities.

POLITICAL-ADMINISTRATIVE DECISION MAKING

Penultimate responsibility for local decision making rests in all four countries with a popularly elected municipal council. Elections to these bodies are currently held at regular four year intervals with seats being allocated according to principles of proportional representation. In Sweden these elections now occur on the same day as national parliamentary elections, whereas in the other three countries local elections are generally held separately from national elections. The 2003 local election in Denmark was an exception in this respect, falling as it did at the same time as parliamentary elections which were called on short notice. As is evident in Figure 10.1, this had an obvious impact on turnout for local elections; participation jumped by nearly 15 percentage points compared with the previous local elections in Denmark. This was an outcome that stands in stark contrast to the general tendency of declining electoral participation evident in the other three countries in recent decades. This tendency has been most pronounced in Finland, where turnout has dropped by more than 20 per cent in the period since the early 1980s. But even if not quite so dramatic, both Norway and Sweden have likewise experienced significant drops in local electoral participation during the same period (14 per cent in Norway and nearly 12 per cent in Sweden).

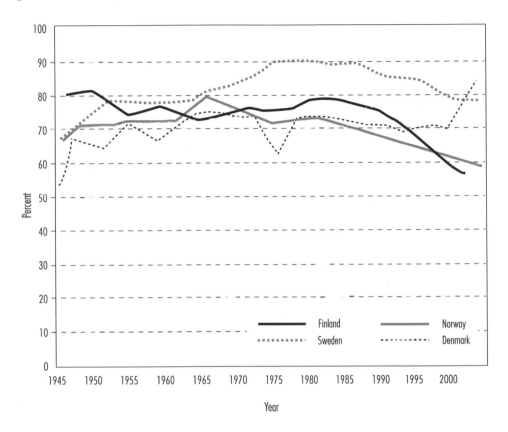

Figure 10.1  Turnout for local elections in four Nordic countries, 1945–2003. In per cent

In each of the countries the number of council members elected is related to municipal size according to nationally determined guidelines. Again, Denmark distinguishes itself inasmuch as local councils tend to be smaller. As a result the ratio between citizens and council members is substantially greater in Denmark than is the case in the other three countries (cf. Lidström 2003:207). Finland also distinguishes itself, albeit in another respect, insofar as there is a stronger element of personalized voting in local elections. In the other three countries voting is primarily based on party lists. Despite this difference, local branches of the national parties tend to dominate local politics in all four countries, although there are many examples of individuals being elected from lists of candidates put forth by local groupings. As a rule these local lists tend to reflect either a specific policy issue or a geographic division within the municipality.

Once elected, the municipal councils determine the internal organization and operation of local government, again within nationally set guidelines. Some country-specific variations are to be found, but the major tendencies and features were quite similar in all four countries at the beginning of the 1990s. Thus, the municipal council commonly appointed various committees and boards, one having overarching executive responsibility for coordination and preparation of matters for the municipal council, the others having responsibility for functionally defined areas of municipal activity. It is particularly with respect to the character of these latter bodies exercising specialized functional responsibilities that variations among the countries are most evident. In Denmark and Norway, for example, board members are appointed by and from among elected council members, while in Finland and Sweden members are appointed by the council but may also – and frequently do – include non-elected representatives as well. The number of such boards is in all countries decided by the council, with the trend being toward a reduction in their number.

The manner in which political-administrative leadership is organized is also a point of significant differentiation among the four countries. In Denmark the mayor (*borgmester*), who is elected by and among the council members, has a much stronger administrative role than his or her elected counterparts in the other countries. The Danish mayor is formally above the municipal chief executive officer (CEO) and has primary executive responsibility, whereas in Finland and Norway political and administrative leadership is clearly separated. In the latter two countries CEOs are appointed by the council and serve either for a fixed period or indefinitely. Sweden, by comparison, falls somewhere between these two models since some of the council members are employed on a full-time basis in connection with their responsibilities as heads of municipal committees or boards, and the relative importance of political leaders vis-à-vis CEOs varies somewhat from one municipality to another.

Finally it may be noted that in the course of time local government administration in all of the countries has become highly professionalized. In part this reflects a general secular trend, but the transformation was also a deed of necessity in light of the expansion of local government responsibilities and activities in the post-war period.

## Recent Developments

The Nordic model of local government has come under increasing pressure in recent decades. A complaint frequently heard from the late 1970s to the present is not only that there has been a mismatch between the expectations placed on local government and the resources available, but that national prescriptions have been poorly suited to local conditions, often inhibiting more effective responses to local needs and problems. Indeed, criticism of excessively detailed central government control of local authorities was one of the motivating forces underlying initiation of what was termed the "free-commune experiments" in all four countries during the 1980s (cf. Baldersheim and Stava 1993; Baldersheim and Ståhlberg 1994; Rose 1990). The essence of these experimental programmes was to free a selected set of local authorities from prevailing norms and regulations, permitting them to experiment with alternative means for dealing with local tasks and responsibilities. These programmes were an important backdrop to many of the reforms and changes relating to local government which emerged in all four Nordic countries during the 1990s.

Recent developments in local government in the Nordic countries have been influenced by more than the criticisms of local officials however. Equally, if not more important, was a set of changes in the broader context of local government. Fundamental in this regard was an economic downturn that affected all of the countries. Worst hit was Finland where, following the collapse of the Soviet Union, which had been a major trading partner, unemployment soared to nearly 20 per cent in the early 1990s. But to varying degrees the other three countries experienced economic decline and rising unemployment as well. As the decade drew to a close, unemployment levels had declined in all of the countries, yet nonetheless remained a problem, especially in Finland and Sweden.

For Finland and Sweden, membership in the European Union was part of a larger strategy in coming to grips with this new reality. Norway, by comparison, turned down EU membership, relying instead on continued membership in the European Free Trade Association (EFTA), and the European Economic Space (EES) agreement on economic cooperation between EU and EFTA countries that had been signed previously (cf. Jenssen et al. 1998). Despite these differences, all four countries have experienced the effects of the four freedoms upon which the EU is built – freedom in movement of individuals, capital, services and products. Being countries with relatively small population bases and hence domestic markets, this situation has had a noticeable impact, contributing in varying degrees to a significant restructuring of social as well as economic life in all four countries. Most noteworthy in this respect has been increased demographic mobility. Migratory tendencies have largely followed classic patterns of movement from more peripheral areas towards urban or regional centres, particularly to those where new production facilities based on high technology have been located. Such tendencies not only flew in the face of traditional settlement policies, whereby central authorities sought to maintain a more widely spread population pattern; they also presented substantial challenges to local authorities faced with new demands for basic infrastructural facilities and the provision of social services.

On a more secular note, the Nordic societies have also been subject to forces that have brought about a shift in fundamental value orientations similar to those observed in many other countries. Contributing to this change is what has been termed the transition from Fordism to post-Fordism – that is the introduction of new production techniques based on high technology and on individualized commodities, new business paradigms and forms of labour organization, new consumption patterns and an increased emphasis on the individual as consumer. Accompanying this transition, a more pronounced consumer orientation to local government has been evident among residents of all four countries (cf. Montin and Elander 1995; Rose 1999).

These changes in the environment have contributed to a number of developments that, if not constituting an outright revolution, have at least altered the organization and operation of Nordic local government. These developments may be summarized under four headings, each of which deserve brief discussion: (1) pressure for structural reform and reallocation of responsibilities; (2) changes in internal organization; (3) changes in the modes of operation; and (4) changes in policy perspectives.

PRESSURE FOR STRUCTURAL REFORM AND REALLOCATION OF RESPONSIBILITIES
One of the most prominent developments has been a renewed pressure for the restructuring of local government or, in the absence of this, a reallocation of responsibilities and competencies for providing selected public services. By no means has the question of restructuring local government solely been an issue in Finland and Norway, where a large number of relatively small municipalities have existed, nor has it only been concerned with municipal amalgamation. In Sweden, for example, there have even been a few instances in which new municipalities have been formed by splitting older units apart. Thus,

whereas there were 284 primary municipalities in 1990, by 2000 there were 289. In the other three countries, however, the principal emphasis has rather been on reducing the number of sub-national governments. In Denmark, for example, a public commission appointed with a mandate to evaluate the structure of local government issued its report early in 2004, recommending a comprehensive reform of the public sector (Strukturkommissionen 2004). The government proposal subsequently submitted to parliament endorsed the principle features of the commission report, a proposal which, if adopted, would involve increasing the size of municipalities (a minimum of 30,000 inhabitants is suggested), replacing the current structure of county government with a larger regional form of government, and transfer of some responsibilities from one level of government to another.

This proposal reflects thinking found in all four countries, especially with respect to the role of regional government and a need to assess where responsibilities for certain tasks should be located. Discussions and developments regarding these issues are treated in greater detail in the following chapter.


CHANGES IN THE ORGANIZATION OF LOCAL GOVERNMENT

Independent of debates over the territorial structure and allocation of responsibilities among different levels of government, a pronounced shift has also occurred with respect to the internal organization of local government. Most important has been a philosophy of greater flexibility that has been prevalent in much of the new legislation and regulations pertaining to local government enacted in recent years. Rather than requiring specific bodies or organizational forms, local authorities have been granted greater discretion to determine their own internal organization. The overarching principle is now that local authorities should accomplish the tasks assigned to them; how they choose to organize themselves is less critical. To be sure, there are still guidelines regarding the existence and composition of certain bodies, such as municipal or county councils and executive boards, but the number and character of many other bodies has been made a matter of local prerogative. As a result, in most authorities the number of committees and boards has been reduced either by total elimination or by combining then with other bodies.[44]

At the same time there have also been experiments, particularly in the largest municipalities, with various forms of decentralization – both administrative and political (cf. Bäck et al. 2004). In part these developments have been motivated by a desire to achieve an organization better suited to the activities of local government, but there has also been a hope that these arrangements would facilitate and stimulate citizen involvement. In Oslo there have even been experiments with direct election to district councils.

The past decade likewise saw increased interest in new types of local government bodies. Particularly important in this respect was the possibility of creating municipal companies. The use of municipal companies has been seen to offer special advantages in areas where there is a combination of administration and business activity, such as is the case with respect to sanitation services, transportation, and public housing. Developmental activities have likewise been a new field for the creation of municipal companies. Moving a step beyond these municipal companies, many municipalities have also sought to establish and exploit public-private partnerships for pursuing local interests. Whereas the former have been seen as especially relevant for authorities pursuing local development policies, public-private partnerships have been used in connection with a wider spectrum of activities (cf. Lundqvist 1998, Pierre 1998).[45]

CHANGES IN THE MODES OF OPERATION

As these last remarks suggest, there has also been a marked change in the modes of operation within Nordic local government during the 1990s. Many, but certainly not all, of these changes can be placed under the umbrella concept of New Public Management. In part, this shift is a result of larger national and international trends relating to deregulation and increased competition (see Chapter 2, this volume). Rather than having municipal electricity companies holding monopoly status on the provision of electrical services, for example, residents are now able to shop around for electricity providers. More characteristic of the new situation and mind-set, however, is the fact that elements of competition and choice are to be found in areas where local authorities previously were the sole provider *and* producer of goods and services. Outsourcing and adoption of purchaser-provider models have become quite commonplace. Accompanying and in part driving this development has been a desire to set clearer boundaries between "politics" and "administration". This philosophy, embodying a strong emphasis on management by objectives, has been especially prevalent in Finland, Sweden and Norway (cf. Naschold 1995). In implementing this philosophy a variety of quality control techniques have been tested and adopted in different settings. Most salient in this respect is benchmarking, but systematic evaluation and quality control inventories are also commonplace.

Another facet of the NPM philosophy that has been increasingly evident is a strengthened consumer orientation. Local governments have to varying degrees developed citizen charters for selected services, carried out customer surveys and instituted other mechanisms to ensure feedback regarding service satisfaction. The use of more general citizen surveys and, in some instances, citizen panels or juries, has also been evident, although these, and the use of voucher schemes, are still much less common than other NPM practices.

Use of new information technology (IT), both as a means of informing local residents and as a means of stimulating citizen involvement, has also had relatively limited distribution and utility to date. A few local authorities have made concerted efforts to exploit these opportunities, often with backing from external sponsors, but these are exceptions rather than the rule. To the extent these technologies are more widely implemented, there appears to be a positive (albeit weak) relationship with the size of the local authority, and the most common forms of technology used are internet home pages and electronic mail, technologies that are well known in all four countries. For internal purposes, however, IT is very widespread, and the turn of the century has been a period of rapid expansion that is likely to continue, providing greater benefits for the public at large in the near future.

### CHANGES IN POLICY PERSPECTIVES

The developments described up to this point are interwoven with two fundamental changes in policy outlooks on the part of local authorities in the Nordic countries. One of these changes concerns internationalization. By no means had local governments operated in isolation from the international environment previously. But the 1990s was marked by a notable increase in the international orientation of local authorities. This is evident in many respects – perhaps foremost by the expansion of "twinning relations" with local governments in other countries, strong participation in various EU-sponsored projects, a sharp increase in memberships in European and international organizations, and the development of local government planning documents containing a solid international component.

The second noteworthy change in policy outlooks is a shift in emphasis from a primary concern with service delivery to a greater focus on local economic development. In part this is apparent in the projects of international cooperation and cross-border alliances just mentioned. Even more significant, however, are the new constellations and activities to be observed at the municipal, inter-municipal and regional levels. One example in this regard is the use of public-private partnerships in the creation of competence centres within such high tech fields as information and biotechnology. Public-private partnerships have also been used for other purposes, including the realization of sports facilities, cultural events and the building of roads. All of this is not to say that the role of local authorities as important providers if not actual producers of a wide range of services has been forgotten. The point is merely that there has been a clear and noteworthy shift in the relative priorities of many local authorities.

## Nordic Local Government – at a Crossroads?

As this review suggests, the Nordic model of local government is currently undergoing transformation. It is, however, a transformation characterized by evolution more than revolution. As such, this transformation is part of a process which dates from the years immediately following World War II and has been ongoing ever since (cf. Bogason 1990/91; Gustafsson 1990/91; Hansen 1990/91). It is a process in which local government in all four Nordic countries has been seen as an important component – or perhaps more correctly stated, an *active tool* – in the pursuit of national policy goals. The fundamentals of the Nordic model of local government – self-governing units operating with nominally generous grants of discretionary authority within a unitary state, universalism as a principle of service provision, taxed based financing and the redistribution of resources – have not only prevailed during this transformation; they have shown their robustness in a period of severe trials (cf. Kautto et al. 1999, 2001).

To understand and explain this situation, several factors are important. Foremost has been a strong egalitarian value orientation among the public (cf. Graubard 1986), an orientation which, at least until recent years, found expression in strong support for social democratic parties. With relatively broad political support, these parties have pursued policies reflecting this value orientation and in doing so have frequently chosen local government as an agent for policy implementation. Local government, in short, has been treated as an integral part of a larger national political-administrative system. In this respect the Nordic countries epitomize what has been termed an *integration* as opposed to *autonomous* model of local government (cf. Kjellberg 1988:40–42). The former – an integration model – emphasizes local and central government as two intimately connected spheres with the division of responsibilities and authority being seen in a flexible, pragmatic manner, whereas the latter – an autonomous model – emphasizes the distinctness of the two spheres, a philosophy more characteristic of, for example, Switzerland.

Beyond this, however, it is also important to underline that the Nordic model has built upon what is termed a *generalist* rather than *specialist* philosophy and perspective of local government. Under a generalist philosophy responsibilities for multiple tasks are collected and vested in one and the same authority. A specialist philosophy, by comparison, tends to distinguish and differentiate responsibility for various tasks, in part based on a belief that differences in the nature of specific tasks make it more appropriate to organize and pursue these through more narrowly defined, specialized authorities. It has been a clear preference for the former which, at least up to the present, has predominated in the Nordic countries. It is the combination of a generalist philosophy and an integrationist model of government that led to such a marked "*municipalization*" of the public sector in the Nordic countries in the last half of the previous century. Local governments, moreover, have been not merely subservient actors in this setting; they have rather been active partners, initiating structural innovation in several instances, thereby facilitating the change from an industrial to an information age. Indeed, developments in the sphere of local government within the Nordic countries have been interpreted as offering a genuine third way, solidly anchored between hierarchical steering and market liberalism (cf. Klausen and Ståhlberg 1998).

Against this overall positive picture, it is nonetheless possible to point to conditions which raise serious questions about the future of local government in the Nordic countries. Perhaps foremost among these in the minds of many observers is a tendency of long-term decline in electoral participation, evident in Figure 10.1, and, in much the same vein, increased problems of recruitment to local political parties. To be sure, these are not developments which are limited solely to local government, but they are more pronounced at the local level than they are nationally. These tendencies, moreover, would appear to be part of a pattern in which citizens increasingly engage in non-electoral forms of political activity not just as a supplement to, but in many cases as an alternative to electoral participation (cf. Bjørklund 2002).

At this point it is difficult, if not impossible, to predict what these developments portend for the future. In the face of increasingly strong emphasis placed on the idea of efficiency in the public sector, there are reasonable grounds to ask whether local government stands at a crossroads. Is the time in which local government was valued as a local political community and arena of local decision making, a meeting ground where democratic values were re-

alized and transmitted, a bygone era? Local government in the Nordic countries, just as elsewhere, has commonly been justified historically precisely because it offered a propitious setting for the pursuit of three values – autonomy,
democracy, and efficiency (cf. Sharpe 1970). In recent years, however, it would
seem that notions of efficiency, especially cost efficiency rather than allocation
efficiency, have come to predominate discussions of local government. Some
argue that this is not a cause of great concern since other settings are available
where the values of autonomy and democracy may be pursued and inculcated
(cf. Kjellberg 1995). For others this is not so apparent. That the issue is a matter
of critical importance on which the future of Nordic local government rests is
in any event underlined by the fact that in both Norway and Sweden public
commissions have been appointed in recent years to consider the status of
local democracy. There have increasingly been discussions of whether it may
be time to abandon the notion of generalist municipalities, all of which have
equal status and responsibilities, and rather differentiate more among the
kinds of tasks and services to be provided by various local authorities. If this
occurs it will be time to speak of more than a gradual transformation in the
Nordic model of local government and politics. But which way the road will
lead remains to be seen.

# Chapter 11: Nordic Regions in a European Perspective

*Harald Baldersheim*

Since the mid-1970s regions have become a more important level of government in many European states, including the Nordic countries.[46] The advocates of regions have even envisioned the emergence of a "Europe of the Regions" (Sharpe 1993; Kohler-Koch 1998; Keating and Loughlin 1997; Wagstaff 1999). The distribution of powers and functions between the state and regionally elected bodies is a long-standing point of contention in many countries. The weight of regions in public decision making usually reflects the balance of power between national and regional elites at any given time. The historical development of the nation-state has largely meant the subordination of regions to a national centre (Rokkan and Urwin 1983). In some countries the dominance of a national centre is such a long-established historical fact that it is taken as the natural order of things. In other countries, national unity is a more recent achievement, e. g. Italy and Belgium. Since the fall of the Berlin Wall in 1989, Europe has witnessed the break-away of regions and disintegration of states (Czechoslovakia, Yugoslavia). In other countries, more discrete processes of elite bargaining have led to an enhanced status for regions. The Nordic model of regionalism has been one in which regions (governed by elected councils) have served the nation-state (and nation-building) as bodies for welfare service implementation and also, to varying degrees, agents of economic modernisation. The fortunes of the regions have reflected the vicissitudes of nation-building.

Why is regionalism mounting in an era when European integration and borderless modernity seem to be the order of the day? Should not regional distinctions and sentiments be expected to fade away in such an environment? Students of the regionalist phenomenon point to a number of forces that may account for its resurgence: The most common arguments refer to functional necessities, the overloaded welfare state, European integration and the pull from Brussels, globalisation, and the rise of identity politics (Sharpe 1993). To what extent do these forces also shape Nordic regions?

Functional necessities refer to technical requirements related to service provision and planning, which may make municipalities too small to perform certain tasks (e.g., run hospitals or public transport); instead of amalgamating municipalities such tasks could be transferred to regions to be managed jointly across larger areas. As technical innovation and professional development are never-ending processes there will always be pressure for larger regions. *Is enlargement of regions on the agenda in the Nordic countries in response to technical requirements of service provision?*

Many European countries are experiencing welfare overload at the centre and are trying to manage commitments by cutting back on benefits and transferring responsibilities to lower government levels where demands may hopefully be met more efficiently; this is, of course, also a strategy for sharing the political burden of cutbacks. Are the Nordic countries transferring welfare responsibilities to the regions as part of a retrenching effort?

European integration entails not only a softening of national borders but also a "pull from Brussels" in a regionalist direction. The European Union has set up the structural or cohesion funds to help the development of backward areas of the member countries. These funds are distributed on the basis of applications from regional authorities; applications are expected to be drawn up by elected regional bodies, not state officials. This requirement has energised elected bodies in many regions and has meant, furthermore, that countries without a tradition of regional democracy have had to introduce such bodies in order to be eligible for EU funding of regional development (e.g., Ireland and Greece). Many regions have set up their own offices in Brussels in order to be able to lobby more effectively when they feel their interests to be vitally affected by European decisions. The European Union has acquired a further regional dimension through the establishment of the Committee of the Regions with seats for representatives of regions and local government in member states. This body has an advisory status to the Council of Ministers and the Commission with regard to regional issues that emerge in the decision process of the EU and strives to express the aspirations of European regions (Wagstaff 1999). The density and vibrancy of transactions between regions and various EU bodies have led scholars to formulate theories on the emergence of a new system of "multi-level governance" (Marks et al. 1994). *How strongly is the pull from Brussels felt in the Nordic regions, and are the Nordic regions responding?*

Globalisation may, paradoxically, drive a specific form of regionalism, "developmental regionalism" (Amin and Thrift 1994, Storper 1997). As industrial production is increasingly transferred to low-cost countries in the Third World, traditional modes of dirigiste development become obsolete in a world of foot-loose capitalism (Ohmae 1990). The state can no longer easily guide industrial jobs to regions with the greatest need. Regions must therefore try to marshal their own inventive and intellectual resources to sustain employment and welfare provisions (Ratti, Bramanati and Gordon 1997). This is known as "the endogenous model of development" (Keating 1997, Braczyk, Cooke and. Heidenreich 1998). This function is difficult to perform from the capital on behalf of regions; elected development boards composed of politicians with thorough knowledge of local circumstances will normally do a better job. The emergence of endogenous development has consequently meant another boost for regions. *How active are the Nordic regions as policy-makers, and which policies are favoured for endogenous development in a global environment?*

The rise of identity politics may be driving the most conspicuous expressions of regionalism in the form of increasing awareness in many regions of the region's cultural specificity and heritage (Harvie 1994). Historically, nation-building usually meant the gradual integration of culturally heterogeneous regions into a common cultural framework (especially a common language), the cement of national unity (Lipset and Rokkan 1967). This process worked out more completely in some countries than in others (Rokkan and Urwin 1983). The Scandinavian countries are examples of countries that achieved a high level of cultural homogeneity at an early stage of nation-building, whereas palpable regional contrasts persisted in Spain, Italy or Switzerland. Since the 1980s, many countries have given increasing official recognition to their regional heterogeneity, especially in the form of linguistic and cultural home rule. France, for example, today recognises four official languages; Spain introduced the concept of differentiated regional autonomy in its 1976 constitution, with the highest level of autonomy granted to the old cultural communities of Catalonia, the Basque country and Galicia. Great Britain introduced regional parliaments for Scotland, Wales and Northern Ireland in 1998. Belgium has granted high levels of autonomy to its three cultural communities, etc. *How strong are regional identities in the Nordic countries? To what extent are demands for autonomy and independence part of regionalist attitudes among Nordic regions?*

The above questions in italics will guide the presentations and discussions in the remainder of the chapter. First, however, the basic outline of the institutions of territorial governance in the Nordic countries is given.

## Institutions of Territorial Governance in the Nordic Countries

The Nordic countries (cf. map 1) are quite similar in terms of their territorial divisions, though there are some intriguing differences, too. First of all, three of the countries (Denmark, Norway, Sweden) have a two-tier system of local self-government: communes and county councils, both of which are directly elected. The major responsibilities of the second tier are hospitals, secondary education, public transport and secondary highways (in Norway, hospital management was taken over by central government in 2002). In Finland, these functions are managed through a system of special-purpose districts formed among collaborating municipalities; Finland has no directly elected county councils. In these four countries, local and regional units of self-government form an important part of public administration, accounting for around half of all public expenditure and employing nearly two-thirds of all public employees (cf. Chapter 10 in this volume for a detailed discussion of divisions of functions and financial foundations of local government).

Table 11.1  The Territorial Organisation of the Nordic Countries 2004[47]

|  | Denmark | Finland | Iceland | Norway | Sweden |
|---|---|---|---|---|---|
| Local self-govt. units | 271 communes | 452 communes | 104 communes | 434 communes | 289 communes |
| Regional self-govt. units | 14 county councils | 252 inter-communal boards 38 service districts 20 planning districts |  | 19 county councils | 18 county councils 2 enlarged regions 1 municipal community (Gotland) |
| National field administrations | 14 counties | 6 counties 15 employment districts | 27 counties | 18 counties | 21 counties |
| Home rule areas | Faeroe Islands, Greenland | Åland Islands |  | (Saami demands in Finnmark) |  |
| Special districts |  |  |  | Spitsbergen (Svalbard) |  |

In Denmark, Norway and Sweden, state district administrations largely follow the geographical boundaries of the county councils (although there are many exceptions to this rule). These state district administrations are co-ordinated by a district governor or prefect appointed by central government. Finland also has this prefectural government. The prefect also has powers of supervision in relation to communes. The balance of power between prefects as the state's representatives and the elected regional councils has varied in the three Scandinavian countries: in Denmark the councils have traditionally been the more dominant actors; in Sweden the prefects have been the leading figures; whereas the situation has been more balanced in Norway (Mydske and Disch 2000:6). In Finland, naturally, with no elected regional councils, the regional scene has been dominated by the prefects and other strong state district administrations. In a survey of regional councillors conducted in 1999 the majority of Norwegian and Danish councillors agreed that the state had increased its influence in the affairs of the regional councils in later years, while only a minority of Swedish councillors felt the same (Ejersbo 2000:39), which may suggest that the development of regions is by no means unidirectional even in homogeneous Scandinavia.

The main financial sources of regions (counties) in Denmark, Norway and Sweden are the regional income tax and state transfers. The special-purpose Finnish regions (the inter-municipal boards) are financed by contributions from the respective municipalities of which they are composed.

For historic reasons Denmark and Finland have areas that have been granted extensive home rule; in the case of Åland (a group of Swedish-speaking islands situated mid-way between Stockholm and Helsinki), since the First World War, and in the cases of Denmark's overseas territories of the Faeroe Islands and Greenland, since 1948 and 1978 respectively. Greenland has opted out of the EU despite Denmark's continued membership, and the Faeroe Islands never joined the EEC or the EU. Under Finland's accession treaty to the EU, Åland is granted a special status. In other matters of foreign and defence policy, they remain subject to the national regulations (in recent years they have obtained the right, under certain restrictions, to conclude treaties with other states). Home rule status includes, furthermore, that these territories have their own legislative assemblies with powers over education, social issues and economic development. All three territories have their respective executives appointed by the elected assemblies. In the case of Åland the mainland government is represented on the island through the prefect, whose authority largely corresponds with that of other prefects in other Finnish regions. In the Faeroes there is no similar mainland executive presence. Åland maintains restrictions on the right of outsiders to acquire property and permanent residence on the island. To get permanent residence and own property, proficiency in the Swedish language is required. No similar regulations are found for Greenland or the Faeroes, although language issues have been a source of contention also in the former territory. In 2003 a "partnership agreement" between Greenland and the Danish state was outlined by a Self-Government Commission, envisioning a development from home rule to "self-government" inside a community of two equal partners.

In Norway, voices are heard among the Saami population demanding extended control over territories in Finnmark regarded as ancestral lands; these claims are, however, met with scepticism among segments of the remaining population in Finnmark and only modest elements of home rule have been granted to the Saami population.

The remainder of the chapter will focus largely on developments in the mainland regions of Denmark, Finland, Norway and Sweden.

## The Shifting Powers and Functions of Regional Institutions – the Tug-of-war between Abolitionists and Revivalists

Are enlargement of regions and transfer of welfare functions issues in the Nordic countries? Regional institutions were recast in the 1990s in all the Nordic countries, perhaps most conspicuously in Finland and Sweden in the wake of their EU accession. The debate on regional powers focussed in particular on the role of regions in *economic development policies* and this is where the most intense battles have been fought (Baldersheim and Ståhlberg 1998, Sandberg and Ståhlberg 2000). In the 2000s conflicts over the status of regions intensified also in Denmark and Norway.

In Finland, responsibility for regional development has traditionally been allocated to state district agencies, whereas local government bodies have been fairly weak in this field, partly a reflection of the absence of directly elected regional bodies. The Finnish institutional pattern could be characterised as one of *fragmented state district* administration. The 1990s saw a number of modifications to this pattern, the most important of which was the transfer in 1994 of responsibility for regional development from regional state authorities to 19 *regional councils* charged with working out development policies for their respective regions (these councils are composed of representatives of the municipalities of the area, and thus only indirectly elected, continuing Finland's tradition of inter-municipal boards for regional affairs rather than general-competence regional bodies directly elected). Although this was, in the Finnish context, an important step towards establishing more powerful self-governing regions, many instruments vital for the implementation of these policies remained in the hands of various regional state bodies.

Furthermore, the 11 mainland *state* counties were amalgamated into five

## Map 1: Regional divisions, the Nordic countries

©NLS 1996

county administrations, and so the previous close correspondence between state and self-governmental boundaries was relaxed. Another part of the reform programme was an amalgamation of 77 regional state administrations into 15 new *Employment and Economic Development Centres*. These state administrations work in close co-operation with the regional councils and manage most of the EU structural fund money allocated to Finland. They are primarily regional implementation agencies for three, often competing, central ministries.

In Sweden, at the start of the 1990s, regional development instruments were largely concentrated in the hands of the prefect or regional governor, i.e., the head of the state district administration. Sweden exemplified the *integrated state district model*. Around 1990, even the *need* for democratically elected regions was questioned. The prospect of EU membership changed the course of the public debate. A regional experiment was launched, where new divisions of functions between state and regional bodies were tested. The experimenting regions were given additional development powers through a transfer of tasks from the state county administration. Two "super-regions" were established, amalgamating the regional councils in Skåne (South Sweden) and Västra Götaland (West Sweden) respectively. A third experimental region was Kalmar (East) and a fourth the municipality of Gotland (an island in the Baltic Sea). The "super-regions" were run by directly elected councils whereas the Kalmar case consisted of a joint municipal board appointed by municipalities in the area plus representatives for the county council. In Gotland, the regional development functions were transferred to the municipality. What is of particular interest in the Swedish case is that the idea of bottom-up style experimentation spread rapidly to other regions. The Swedish regional experiment was initiated from below, by regions and municipalities.

The developmental capacity of Swedish regions was further enhanced through central governmental intervention. In 1998, the government introduced a new regional growth agreement process, modelled after the programming concept of the European administration of structural funds. Regional growth programmes are set up by regional and local partnerships, including public as well as private partners. In non-experimenting regions, the programming process has been anchored in the regional state administration, while the experimenting regions manage the process through their own development organisation. Experiences in the first programming process, which was concluded early in 2000, were rather mixed. However, the important thing about the process may be the process itself. Regional actors from different walks of life could be brought together and gain familiarity with a new way of pooling regional resources.

Box 1   *Vestre Götaland's web presentation*

**Region Västra Götaland – a pioneer region in Sweden**

Region Västra Götaland came into being in 1999 by merging three former county councils and including parts of Göteborg's decision-making functions, mainly those concerned with healthcare. With time, the former historic county borders became an obstacle to mutual interests in fields like public transport and catchment areas for healthcare. The planning procedure for the new, considerably larger region was carried out through political action rather than a government inquiry. Healthcare is one of the region's major issues – as in all Swedish county councils accounting for some 90% of the region's budget, the basis of which is the region's right to levy taxes. Region Västra Götaland is responsible for the overall management of healthcare – hospitals, primary healthcare, specialized dental healthcare and free dental care for children and young people. A majority of the region's 48,000 employees are found in healthcare. The other major responsibility concerns regional development – normally a Government responsibility exercised through the county administrations. The region shoulders responsibility for business development, public transport and communications, international issues, culture, tourism, environmental issues, higher education and research. A ten-point regional strategy sets out the objectives – leading position as an IT region, prominent in know-how development and expertise, in eco-friendly technologies, culture and tourism, an internationally recognised partner and a model for equal opportunities and integration.

The 149 Regional Councillors appoint the 17 Members on the Regional Executive Board. The Executive Board prepares proposals for the Council with the assistance of a Health and Medical Care Executive Board, 12 local healthcare committees, provision committees to mention some. Four patients' committees report directly to the Council. Regional development, environment and culture each has a committee of 15 regional representatives working with another 12 municipally elected representatives in drafting committees thus providing a wider base for public opinion.

http://www16.vgregion.se

In comparison with Finland and Sweden, regional institutions in Denmark were subjected to fewer changes during the 1990s. In the preceding decade, the state reduced its regional development programmes substantially, leaving the field open to *local government initiatives*. The trend during the 1990s was one of gradual enhancement of the developmental role of regions. As in Sweden, there was a debate, in the early 1990s, on the need for regional self-government institutions. This discussion subsided after a while. The regional councils became important instruments in the administration of the structural funds, both regarding programme development as well as implementation. However, a Commission of Inquiry (*Rapport fra Strukturkommissionen*, 2003) recently concluded that there was a need for large-scale amalgamation of municipalities as well as regions. The liberal-conservative Government of the day (Spring 2004) followed up the Commission's views with a proposal to abolish the county councils in their present form. Responsibility for hospitals was to be taken over by five health regions (the latter element of the proposal is a replica of the Norwegian health reform of 2002). The minimum size of municipalities was stipulated at 30,000 inhabitants; municipalities were to take over a number of existing county council responsibilities, other functions, such as secondary schools, were to be transferred to the state. Predictably, these proposals have proven highly controversial and the outcome is uncertain at the time of writing.

Norway seemed to be something of a deviant case in the Nordic setting during the 1990s. This is where elected regional councils previously had the greatest say over regional economic development policies. However, voices in favour of abolishing the regions altogether became stronger. The county councils lost, first, responsibility for innovation support funds aimed at local firms, and then their most important function in terms of budgets and manpower, hospitals, which were transferred to the state in 2002, despite a favourable review by a Commission of Public Inquiry (NOU 2000:2). In compensation for the latter loss, the functions of the councils as regional development agents were to be strengthened. The Norwegian debate has had more overtones of centralism and etatism than the parallel debates in Finland and Sweden and the emphasis has been less on developmental policy and more on shortcomings with regard to service provision, in particular by hospitals. The Norwegian discourse may reflect a situation in which European regional competition is not viewed with the same urgency as in the new member states of Finland and Sweden, countries that also lack the comfortable oil funds of Norway.

However, in the early 2000s, Norway has pursued a parallel, bottom-up and self-initiated process of enlargement and experimentation in which county councils seek to pool their resources and ask to take over state functions, particularly as regards transport, highways and higher education. Discussions on amalgamation or pooling of resources are taking place among county councils in all parts of the country, i.e., eastern, southern, western, mid and northern Norway, involving from two to eight councils. The two extreme outcomes envisioned in discussions on the future of the regional level of governance are the complete abolition of regional councils on the one hand and the consolidation of the regional level into five super-regions on the other hand. The discussion is highly politically charged, with parties on the right favouring abolition, parties in the middle preferring the status quo, while many social democrats are in favour of larger regions.

Box 2  *The county council of Hedmark's web-presentation*

**Hedmark County Council – for you, an inhabitant of Hedmark –**
When you live in Hedmark you can be sure of receiving the high quality services you need, like upper secondary education, cultural activities and public transport, dental care, child and family welfare and industrial development. These are the main responsibilities of the County Council, in addition to managing natural resources, taking care of the environment, preserving the cultural heritage and making county plans.

The County Councillors are elected every fourth year in order to safeguard the needs of the inhabitants. As spokespersons for the people, their task is to develop Hedmark through co-operation and binding partnerships with various local, national and international organisations and bodies. The County Council speaks with the national authorities on behalf of Hedmark and the inland region.

In order to carry out these tasks there is a staff of 2.165 altogether in the County administration and institutions. The County's annual budget for 2002 amounts to NOK 1,6 billion.

Hedmark is luxuriant, with respect both to its nature and its inhabitants. The people of Hedmark are knowledgeable and able. This is something the County wishes to show, nourish and develop. It is important to plan, arrange and develop high quality activities and services, in addition to supporting and encouraging even greater creativity.

> *Our hope is that even more people will come and settle in Hedmark!*
>
> *The Chairman of the County Council, the County Council and the County Executive Board*
>
> Hedmark County is run by a democratically chosen County Council. The inhabitants elect a new Council every 4 years. The Council is presided over by a Chairman, who for the period of 2003–2007 is *Siri Austeng*. The County Council is divided into three committees with separate areas of responsibility: Education and Competence, Industry, Business and Culture, and finally Public transport, the Environment and Planning.
>
> The Chairman of the County Council, the Deputy Chairman, the committee leaders and the group leaders of the largest political opposition parties together make up the County Executive Board. The Chairman of the County Council and the Executive Board are responsible for the day-to-day political administration of Hedmark County.
>
> http://www.hedmark-f.kommune.no

The answer to the first two questions posed at the outset is that *enlargement* of regions has taken place in the Nordic countries, mainly in Finland and Sweden, while enlargement-debates are heating up in Norway and Denmark. *Transferring more welfare functions* to regions has not been an issue, however. Enlargement has been seen as a response primarily to requirements related to more say for regions in *economic development policies*. The latter requirement is driven both by requirements from Brussels regarding the management of structural fund money and by pressures from the global economy. The internationalisation of regions and the policies that regions seek to develop in responding to such pressures will be outlined below.

## The Pull from Brussels? The Internationalisation of Nordic Regions

As indicated above, regions are involved in various international activities (Östhol 1996, Goldsmith and Klaussen 1997). What are these activities precisely? The internationalisation of regions was surveyed in Finland, Norway and

Sweden (Baldersheim et al. 2001). The results (table 2) showed that all regions were involved in international co-operative ventures in one way or another, and in most cases in many ways. Most regions were involved in bilateral as well as multilateral projects. They all had partners across the border. But, of course, the volume and intensity of such co-operation varied substantially. The table below lists the most common types of international initiatives by country.

Table 11.2 *International activities of regions in Finland, Norway and Sweden. Pct. of regions with activity indicated 1998*

|  | Finland (20 regions) | Norway (19 regions) | Sweden (21 regions) |
|---|---|---|---|
| Developed internationalisation strategy | 25 | 94 | 71 |
| Established unit for international affairs | 31 | 69 | 63 |
| Functionaries with special responsibilities for international affairs | 100 | 88 | 96 |
| Offered language courses to politicians and officers | 88 | 38 | 63 |
| Offered courses on administrative systems of other countries | 25 | 19 | 13 |
| Courses in EU affairs | 81 | 50 | 70 |
| Courses on foreign cultures and traditions | 44 | 38 | 13 |
| International personnel exchanges | 38 | 94 | 71 |
| Co-operative ventures with other regions | 75 | 73 | 52 |
| Employed joint personnel with other regions | 100 | 50 | 57 |
| Unofficial lobbying regarding international issues | 88 | * | 88 |
| Managing own EU projects | 93 | * | 80 |
| Taken own initiatives to obtain EU projects | 81 | 60 | 75 |
| Lobbying office in Brussels | 75 | 6 | 100 |
| Study visit to regions in other countries | 100 | 94 | 92 |
| Sent official representatives to international meetings of regions | 94 | 100 | 96 |

Source: Baldersheim et al. 2001

The list of activities that regions engage in is long, ranging from twinning visits to courses in foreign languages for politicians and functionaries. The pull from Brussels is, of course, apparent in initiatives such as establishing lobbying offices in Brussels, offering courses in EU affairs, producing applications to obtain EU funding or taking on the management of EU projects. Joint ventures with other regions have been stimulated by successive generations of the Interreg funds intended to stimulate co-operation between regions across national borders. More summary indices of internationalisation (Baldersheim et al. 2001) suggest that the overall level of international participation was somewhat lower in Norwegian regions than in those of Finland and Sweden. Much of the difference could be put down to Norway's outsider status. Naturally, access to the EU structural funds was not the same for non-member regions. Still, Norwegian regions were involved in a substantial number of EU projects through their partnerships across borders with regions in Sweden, Finland or Denmark or through such multilateral arrangements as the North Sea Commission. In conclusion, the pull of Brussels was certainly felt in the Nordic regions. The surprising finding is that there was not *more* variation in the regions' responses to international pressures.

## Policy Responses to Globalisation: Choice of Regional Development Strategies

Most European countries have areas that lag behind the rest of the country in terms of economic development, availability of jobs and levels of income. Most countries have established policies intended to boost development and economic growth in such backward areas. European Union resources are redistributed among regions and across national boundaries by the structural funds. The richest parts of a country are often found in and around the capital, for example Paris and Île de France or London and the south of England. Italy, Spain and Germany exhibit different patterns of disparities, however, where the richest and most competitive areas are not the capital districts, but Lombardy, Catalonia and Hamburg respectively (European Competitiveness Index 2004).

Regional disparities are also found in the Nordic countries. Map 2 shows the distribution of population change between regions. In Norway, Sweden and Finland there is a north–south gradient where populations decline in the north and mount, along with jobs, in the south, especially around the capitals. Denmark has a west–east gradient, with declining areas along its western seaboard. It should also be pointed out, however, that despite regional disparities in the Nordic countries, the actual levels of income and employment are higher than in most other West European countries, so even in the Nordic peripheries, the level of welfare may still be envied by the rest of Europe.

Map 2: Population change 1995–99, European regions

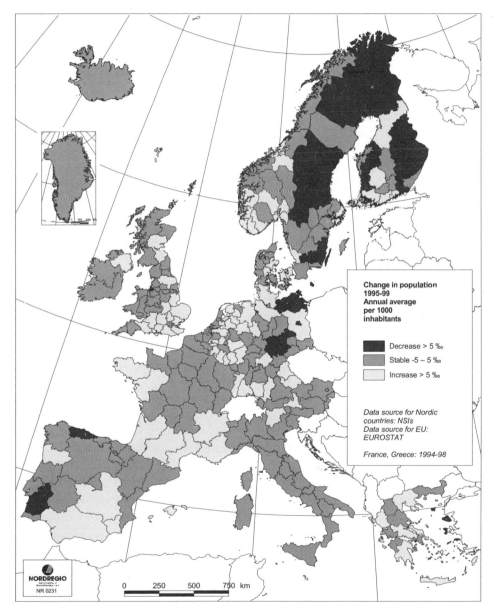

Change in population
1995-99
Annual average
per 1000
inhabitants

Decrease > 5 ‰

Stable -5 – 5 ‰

Increase > 5 ‰

Data source for Nordic
countries: NSIs
Data source for EU:
EUROSTAT

France, Greece: 1994-98

0    250    500    750 km

NORDREGIO
NR 0231

© NLS

As mentioned above, in the world of footloose capitalism nation-states have fewer instruments to affect the distribution of jobs. "Increasing competition" is a frequently used term to describe one consequence for the regions of globalisation and European integration. Regions try to develop their own policies and shape their own futures. This is also the case in the Nordic countries (Asheim and Mariussen 2003). Have the Nordic regions any clear policy options in mind to help them face such a situation? What would competitive policies for regions (and cities) probably provide for? A) Third-stage modernisation (gearing up for the information economy, as suggested by Clarke and Gaile [1998]), or traditional service provision? B) Internationalism and cross-border networks (Goldsmith and Klausen 1998) or go-it-alone? C) Active multi-level governance: pursuits of partnerships across levels of government, or a preference for redistribution/decentralisation of functions?

Some answers can be given on the basis of information from a survey of regional policy-makers in Denmark, Finland, Norway and Sweden. The respondents were asked to take a stand on a series of policy options that could be of potential value in dealing with a climate of increasing competition. The survey covered the policy-makers (elected politicians serving on the policy committee[48]) of all Nordic regions.

What sort of *policies* did the policy-makers see as relevant responses in order to promote the interests of their respective areas? Respondents were given a list of 18 different policy options and asked to state their preferences for these options. Based on factor analysis these alternatives can be divided into four categories (cf. box 3).

Box 3  *Policy choices for regions*

Internationalisation, e.g. cross-border alliances, learning languages, etc.

"New" modernisation, e.g. better electronic communications, upgrading R&D and educational facilities, alliances universities-business

Functional decentralisation, i.e. more functions to regions and/or cities

Better service provision, i.e. in health, education, etc. services

Regional policy-makers in *all four countries*, most of all in Finland, but also in the other three countries, put *modernisation* strategies at or near the top. The challenges of the emergent information economy were taken very seriously. In Finland and Denmark, policies of institutional reconstruction and functional redistribution took second place. Norway and Sweden put more faith in improving service provision than Finns and Danes. The various forms of internationalisation received less support, including such measures as cross-border alliances and improving the capacities of elected members and civil servants to engage in international contacts. However, this sort of activity was not discarded by the regions; more than two-thirds of elected members in all countries favoured such initiatives.

It should be pointed out, furthermore, that policy-makers also disagreed over policy choices. New development policies represented new dimensions of conflict inside the respective councils. This was so in particular with regard to policies of active internationalisation. On the whole, two-thirds of the councillors supported the latter type of strategies, in some councils more, in others less. The opponents of internationalisation preferred the councils to concentrate on the traditional programmes of welfare provision. Thus, globalisation and the concomitant regional responses created new cleavages in the Nordic welfare states.

## Do the Nordics Love Their Regions? Will the Regional Elites Fight for Their Regions?

Region-building activities are driven by the ideas, attitudes and sentiments of regionalists. How strong or uniform are such attitudes? Are they strong enough and so compatible as to guarantee a continued regionalist development? In order to answer these questions two sets of data will be presented. The first set indicates the subjective attachment of people to the regions where they live, i.e., their regional identity. The second set probes the attitudes of regional policy-makers on the role and independence of regions in relation to the state.

To what extent is regionalism in the Nordic countries driven by identity politics? How strong are regional identities, and where are the strongest identities found? As pointed out above, a few areas have been granted home rule (Greenland, the Faeroe Islands and Åland) against a background of cultural and economic distinctiveness. Saami districts in Northern Norway have voiced similar claims. These communities could be said to represent "nations without a state", like Scotland, Catalonia or Quebec (Keating 1988), and possess distinctive cultural profiles that can be mobilised politically. What about other Nordic regions? To what extent do populations in say Western Norway or Northern Sweden feel strongly about their regional roots? Do they feel a special attachment to their regions?

The attachment of people to their regions is highlighted in table 3, comparing the Nordic countries to a selection of other European countries. Interestingly, people in most European countries feel quite attached to their respective regions, with Portugal and Austria as the leaders in this respect, while people in the UK and the Netherlands seem to care less about their home regions. The level of regional attachment is quite high in the Nordic countries, with the exception of the Finns. The Finns are in the same indifferent category as the Dutch and the British, whereas the other three countries demonstrate high regional affinities. Why the Finns identify less with their regions is not easy to explain. The same lack of identification has previously also been found with regard to places closer at hand, like the municipality, another Finnish exception which has baffled students of Nordic local politics (Rose and Ståhlberg 2000). At least in the three *Scandinavian* countries popular sentiments would suggest support for wider regionalisation.

There are also variations among regions as to the attachment of their inhabitants to their regions. Table 3 lists the regions (NUTS 2 regions) with highest and lowest level of attachment in the respective countries. Interestingly, some well-known historical lands appear in the data in the table, such as Alsace and Burgenland (the presence of historical lands, Catalonia, Wales, Flanders, etc., among leading identity regions is even more pronounced when the data are grouped for larger areas; figures not presented). As a general rule, in the Nordic countries it seems that the level of attachment is highest in more peripheral regions, but the opposite is not necessarily true: that people have low attachment to the capital city areas, although the Danish case fits such a pattern. The Swedish region with the highest attachment score, Gotland, is an island in the Baltic Sea, whereas the leading Norwegian identity region, Troms, is situated in the far North (the neighbouring region, Finnmark, situated even further North, has an almost equally strong score). The strongest Finnish scorer also has a somewhat isolated location on the Eastern border. These are the regions we can expect to lead the crusades for regionalisation and national policies in favour of peripheral regions.

Table 11.3 Subjective regional attachment. Eurobarometer survey 1995 (Norway 1993*)

| | Pct. "very attached"; national mean | Area of residence of respondents with highest/lowest regional attachment | Mean score difference highest/lowest |
|---|---|---|---|
| Sweden | 60 | Gotland/Västmanland | 0.8 |
| Norway* | 59 | Troms/Hedmark | 0.4 |
| Denmark | 56 | Funen/Copenhagen area | 0.1** |
| Finland | 38 | Pohjois-Karjala/Etela-Savo | 0.7 |
| Portugal | 73 | Algarve/Azores | 0.7 |
| Austria | 70 | Burgenland/Salzburg | 0.4 |
| Spain | 69 | Asturias/Castilla-Leon | 0.7 |
| Belgium | 61 | Brabant flamand/ Brabant wallon | 0.5 |
| Germany | 60 | Schwerin/Weser Ems | 0.6 |
| Italy | 53 | Trentino/Lazio | 0.7 |
| France | 51 | Alsace/Poitou-Charentes | 0.7 |
| UK | 46 | Shropshire+Staffordshire/ Berkshire+Buckinghamshire+Oxfordshire | 0.8 |
| Netherlands | 35 | Limburg/Groningen | 0.5 |
| EU total | 57 | Gotland/Groningen | 1.3 |

Q: People may feel different degrees of attachment to their town or village, to their region, to their country, to the European Union or to Europe as a whole. Please tell me
how attached you feel to your region? Alternatives: 1 very attached, 2 fairly attached, 3
not very attached, 4 not at all attached, 5 DK.

* The Norwegian survey was somewhat differently designed as "region" was specified
as both "province/landsdel" and "county/fylke" and responses about both were elic-
ited; the percentage given refers to province/landsdel; attachment to the county,
which is the smaller of the two entities was somewhat lower (cf. Rose and Skare 1996).
In the Eurobarometer survey it was left to the respondent to specify region of attachment.

** For Denmark, data could be broken down into four regions only; data for the other
countries allow for a finer grained regional analysis at NUTS 2 level.

Whether or not such crusades will succeed may depend upon how different these regions are from the rest of their respective countries. If the remaining regions do not feel a regional dimension to be important they may not favour regionally differentiated policies or transfer of powers to regions. How different are the leading identity regions? Does regional attachment peak in a few regions while the rest are indifferent? Or is regional attachment a fairly uniformly distributed sentiment?

Among the Nordic countries, regional attachment is strongest in Sweden. The difference between attachment scores for the highest and lowest is 0.8, but only 0.4 in Norway (the Danish data are disregarded in this respect because of problems of comparability). Theoretically, the differences could range from 0 to 4, so the contrasts have to be considered as moderate (the Nordic contrasts are similar to the range found elsewhere in Europe). So the claims of regionalists in identity regions are not unlikely to find sympathetic listeners in other regions.

Turning now to the second set of questions indicated above, what are the views of the *elite* on the future role of regions in national and European decision-making? It was pointed out above, that the division of functions and powers to regions has caused recurring controversy, especially with regard to responsibility for regional development. The policy-makers of the Nordic regions were surveyed (cf. footnote 4) also with regard to their views on the role of the regions in national settings, in Nordic co-operation and in European integration. How strong were regionalist sentiments among the regional policy-makers? How unified or split were they in their views? Could greater regionalisation be expected to lead to conflict among regional groupings, or were they likely to present a unified front of regionalist demands towards the state? How attitudes were distributed among regional councillors is spelt out in box 4.

"State regionalism" is a mind-set built around a desire to see central authorities do more to protect regions from the impacts of globalisation and competition, and not wider autonomy per se. "Regional activism" correlates with a preference for more independence in national decision-making whereas "Euro-regionalism" favours regional activism and European integration, which it sees as a key to opportunity for regions. Interestingly, state regionalism is negatively correlated with the two former sets of attitudes seeking protection from competition under the umbrella of a strong nation-state; further regional autonomy is viewed with suspicion.

Box 4: *Attitudes to the role of regions among regional policy-makers*

State regionalism: regional interests can only be defended by strong nation-states; nation-states should bear the main responsibility in European structural policy; regions should not have more independence in
European co-operation; regional co-operation in Europe is over-bureauc-
ratised; there are too many organisations claiming to represent regions in
Europe.

Regional activism: regions should count more in national decision-
making; it's time for regions to have their own "foreign policy"; regions
should have more to say in European decision-making; integration has
increased regional competition.

Euro-regionalism, indicated by statements such as: regions are important in European integration; the European Union's regional initiatives
are helpful for regions; the advantages of co-operation between European regions outweigh the costs; regions have a lot to gain by co-oper
ating with each other.

The general trend goes markedly in favour of *Euro-regionalism* and with only
limited support for *state regionalism*. Around half of those surveyed could be
said to be Euro-regionalists, with only a fifth state regionalists. There were interesting variations between countries, however. Regional policy-makers in
Finland supported stronger regions in European decision-making and wished
to pursue a regional foreign policy. The regions were seen as too weak within
the national setting. The outstanding feature of Finnish policy-makers was
their strong support for regional activism. Such sentiments were weaker in the
other countries. Danish regional politicians were clearly more Euro-regionalists than their counterparts in the other countries. The longer experience of
European co-operation may have turned many Danish regional politicians
into Euro-regionalists, seeing much to gain from closer collaboration with regions from other countries and through membership in European organisations such as the Association of European Regions.

Norway had the largest proportion of state regionalists (25 per cent), but
this group was quite large in Sweden also, which might reflect tensions between those who wanted to build on the new regional movement as it was ex-

pressed through the regional experiments (see above) and those who wanted to maintain a strong developmental capacity within the traditional state–county administration.

## Conclusions

What are the answers to the five questions outlined in the introductory section?

*Is enlargement of regions on the agenda in the Nordic countries in response to technical requirements of service provision?* Enlargement took place in Finland and Sweden in order to create more effective development regions in preparation of EU accession. Debates in Denmark and Norway have been less favourable with regard to the role of regions, where service provision rather than development has been the focus of concern; right-wing parties would like to see regions eliminated altogether to promote "debureaucratisation".

*Are welfare responsibilities being transferred to regions as a part of cutback strategies in the Nordic countries?* Since the 1990s a crisis of public finances has led the state to look for ways of curbing welfare expenditures, especially in Finland and Sweden. Transfers to regions and municipalities have been cut. This was one of several reasons why regions wanted to stimulate economic growth and create jobs. They have tried to take on extended roles in economic development assistance, which again has led to strategies to enlarge regions or pool resources. Transfer of functions is taking place in the field of economic development, not welfare or service provision. The developmental role of regions is being enhanced most clearly in Sweden. The pattern of state control over regional development instruments is not seriously challenged in Finland while the Norwegian model of county council eminence in regional development has been reduced. In the latter case, welfare functions are actually being transferred to the state, no doubt as a reflection of state fiscal strength.

*How strongly is the pull from Brussels felt in the Nordic regions, and are Nordic regions responding?* The impact of European integration is naturally felt most by the new member states, Finland and Sweden, where much has been done to get regional structures to comply with requirements from Brussels, especially with regard to the management of the structural funds. As mentioned, some regions have been enlarged and new patterns of co-operation between levels of government have emerged, especially as regards relations between county councils and municipalities – a series of multi-level initiatives have been taken. Norway has not been untouched by the new developments in its neighbouring countries, and Norwegian regions have grasped many of the opportunities presented by, i.a., the Interreg programmes to become partners in border-crossing ventures with Swedish, Danish and Finnish regions. Generally speaking, the role of regions in regional economic development has been boosted by Brussels. This does not mean that nation-states are withering away under the pressure of European integration, however. It is a rather an indication of strategic adaptation to European institutions as active regions represent efficient means of gaining access to European funds.

*How active are the Nordic regions as policy makers, and which policies are favoured for endogenous development in a global environment?* Nordic regions try to supplement the role of service producer with that of the development corporation. In the Norwegian case this means maintaining the county's historic role as agent of modernisation. The most urgent policies of modernisation are concerns for facilitating peripheral communities' move into the information economy, which also entails an emphasis on international and cross-border co-operation. These policies do not enjoy unqualified support, however. Some policymakers would prefer to concentrate on classic welfare challenges rather than high-tech or international adventures. New times bring new conflicts.

*How strong are regional identities in the Nordic countries? To what extent are demands for autonomy and independence part of regionalist attitudes among Nordic regions?* In a European perspective regional attachment is fairly strong among the Nordic peoples, with the exception of Finland where regional roots seem to matter less. More regionalisation would harmonise with popular attitudes. At the elite level, regional policy-makers are actively pressing for accelerated transfer of powers and functions to the regions. Interestingly, the majority is remarkably aligned with pro-European attitudes on regionalism. Regionalists love Brussels. However, there are also advocates of a strong state hand to guide regions. And the latter are more euro-sceptics. Here, too, new cleavages are emerging.

To sum up, up to the mid-1990s, regions in the Nordic countries could be said to espouse a Scandinavian-plus-Finnish model of regional governance. Regional authorities in Denmark, Norway and Sweden were popularly elected, they had independent taxation powers and a wide range of responsibilities, although healthcare and the running of hospitals remained their dominant duty. However, region-building was considered an important component of nation-building and too important to be left completely to regionally elected councils; the state retained the upper hand. This was most obvious in Finland, which had (and has) a highly fragmented regional level with indirectly elected special-purpose boards while the dominant actors were (and are) state district agencies. The Finnish "deviation" might be attributed to the existence of two linguistic communities (Finnish and Swedish), which were successfully integrated at the national level but might have proven uneasy bedfellows at the regional level on popularly elected councils. These "models" were somewhat modified when Sweden and Finland acceded to the EU, with the introduction of bottom-up decision-making on economic development. In the 2000s, regions have come under strong pressure in Denmark and Norway. In the former country, the incumbent government has proposed eliminating them. In Norway, the county councils are losing their erstwhile responsibilities and are steadily being undermined. At the same time, regions are seeking to pool resources and establish larger constellations, which may be embryonic "super-regions".

Some of the developments occurring in Denmark and Norway may point towards a "Finlandization" of regional governance and thus a goodbye to the Scandinavian model. At the time of writing it is difficult to say whether the Nordic countries are parting ways entirely, or simply travelling to the same destination along different routes. Classical analysis of regionalism would portray it as an expression of a centre–periphery conflict. Does the (possible) demise of regions suggest the final victory of the centre over the periphery, or the end of the nation-state as we have known it?

# Chapter 12: The Welfare State – Still Viable?

*Anton Steen*

Over the past twenty to thirty years the Nordic countries have scored relatively well on indicators like well-being, equal income distribution and "just society". An active government, willing to engage with market forces to further its redistributional aims, is one of the most frequently cited explanations. The Nordic countries tend to be lumped together under a particular governance model or regime, generally known as the "Nordic" or "Scandinavian" welfare state model. That said, an active state could never single-handedly have kept the wheels running without the resources provided by an efficient capitalist economy through taxation, on top of which comes the input of families and voluntary organizations, both substantial providers of welfare but not so easy to measure. The Nordic "welfare state" is probably best described in terms of "welfare capitalism", i.e., a particular way of organizing not only state but also the capitalist economy and societal institutions (Goodin et. al. 1999). Overall, the Nordic model can be conceived as a set of "social contracts" between state and society (Flora 1986, Arter 1999); legitimating state intervention to address and redress inequalities among social groups.

How similar are the Nordic countries when it comes to welfare? Are there so many common traits that we can identify a model, and are these similarities sufficiently different from other welfare state models to talk about a specific Nordic model? The literature diverges considerably in this matter with answers differing according to which aspects of the welfare state are selected for study, and the time frame involved. During the 1990s, privatization ideology and internationalization put the welfare state under pressure. What did this wave of liberalism mean for the basic "social contracts" underpinning the Nordic welfare states? Are they stable, fragmenting or only renegotiated to new circumstances?

In this chapter I examine the "Nordic model" in terms of a political project; as an ambitious modern state; and as a set of social programmes. I look at the effects of this type of state on income redistribution, levels of public support and gender equality before dealing with the impact of internationalization on the welfare states. Finally, I discuss the impact of recent history on the "social contracts".

## Perspectives on the "Welfare State"

The Nordic welfare state may be regarded as *a type of political regime* based on a broad political compromise between the state, the labour movement and the capitalists. The welfare state may also be identified as a set of *comprehensive policies*, including market intervention. Accordingly, governance affects many aspects of people's lives, not only social security rights but also equality of opportunities, like a free health service, free education, and redistribution of wealth among social classes, industries, regions and gender. Finally, the welfare state is associated with universal, high cost *"social policies"* consisting of a "package" of cash benefits and services.

### THE NORDIC WELFARE STATES AS A PARTICULAR POLITICAL REGIME

The Nordic countries viewed as a single political regime comply with what Esping-Andersen (1990) termed a "social-democratic welfare regime", and the similarities between them are numerous and significant. Broad political mobilization in and by social democratic parties distinguishes this regime from "conservative" and "liberal" welfare regimes. Substantial support in parliamentary elections, government formations, a high level of blue and white collar unionization and corporativism between the government, trade unions and farmers' organizations have laid the foundation for "decommodification policies". The main idea is that the economic and social welfare of the citizens should not depend solely on the demand for labour in the market. The state should accept responsibility to provide welfare for those without "commodity value" in the labour market, due to illness, old age or other causes.

However, although the social democratic parties were a leading force in Nordic politics, they seldom enjoyed parliamentary majorities. Another essential reform pillar involved finding a middle-ground with other parties: consensual policy-making. Before, but particularly just after WWII and particularly in Norway, all the main political parties were agreed on the desirability of expanding the welfare state (Kuhnle 1983; Hatland 1992). Universal welfare measures were enacted on the basis of broad political consensus, to counteract market shortcomings; provide a sufficient tax basis to finance the welfare state; and create a negotiating platform with the owners of capital in a corporativist bargaining system.

More often than not, the Nordic social democratic parties accepted compromises on welfare policy with the non-socialist political parties. It is arguable that the political basis of the Nordic welfare model can be traced back to the historical shift in political strategy of the social democratic parties at the beginning of the 1930s. The economic depression spurred parliamentary co-operation in so-called "Red–Green alliances", between dominant social democratic and the smaller agrarian parties. The social democratic parties substituted parliamentary majoritarianism for their revolutionary strategy. They cultivated political unity among workers, peasants and the rising white-collar workforce, naturally leading to a wide acceptance of *universalism* as a distributional principle (Esping-Andersen 1985).

The strength of the Nordic social democratic parties has varied considerably over the years. Danish social democratic aspirations were constrained by influential liberal and conservative parties. Although few conflicts erupted over specific reforms, getting them enacted did not necessarily imply consensus. While Danish social democrats did expand the welfare state, success came more through liberal notions of public responsibility than in the other Nordic countries. Consequently, the Danish welfare state was never a "typical" social democratic welfare regime, like Norway and Sweden, whose social democratic parties enjoyed a much deeper hegemony.

Although the Swedish and Norwegian welfare states are largely similar, the political circumstances under which the reforms were enacted differed notably. The Norwegians achieved their post-WWII welfare reforms through consensus with the non-socialist parties and should hardly be seen as a specifically social democratic accomplishment. Others stress the importance of ideological change, away from liberalism, which affected all political parties in the late 1930s as a response to the economic depression and social problems.

Some of the major Swedish reforms, e.g., the radical 1948 pension reform with universal coverage and flat-rate benefits, succeeded only in the face of staunch non-socialist opposition. Issues and political fronts followed traditional class cleavages (Esping-Andersen 1985). When the Norwegian social democrats came up with a similar pension scheme some years later, the non-socialist government gave its blessing and the bill was passed unanimously in 1967. At

about the same time, Denmark was ruminating over yet another pension reform; in the event, it turned out to be a much more modest affair, because employers were unwilling to adequately fund the retirement benefit. Another major, uncontroversial Norwegian reform was prompted by the labour movement
who wanted universal, standardized family allowances. It was implemented in
1946, with Sweden and Denmark following shortly thereafter.

THE NORDIC WELFARE STATES AS AN INSTRUMENT OF REDISTRIBUTION
We get an idea of how far-reaching the welfare state was with its multi-secto-
ral ambitions in the countries' budgets. Budgets of the Nordic countries have
peaked at nearly 50 per cent of GNP. A high proportion of the labour force is
state employed. Composites of public spending have been used to compare
state ambition levels. Results for the Nordic countries compare favourably
with others whose state aspirations and budgets tend to be less ambitious
(Castles 1993, 2002). Steen (1986) and Amoroso (1996) argue that, in addition to
a social policy, a welfare state pursues additional welfare policies, including active redistributive policies, in the labour market, health, education, income
formation and taxation. Powell and Barrientos (2004) include active labour
market policies as a key sector in the "welfare mix". Steen (1995) analyses state
ambitions to make occupational health care services an obligatory responsibility for all private employers in the Nordic countries. In the immediate post-
WWII decades, Norwegian and Swedish agriculture transfers aimed at redis-
tributing resources to bring the farm incomes up to the level of industrial
workers (Steen 1981). All of the Nordic countries took steps to establish equality of results in the distributive process beyond basic social security policies.

The welfare state can be likened to an evolutionary process, which starts by
safeguarding basic security, ensuring equality of opportunity, and ends by
taking on responsibilities for equality of result (Flora and Heidenheimer
1981). In addition to minimum living standards, social needs are articulated in
several interacting policy areas: education policy, income policy, labour market policy, finance and fiscal policy, subsidies to industries and regional policies (Amoroso 1996).

Efforts to intervene in distributional outcomes has profound consequences
for the organization of the state. As Kjellberg (1988) argues, welfare state
expansion in Scandinavia necessitated robust local and regional government,
able to administer the many reforms. The amalgamation of communes and
establishing of closer central–local financial relations were important instruments in the expansion of the welfare state. But the changes required chal-

lenged democratic values, not least in relation to views on the correct balance of state supervision and local autonomy. The process of state–local integration was strongest in Norway and Sweden, while a less ambitious welfare state in Denmark seems to explain the preservation of more local autonomy there.

Public spending in percentage of GDP was about 30 per cent in the Nordic and other western countries in the 1960s, but rose steeply in the Nordic countries in the succeeding decades. US spending remained around the 30 per cent mark until 1995, but by then the Nordic spending was peaking at about 60 per cent, roughly 10 per cent higher than major EU countries (Barth et. al. 2003). The figures show just how much more comprehensive and ambitious state policies in the Nordic countries were than in the EU and the US.

However, differences exist between the four countries. Marklund and Nordlund (1999) analysed public spending per capita between 1980 and 1995 and compared with average spending levels of other OECD countries. They found that spending in all of the Nordic countries exceeded OECD levels. Denmark, Sweden and Norway were markedly ahead, with Finland, at the beginning of the period, close to the OECD average, but closer to its Nordic neighbours before the international recession set in in the early 1990s. The governments of Denmark and Sweden spent about 60 to 80 per cent more than the OECD average. Norwegian spending rose rapidly from about 1980, by the mid-1990s reaching Danish and Swedish levels.

The Norwegian state's favourable financial situation is largely due to oil revenues. The 1990s international recession hit the Nordic countries differently. While Finland and Sweden reacted by cutting public spending, the more propitiously placed Norwegian and Danish governments with their well-balanced budgets and lower net lending, were able to resist cuts. Finnish and Swedish lending approached about 10 per cent of GDP 1992–93. When Finland's prime export market to the east evaporated, its export industries were hit exceptionally hard. Both states were therefore forced to cut spending, not least in the social service sector. Privatization ideology was putting added pressure on the Nordic public sector to cut budgets, reorganize government and leave some traditional state tasks to the market. The effects were dramatic: total public spending relative to GNP fell on average from a 62 per cent high in 1995 to 47 per cent in 2000 (Barth et al. 2003:58). The reduction was notably more moderate in the EU and USA.

The cuts came in a period where the responsibilities of government to provide for mounting unemployment and an aging population, demands for more and better health care, institutions for the elderly and pensions etc., were stretching governments to the bone. Cuts and increases have gone hand in hand in the Nordic countries.

## The Nordic Welfare States as an Intrument of Social Policy

Social policies may be few or many and assistance scarce or generous. Here we look at welfare schemes, their costs and financing. Welfare provisions can be made available to citizens on the basis of needs testing and selective criteria or as a universal right. The limited means-testing types are referred to as "residual"; "universal welfare" obtains when benefits are made available according to rights and residence (Titmuss 1963). In the residual social policy approach the state has obligations only when the market and the family fail to provide basic necessities of life. Schemes are targeted at providing minimum benefits only to the most deserving. The main object of the "social service" state is to mitigate the consequences of the capitalist production system (Briggs 1961). In the extended version, the "universalist welfare state" guarantees bountiful benefits to which all citizens are entitled in the event of injury, illness, unemployment and old age. In the residual version the state may pass social laws but the responsibility for financing rests mainly with the insured. In the universalist version the state shares responsibility with the employers to fund the services.

The first social insurance laws were passed in some Nordic countries more than a century ago and covered mainly accidents at work and sickness. Denmark, and to some extent, Sweden were forerunners, Norwegian social policy legislation followed a little later. Finland has tended to lag behind the others. While the ideas were radical at the time, ambitions in today's standards were modest and only covered a small part of the population. The allowances were meagre, insufficient for subsistence and the insurance schemes were only partly financed by the government.

These years saw several changes: new social groups were included, allowances were increased incrementally, the voluntary premium system was phased out, being replaced by obligatory tax-based financing, and funds management passed from the private sector to the state. Table 12.1 shows which year these selective and insurance-based social laws were enacted, and the year they became universal, offering coverage for the whole population.

Although nominally universal, the provisions vary widely between the countries as to entitlement and level of benefits, criteria for unemployment benefits and sickness allowances. The year of full coverage was not necessarily coeval with the fully developed welfare state. New demographic and other pressures on the welfare state, along with a relatively hefty burden of taxation, mean that changes are still taking place. There is an ongoing discussion concerning the level of welfare benefits, ways of financing and, more generally, the responsibility of the state for individual welfare, e.g., the balance between earnings-related and flat-rate pensions. Despite the debate, the egalitarian principle of universal coverage is firmly entrenched and not seriously questioned.

Table 12.1  Year of introduction of social insurance laws for targeted groups and year of universal coverage

| | Denmark | Finland | Norway | Sweden |
|---|---|---|---|---|
| Accidence | 1898 1916 | 1895 1948 | 1894 1950 | 1901 1916–27 |
| Sickness | 1892 1960 | 1963–67 | 1909 1956 | 1891 1953 |
| Old age | 1891 1956–70 | 1937 1956 | 1936 1956 | 1913 1946 |
| Unemployment | 1907 1967–71 | 1917 1959 | 1906 1938 | 1934 |

Sources: Kuhnle in Flora/Heidenheimer 1981:140; Kuhnle 1983; Flora 1986; Øverby 1996.

New laws tended only to cover certain groups of the population, benefits were means-tested, and a major part of the outlays were financed by contributions from the employers and with employee premiums. The year universal coverage was introduced meant that the entire population was ensured of a minimum level of largely tax-financed benefits, guaranteed by the state.

The early laws were largely inspired by social insurance legislation in Bismarckian Germany. The accident and sickness laws were particularly important and aimed at appeasing the demands of the growing working class and preserve social stability. The gist of the German insurances was their selective character, inasmuch as they only offered cover for industrial workers. It was they, together with the employer, that paid individual premiums into a special fund. Benefit entitlements and the predominating employer/worker-based financing instituted a special type of conservative/corporatist welfare model, which underpinned existing economic differences between social groups.

As the Nordic social democratic parties and the labour unions grew stronger in the 1920s and 30s, political pressure caused the generation of more universalist schemes, widened government responsibilities and the inclusion of more and more social groups. Income testing counted less and less for benefit eligibility, and central and local authorities, along with the employers (especially in Sweden and Finland), became the main economic contributors. True universalism – that is, universally applicable social security entitlements – and the high level of benefits that was institutionalized during the 1950s, made the Nordics stand out from other welfare states.

However, although all elderly persons were entitled to a pension, the provisions only offered a minimum income. For additional incomes people had to rely on personal savings or private pensions. As Øverby (1996) shows, the Nordic political parties and trade unions wanted to see supplementary public pensions related to level of income, or super-annuations, along with occupational pensions and private pensions provided by the market. Denmark has gone furthest in relying on additional private pensions. The set-up of these pensions varies a lot among the countries, the only common denominator being that the state guarantees a fairly generous minimum pension.

The Swedish system of unemployment benefits has mainly been the responsibility of the trade unions and their benefit societies, which explains the late introduction of legislation in this area. Contributions were in principle voluntary, although in practice most unions made them compulsory. From 1974, the trade union-organized insurance scheme for the unemployed expanded as state assistance for unemployed persons not covered by the trade union scheme kicked in (Olson 1986). As Hatland (1999) remarks, the principle of voluntary membership, which also applies to Denmark and Finland, has long traditions in these countries. It must not be mistaken for "liberalism" in welfare policies, but as an institution, expressing co-operation between the trade union movement and the state. Norway is an exception, with its state-dominated compulsory system and universal coverage.

The British model proposed under WWII and instituted just after is said to be the origin of the universal ideal. But the issue had been on the agenda in Scandinavia since the mid-1930s and forwarded by several government appointed committees (Kuhnle 1983). The British post-war universal allowances were rather modest and it was necessary to top them up with other income, like means-tested grants. The German system was based on an employer–em-

ployee corporate relationship preserving ineqalities between industries. The
Nordic model was forged on a combination of inclusive rights following citizenship status and bountiful benefits to safeguard a reasonable standard of
living in case of illness, unemployment or old age irrespective of occupational
status. The institutions of social policy obviously vary between groups of
countries, but does the social democratic type of welfare regime necessarily
mean higher social expenditures?

THE COSTS OF SOCIAL PROGRAMMES
In the 1970s, social spending fluctuated between 20 and 25 per cent of GDP,
reaching 25–30 per cent at the turn of the century. During this period, spending was clearly highest in Sweden and Denmark, with Norway and Finland
making up the rear.

Table 12.2  Social expenditures 1975–2001, as percentage of GDP

|         | 1975 | 1981 | 1987 | 1990 | 1995 | 2001 |
|---------|------|------|------|------|------|------|
| Denmark | 26   | 30   | 28   | 29   | 32   | 30   |
| Finland | 18   | 22   | 26   | 25   | 32   | 26   |
| Norway  | 19   | 22   | 26   | 26   | 27   | 26   |
| Sweden  | 25   | 34   | 35   | 33   | 35   | 31   |

Source: *Social Protection in the Nordic Countries*, Nordic Social Statistical Committee
(NOSOKO), 1987 and 2001.

European states are generally catching up with Scandinavia. In 2000, Germany
spent 30 per cent of their GDP and the UK 27 per cent on social security. Obviously, the Nordics are not alone in having a high level of social expenditure. It
is common also in states with "continental" and "liberal" type welfare provisions. The redistributive effects found in the Nordic countries seem to be
more related to wage structures and taxation system than to social policies.
    Social benefits may be provided as free services or cash payments. While servi-
ces like basic medical care, hospital treatment and education are less vulnerable to
cut-backs, benefits provided through cash payment such as unemployment,
sickness, maternity, disability, old age and family benefits, in particular when
they are means-tested, are more sensitive to changes in economic climate.

Ploug (1999) investigated the development of cash payments in the 1980s and early 1990s and concluded that, except for old-age pensions, compensations in the other fields had fallen, but not dramatically, and the Nordic countries have retrenched, though again to varying degrees. Benefits have been cut, eligibility criteria tightened and benefit periods shortened. But these changes have not been systematic, far less radical, and may most aptly be described as marginal adaptations. Pensions and family (i.e. maternity) benefits have been sheltered from this development. Much of the same stability is found for how social costs are financed. While the employers and the insured had to pay a major share of the early social programmes, in post-WWII Scandinavia, expanding state obligations to compensate the costs have been the trend. If the welfare state had been in a serious crisis one should have expected to a larger extent costs to be charged to the employers and insured. This happened only in Denmark. Table 12.3 illustrates the share of various social expenditures after the turbulent 1990s and how the expenses are compensated for.

The Nordic countries spend approximately the same amount of total social expenditures on *families and children* and, comparing with most other European countries, the share is relatively high. Especially the outlays for these purposes in southern European countries are low, e.g., Greece with 7 per cent, Portugal 6 per cent, Italy 4 per cent and Spain 3 per cent. The Nordic pattern is explained by the rather generous maternity benefits, a family structure with a high proportion of single mothers and women's widespread participation in work life, which necessitates measures for childcare institutions.

The variations in *unemployment* benefits are directly related to the rate of unoccupied and vary considerably over time. As the figures show, in 2000 the less favourable situation in the labour market in Denmark and Finland accounts for the higher share. However, other factors influence expenses: the qualifying conditions requiring a certain earning period and minimum income; the duration of support; and the compensation levels. All these requirements vary among the Nordics, and all have been tightened during the 1990s. Though, as Hatland (1999) points out, the adjustments were modest compared to those put in place by other countries, e.g. the UK, where all earnings-related benefits were abolished and the unemployed had to rely on basic social benefits. Probably the most important measure to reactivate the unemployed are the public labour market schemes in which the authorities pay for obligatory participation of the unemployed in various education and training programmes.

Expenditure on *illness* is high in most countries and normally payable for a maximum of 52 weeks. Norway spends a larger share than other countries, one explanation being the more generous level of benefits.

Table 12.3 Expenditures for social purposes and financing of some major types of social expenditures, in 2000

| | Expenditures for major social purposes as a percentage of total social expenditures, in pct. | | | | Contributions to financing, in pct. | | | |
|---|---|---|---|---|---|---|---|---|
| | Families and children | Unemploy-ment | Illness* | Old age and disability | Public | Employer | Insured | Other |
| Denmark | 13 | 11 | 20 | 50 | 64 | 9 | 20 | 7 |
| Finland | 13 | 10 | 24 | 50 | 43 | 38 | 12 | 7 |
| Norway | 13 | 3 | 34 | 47 | 60 | 24 | 14 | 1 |
| Sweden | 11 | 7 | 27 | 51 | 47 | 40 | 9 | 4 |
| Germany | 11 | 8 | 28 | 50 | | | | |
| U.K. | / | 3 | 26 | 57 | | | | |

Source: *Social Protection in the Nordic Countries*, NOSOKO, 2001. Housing and other social benefits are not included. The percentages do not add up to 100 per cent since a number of social needs are not covered by any specific legislation and therefore difficult to compare between the countries.
* Including paid absence from work in connection with illness, benefits in the event of industrial injury and health services provided by hospitals.

The heavy burden of outlays on *pensions* and early retirement due to disability is a common feature of the Nordic and most other European countries. About half of all social spending relates to these areas. Common to the pension systems in the Nordic countries is that all citizens have a statutory right to a minimum amount of cash payment to cover basic subsistence needs. Supplementary employment pension comes in addition for those who have been active in the labour market. Private pensions are less common, but are becoming more important due to demographic changes.

The expenditures to pensions are growing because of increasing life expectancy. In the case of Norway, spending on old age and disability is expected to grow from 7 per cent of GDP in 2001 to 19 per cent in 2050 (NOU 2004:1).

While the proportion of pensioners is increasing rapidly the share of the population of active work age is decreasing. In Norway the ratio of tax-payers to pensioners was 3.9:1 in 1967, 2.6:1 in 2003, and is estimated to reach 1.6:1 in 2050. The figures forewarn of the imminent clash between pension expenditures and financing. The recommendation of the State Commission who made the report on the future pension system is to extend the period of work and introduce a higher pension age.

The main *sources for financing* the social expenditures are revenue from general taxes, redistributed by the public budgets (state and local), and the special fees paid by the employers and the employees. Due to the more prominent position of corporativist relations in Finland and Sweden, they have traditionally relied more on employer charges than other countries. Denmark saw a remarkable drop in public contributions from 80 per cent in 1990 to 64 per cent in 2000. The fall was compensated for by increasing the contributions and special taxes from the individuals insured from 5 per cent to 20 per cent in the same period. It seems that changes in the Danish welfare system have tended to hike individual responsibilities, more so than in the other Nordic countries. Similar developments, with diminishing contributions from public authorities and increasing individual contributions, are also observed for Finland and Sweden.

Norway's situation is distinguished by a combination of substantial public and employer financing while the share paid by the insured has been stable and modest. The fact that duties nonetheless have to be extracted from the productive sector, one may argue that source of financing does not really matter for the welfare state. However, one should not disregard the symbolic aspect and potential political responses when accounting for who pays for the welfare benefits. It could be argued that the more state-centred Norwegian model of financing enjoys wider political legitimacy than the Finnish and Swedish system where welfare costs more directly affect the employers' interests or the Danish where welfare is partly linked to individual payment.

## Effects of the welfare state

The welfare state is a distributional as well as a political project. A main object of the Nordic states has been to even out income distribution among social groups while laying the foundation for political consensus. The following section discusses the achievements of income equalization and how welfare rights and employment in the public sector may affect future solidarity among the population in general and females in particular.

INCOME DISTRIBUTION

One important indicator of welfare state performance is to what extent incomes differ between social groups. Comparing with other industrialized countries the income differences between occupations in the Nordic countries are relatively modest. However, Esping-Andersen said in 1985 that by the end of the 1970s the Danish labour movement had failed to bring about greater equality between the blue and white collar workforces. The income gap between unskilled and skilled workers and higher functionaries was still very wide. In Sweden, the designated "solidarity" wage policy of the trade union movement actually narrowed the income gap, especially between unskilled and skilled workers. According to Esping-Andersen, Norway, on the whole was the more successful of the three in making incomes more even through its ability to redistribute wealth through progressive taxation and to level out earning differences through wage negotiations. While Norway accomplished redistribution between social classes, and Sweden levelled out incomes among working class strata, the weaker Danish labour movement and less dominating Social Democratic Party were more willing to accept that competence and education should pay off.

Although some variations still exist between Nordic income-groups, as reported by Gustafsson et al. (1999:221, 232), all the evidence points in the direction of decreasing income inequality everywhere up to the early 1980s. In international perspective the redistributive impact of transfers and taxation on disposable incomes was substantial in all Nordic countries. During this period the state actively provided social benefits, charged progressive taxes and influenced wage settlements. It was therefore possible to counteract the gap-widening dynamics of market competition. From the early 1980s and onwards many signs of increasing inequalities once more became visible. Interestingly, the two countries with the most ambitious redistributional policies during the first period, Norway and Sweden, had the most noticeable increase in income inequality from the mid 1980s. Obviously, the effects of redistributional policies are becoming less clear because market forces were given more leeway in wage formation.

But still, income differences between the top and low wage earners in the Nordic countries are modest compared to other OECD countries. In particular, the highest income brackets among the Scandinavian leaders, while being well paid, earn considerably less than colleagues in the US and continental Europe. The Nordics' compressed wage structure correlates closely with degree of coordination in the wage negotiations. Comparing OECD –countries, Barth et al. (2003) find that the more organized the wage earners are in trade unions and the more centralized the wage negotiations, the narrower the income gaps. They argue that a basic egalitarian norm among the general population is used as an important standard in the wage negotiations.

### SOLIDARISM IN RETREAT?

The debate on the welfare state and its responsibilities has at times been quite heated. In the early 1970s some spoke of disillusionment among certain groups stemming from stalled economic growth and disappointment with failed equality measures. There was widespread concern on the political left that the established welfare institutions would suffer. Other allegations came from the new right critics (Heclo 1981), who argued that the costs of financing welfare services was out of control and had become an intolerable tax burden on moderate and even lower income groups. The middle classes were less willing to meet the burden of the welfare state. Some critics argued that the welfare state had failed to live up to its promise, and was incapable of solving distributional problems better than the market. The welfare state regulations fostered bureaucratization and ineffectiveness and seemed more to benefit professionals than the target groups. New political parties, whose main platform was anti-state, were established in Denmark and Norway. The new liberal views of 1980s "Reaganite" and "Thatcherite" market ideology sustained individualistic forces and also affected the other political parties.

Paradoxically, these trends were a result of the success of the welfare state: a high level of education, rising living standards and geographic and social mobility may have promoted individualistic values and undermined public support for financing welfare programmes and social solidarity, as Andersen et al. (1999) argue.

The overall picture of the 1965–95 years is the generally high level of support in all Nordic countries, and the move from buttressing welfare expansion to welfare consolidation. There is no long-term decline in welfare state support and the proportion of the population who want to see a reduction in welfare benefits and services has remained on a modest level in all four countries. For example, since the mid-1970s in Norway, only about 10 per cent have said they would like to see the welfare state dismantled. By 1995, about 20 per cent wanted to expand the social security benefits, while more than 60 per cent said that they should stay where they are.

Support for what were called the early 1970s "tax-revolt" parties fluctuated most in Denmark and Norway, but this "tax backlash" effect lasted no more than a few years. Finland and Sweden were both hit by severe economic recession but only Finland saw a major drop in support for the welfare state. The widespread support for the Swedish welfare state has been astonishingly stable. It seems that neither economic crisis nor liberal ideologies have eroded its legitimacy in the population.

One may assume that universal programmes which include the whole population at some stage of their life will garner more support than selective programmes aimed at covering special needs of particular groups. Accordingly, one would expect to find a hierarchy of support depending on the inclusiveness of the programme. Andersen et al. (1999) find a relatively similar pattern among the Nordic populations, who rank support for welfare provision in the following way: 1. Health service; 2. Public pension; 3. Child care; 4. Child allowance; 5. Sickness insurance; 6. Unemployment benefits; 7. Social assistance; and 8. Housing allowance.

In the first half of the 1990s more than 75 per cent of Danes, Norwegians and Swedes wanted to increase public health service spending, and more than half wanted to increase old-age pensions. The rest preferred no change, while less than 3 per cent wanted cuts made. While very few Finns wanted to see reductions, the proportion supporting an increase is lower probably because of the sense of caution created by the severe economic crisis of these years. In contrast, Norway's favourable economic situation made the population less restrained in their welfare demands. As many as 88 per cent wanted health service expansion and 63 per cent were in favour of higher pensions. About 40 per cent wanted to expand child care.

Increasing sickness insurance had much lower support. For example, only 16 per cent of Norwegians are in favour, which is probably explained by the generous system of sickness insurance still in existence, which compensates 100 per cent of income loss from the first day of sickness. Popular support for increasing unemployment benefits is generally low and directly correlated with unemployment rates in the mid-1990s. Finns and Swedes were considerably more in favour of increasing such benefits than Danes and Norwegians, who were less severely hit by the economic recession. Welfare benefits like social assistance and housing benefits which target specific groups, and traditionally have been associated with a certain social stigma, find less than 20 per cent in support of expansion.

In summary, the public support for the welfare state was highest around the early 1970s, when it went through a consolidation phase after a long period of expansion. We do not see any long-term decline in support for the Nordic welfare state, with particularly high support levels among women, public sector employees, workers, persons with low incomes, the less educated and unemployed. And there are differences between generations, older people are more apt to support pension schemes over child allowances, than the younger generations are. Support obviously differs among the populace according to the inclusiveness of the social programme in question and the overriding economic climate in society. While contrasts in support for the welfare state between income groups is pronounced in Sweden, and also evident in Denmark and Finland, the Norwegian population exhibits attitudes that are considerably less antagonistic.

GENDER AND THE WELFARE STATE

The Nordic countries are often associated with some success in ensuring equal possibilities for both sexes in the labour market. Feminist movements, non-discrimination laws and state supervision of the implementation of these acts have opened both the private and public labour markets to women in an unprecedented way. As Hernes (1987) argues, because of the reproductive function women tend to be more dependent on the state than men, and market and state can in some ways be regarded as gender-specific areas. The transition from generating welfare in the unpaid family sphere to employment in the public sector, in particular in service work, has been especially comprehensive in the Nordic states.

Several empirical studies have identified the large female labour force participation in the Nordic countries. Employed women as a percentage of the female population between 15 and 65 had a participation rate in the Nordic countries of about 75 per cent by the end of the 1980s, (Huber and Stephens 2000). The group of "conservative-corporate welfare states" has a rate of about 50 per cent while the "liberal welfare states" have about 60 per cent. The explanation for the substantial female share of the labour market are the equalization policies of the Nordic governments, compared to the more family-oriented policies of continental "Christian democratic regimes". However, even more important is the interaction effect of women's labour market participation with public delivery of welfare services in health, education and social benefits. Huber and Stephens (2000) argue that while generous unemployment, sickness and retirement benefits may reduce the incentive to work, the social democratic welfare programmes of actively including the female work force mobilize labour.

Making the life of modern families easier, with its combination of parenthood and work, by, for example, generous maternity leave provisions and cheap access to child care has favourable demographic consequences inasmuch as they counteract the problem of aging populations. Further, it seems that high female labour force participation increases the support for the welfare state and reduces the number dependent on it. As Hagen (1999) argues, there exists an intimate bond between the fate of the welfare state and women's interests in basic and generous welfare policies.


## Globalization and Europeanization

Some argue that parallel industrialization and modernization during the 1950s and 1960s urged societies to develop along the same path and adopt similar policies (Wilensky 1975; Flora and Alber 1981). The "convergence thesis" obviously did not hold true for the next decades and its functional logic has been criticized for determinism. However, as Kautto et al. (2001) argue, the thesis has found new actuality after internationalization more directly interfered with the Nordic welfare model. The Nordic states have had to respond to unintended consequences of globalization and adapt to policy-making in supranational bodies, like the EU.

Globalization accelerated after the fall of communism and the spread of market ideology. The free flow of capital, labour mobility, multi-national business corporations operating across national borders and immigration created new pressures limiting distributional ambitions of the state. Contrary to the idea of common welfare expansion following the modernization thesis, the globalization thesis implies convergence around a restructured and more limited welfare state which entrusts more welfare responsibilities to the market, e.g. the international tendency to use the tax system to stimulate private welfare.

Referring to Titmuss' (1963) seminal article, Ervik and Kuhnle (1996) argue that the Nordic states are drifting towards a segmentation of the welfare society. The growing importance of socially biased tax deductions for pension premiums available for middle and high-income groups tends to support an increase in private pension insurance schemes provided by the market and undermine the resource base of the state. Internationalization puts the extraction capability of the welfare state under pressure. Another challenge to the national tax base are the international companies. The possibility of tax evasion may easily erode the redistributional potential of the Nordic welfare state and expose nation-states to "tax-competition" to counteract unemployment (Kautto et al. 2001). However, these strains should not be overestimated. Experience shows that the small and open economies of the Nordic states, rather than being impeded by international trade liberalization, have long responded by developing a welfare state ensuring stable economic and social conditions for long-term investments. As Katzenstein (1985) argues, the comprehensive welfare systems enabled the Nordic countries to tackle social inequalities and restructuring of the economy and provide economic growth better than many protectionist countries.

The rather unpredictable globalization process with its many unintended effects should be separated from more deliberately designed European integration processes. EU political bodies may purposely impose measures to achieve specific aims, e.g. related to standardization of minimum levels of occupational health among the member states. One finds impositions of EU policy on the member states, often supported by interventions from the European Court, in areas of rights connected to labour mobility, gender equality, occupational health, workplace security and imposing of minimum standards on maternity leave and working hours. While these policies have some equalizing effects they are mainly grounded on the idea of alleviating the play of the market forces. Regulations of the labour market have been in place in the Nordic states for decades and guaranteeing rights in most cases above European average. In this field the EU obviously stimulates convergence, which means that other countries, e.g.,. in Southern and Eastern Europe, are starting to "catch up" with Nordic standards (Kautto et al. 2001).

Has the Nordic welfare state become more Europeanized, in the sense that EU regulation directly impinges on national welfare measures? In the field of traditional social policy formation the EU has had minimal direct impact on national activities (Hagen 1999). By stating the principle of "subsidiarity" in the Maastricht Treaty, that tasks should be solved at the lowest administrative level possible, the nation-states have preserved social policy autonomy. EU "social policy" has become more about occupational health and industrial relations, than universal benefits related to citizenship rights. The EU emphasis on labour-market issues has more parallels to the "conservative-corporatist" type of welfare regime than the "social democratic" Nordic regimes. Any supra-national social welfare legislation will impinge on the prerogative of the nation-state to tax and redistribute resources. This precedence cannot be discarded without undermining the legitimacy of the modern nation state to control its own resources. It may explain, according to Hagen (1999), the prevalence of suspicious attitudes to the EU among the Nordic populations.

However, national autonomy in the social policy field does not mean a completely passive EU, but that the method of policy formation is more "open coordination" than legal regulation. The Commission and the Council work out priorities, e.g. defining a minimum level of poverty, which are discussed by the countries and expert committees. The idea is that gradually, as a result of transparency and cooperation, a mutual understanding of the problem will emerge among the participants and pave the way for interstate learning, copying of instruments and goals and efficient implementation of social programs.

## The Nordic Welfare Model: Policy Adjustments and Renegotiating Social Integration

The "all-embracing" post-WWII welfare state obviously has come to a halt. It is too expensive to continue subsidizing special interests like farmers, fishermen and state-owned industries on the same level as before. Parallel with opening for market forces and competition in these sectors, support among the general public for such policies has eroded. Cheaper agricultural products are more important for the consumer than solidarity with farmers' demands for higher subsidies. The Nordic countries' total public expenditures have reached the ceiling. This development has been possible because there have been no major protests of note. The same may be said about various programmes for increasing public efficiency. The liberalist-inspired ideas of New Public Management (cf. Chapter 2, this volume) questioned what should be the appropriate responsibilities of the state. Market principles, deregulation and privatization of public tasks obviously have reduced the post-war trend of a continually increasing public sector.

On the other hand, the core responsibilities of the welfare state, the basic social benefits and services, including education and other collective goods, appeal to the rights and welfare of the whole or major parts of the population and are therefore less amenable to change. As demonstrated by Ploug (1999), cuts in social services during the 1990s were not dramatic, but serious enough for those who were hit. The number of social programmes has not been reduced, but some programmes tend to be less generous at the turn of the millennium than in the expansionist 1970s and 80s. Most importantly, the principle of universality in coverage is strongly institutionalized. However, the ability to shelter the welfare programs is not restricted to the Nordic countries. As Castles (2002) illustrates, neither on the continent nor in English-speaking countries is there evidence of massive cutbacks in state welfare.

Peter Flora (1986), writing in the middle of the 1980s, argued that the future welfare state would have to meet three challenges in order to preserve social integration: the requirements of the new middle class and the necessity of a new "contract" between state and citizens; the changing gender division of labour and the necessity of a "gender contract"; and the aging of the populations necessitating a new "generation contract".

A common international trend for the state's relations with the middle class is that non-governmental welfare becomes more important to this well-to-do group. As Kuhnle (2000) remarks, the increasing number of prosperous citizens in the Nordic countries may limit the demand for state welfare since they will cover their needs through private pension insurance schemes and health services. Such a development opens for larger inequalities and the possible disruption of future political consensus on who shall carry the burdens of a redistributive welfare system. In this respect the traditional "state–citizen contract" is in the process of renegotiation of benefits and burdens.

The "social democratic type" of welfare state has also been challenged by the decline of the working class, the volatility of voters, the reduced electoral support for the social democratic parties and the diminishing power of the trade unions. On the other hand, as opinion polls illustrate, the support for social policies is widespread among the general population. It seems unlikely that any of the major parties, even those propagating a market liberalist programme, would dispute welfare benefits associated with strategic voter groups, e.g. women or pensioners. The welfare state is stable because it is embedded in the needs of the general public which directly adhere to the preservation of institutionalized rights. The challenge seems more a question of introducing larger flexibility for some groups rather than renegotiating the basic "contract".

The "gender contract", providing equal opportunities for employment and education for women and men and improving the conditions for parents with small children, has developed a new support base. Particularly, structural changes in the labour market produced by the welfare state itself, with the large proportion of females employed in the public sector, have laid a solid political foundation for the future welfare state.

Turning to the "generation contract", the prospects may look less straightforward. As the size of age cohorts change in favour of pensioners, the older generation will not only become more costly for the state but will also gain in political importance. Pension systems on a "pay as you go" basis where the working part of the population pay contributions through taxes and fees and senior citizens draw pensions mean a major redistributive machinery with considerable explosive potential (Flora 1986). Not only in the Nordic countries but also on the continent governments are facing a formidable challenge in negotiating a new "contract" that is accepted by all generations which society can afford.

Opinion polls from 2001 (NSD/Eurobarometer) show there is no "either or" for the general public in the Nordic countries. Although resulting in higher taxes, a large majority of the older, middle aged and younger want to preserve the present level of public pensions and not increase the age of retirement. A main challenge not only for the Nordic countries is to negotiate the distribution of the increasing tax burden due to increasing pension costs. The "state-citizen contract", the "gender contract" and the "generation contract" are highly intertwined. More scant state resources following the renegotiated "state-citizen contract" and higher expenditures due to the gender revolution, directly impinge on financing the demands from the elderly generation. It remains to be seen if these new forms of redistribution will erode the basic social integration of the Nordic societies.

# Chapter 13: Security Policies from Constraints to Choice

*Tore Nyhamar*

The Nordic region is a security community. That the Nordic countries should use military force on each other is unthinkable, no matter what the nature of their disputes might be. This is a fairly recent development. The last war between two Nordic countries, the 1814 Norwegian–Swedish war, resulted in a Swedish victory that ensured a union between the two countries. The last time the inter-Nordic use of military force was seriously considered was in 1905, when this union was peacefully dissolved. Historically, however, relations between the Nordic countries have been shaped by war, particularly between Denmark and Sweden. Indeed, the development and increase in state power in the Nordic countries were caused by military necessities created by incessant warfare. The Danish–Swedish struggle for regional dominance in the period 1563–1720 involved seven wars. During this period, Denmark dominated Norway and Sweden dominated Finland, so the whole region was affected by these wars. The Great Nordic War of 1709–20 pitted Sweden (and Finland) against a coalition of Denmark-Norway and Russia. The war ended Sweden's claim to be a European great power. Since 1720, all the Nordic countries have remained minor powers on the international stage. As such, the Nordic states have had to adapt to constraints that are usually beyond their control.

The term "security policy" came into being after 1945. Before World War II, the distinction was only between the foreign policy and the defence policy of a state. Foreign policy is the actions a state performs that are motivated by or affect its surroundings. Defence policy is the direct or indirect use of military force by a state to secure it from threats. Security policy is the integrated foreign and defence policy, seeking to optimally handle military threats. The attempt to integrate state policy in order to optimally handle security threats is a general trend and not a peculiarly Nordic phenomenon. However, the need for a dedicated security policy also had local roots, particularly in the Danish,

Norwegian and Finnish policies prior to World War II. The Norwegian pre-war foreign policy of neutrality failed to prevent an attack from Germany in 1940. An important reason for this was that the military premises of the neutrality policy had been rendered obsolete by the evolution in airpower that had made Norwegian territory of import to the great powers. However, the separate pre-war compartmentalisation of foreign and defence policy prevented this insight from reaching the foreign policy leadership. Another example from the same period concerns Finland. As in Norway, Finnish foreign policy in 1939 failed to take into account the military realities of the day. In spite of widespread international sympathy, the Finns found themselves alone in fighting off the territorial demands of Soviet leader Stalin. Their defeat in the 1939–40 Winter War by the Soviet Union was a defining moment in Finnish security policy. The perception that came to prevail after World War II, i.e., that the Nordic countries could not afford not to integrate all available means to achieve security as far as possible, therefore had several roots.

The chapter is structured as follows. The first part discusses how the Cold War affected the security choices of the Nordic states. The next section sets forth the security choices of each Nordic country after the Cold War. The final part summarises the article and compares inter-Nordic similarities and differences and Norden with Europe.

## The Cold War: Small States Facing Big Geopolitical Constraints

The Nordic countries had different security policy orientations during the Cold War. As small players on the international stage, they had to accept that the US–Soviet confrontation was superimposed on all other international relationships, even in their peaceful region of the world. Finland was the country most profoundly dominated by a superpower; its very independence came perilously close to annihilation by the Soviet Union between 1944 and 1948. After having joined Germany in the war against the Soviet Union in 1941 to regain territory lost in the Winter War, Finland managed to switch sides and forcefully drove German forces off its own territory and into Norway in 1944–45. The fear of another Soviet or Russian attack has dominated Finnish security policy ever since. President Paasikivi (1946–56) formulated the Finnish Cold War strategy. In order to maintain the widest possible internal autonomy, Finland had to assure the Soviet Union that its territory would not be used for a military attack against Soviet territory. In the words of his successor, President Kekkonen, "the nation had to come to grips with the realities of power and find a way to live in friendship with the Soviet Union." The Friendship, Cooperation and Assistance Treaty of 1948 was the main vehicle to achieve this. The constraints imposed on Finnish freedom of action in foreign policy that the Treaty implied were considerable, but were seen as an inevitable part of the deal as Finnish security policy tried to strike a balance between reassuring the Russians and preserving internal autonomy.

Unlike Finland, balancing the Soviet Union was a realistic option for the remaining Nordic countries. The communist coup in Czechoslovakia in February/March 1948 created fear of Soviet intentions in all of the Nordic countries. In Norway, the concern of key decision-makers was heightened by dispatches dated March 5–8 1948, indicating that the Soviet was about to offer Norway a treaty similar to the one the Finns had found themselves forced to sign (Eriksen 1981:200). The events of February/March 1948 compelled all Nordic states (except Finland) to reconsider the policy of non-alignment they had pursued up to then. Change did not come lightly. In fact, Denmark, Norway and Sweden first attempted to create a Scandinavian pact in order to remain neutral in the emerging Cold War. The attempt failed. The Swedes would not accept the Western ties Norway found to be essential, and the USA, on its side, would not provide arms to a neutral Scandinavian defence organization. This made the proposed structure too weak for Norwegian comfort. Denmark, Norway and Iceland thus elected to help forge the 1949 North Atlantic Treaty Organisation (NATO), of which they are founding members. Sweden remained non-aligned, aiming to stay neutral in case of war.

These different attitudes to Western security ties during the Cold War are explained by three factors. First, a policy of neutrality had successfully kept Sweden out of both World Wars. Indeed, the country had been at peace since 1814. In Norway and Denmark, on the other hand, the policy of neutrality was very much discredited by the recent experience of five years of Nazi occupation. Second, Sweden perceived its territory to be of relatively modest strategic importance and was furthermore concerned to avoid causing added Soviet pressure on Finland. One feared that if Sweden retained close formal links with the Western powers, the Soviets might take action against Finland to foil any attack across Finnish territory. On the other hand, Denmark's proximity to the European central front made it a natural member of any Western defence alliance. Norwegian territory had assumed new importance in securing the sea lanes along which American forces and equipment could be moved across the Atlantic in order to contain the Soviet Union. Third, emerging unscathed from World War II, Sweden was economically and militarily much stronger than Norway and Denmark in 1949. It could realistically opt to be sufficiently strong militarily to deter Soviet attack.

During the entire Cold War – from 1949 to 1989 – the security alignments of the Nordic countries remained stable. Norway, Denmark and Iceland belonged to NATO, the Western security alliance. Sweden and Finland were non-aligned, aiming to stay neutral in case of war. However, although their choice of alignments differed, all of the Nordics shared a desire to strike a balance between Soviet deterrence and reassurance. Thus, Norway and Denmark both imposed restrictions on their memberships of NATO. Neither country was willing to permit NATO or any NATO country to establish and/or man permanent bases on their territory. Nor were they willing to accept nuclear weapons on their territories. In addition, Norway imposed restrictions on military exercises with allied participation on Norwegian soil, especially in proximity to the Russian border. These restrictions applied throughout the Cold War and were meant to reassure the Soviet Union that an attack from the West involving Norwegian and Danish (and, indirectly, Swedish and Finnish) territory would not take place. The thinking was that this would reduce the potential Soviet utility from controlling Nordic territory, and ergo, reduce the risk of a Soviet move to gain control, thereby improving Nordic security.

DETERRENCE AND ASSURANCE

This policy of self-imposed restrictions was maintained throughout the Cold War, but the policy was dynamic inasmuch as all new issues were considered in light of their impact on both deterrence and reassurance. Some of the fiercest domestic security policy debates raged precisely over how to strike that balance. For example, when NATO decided to deploy Pershing and ground-to-air cruise missiles in Europe, it put a considerable strain on both the Danish and Norwegian labour-led governments of the late 1970s and early 1980s. Denmark's attempts to delay the decision in late 1979 in order to negotiate further with the Soviets, and the Danish *Folketing*'s recurring attempts to undermine Danish funding participation, irritated Washington considerably. The decision to modernize NATO's nuclear arsenal had been coupled with the negotiations with the Soviets on the SS-20 missiles. If agreement could not be reached with the Soviets about them, NATO would deploy new missiles. Denmark earned a certain notoriety for trying to insert "footnotes" into NATO communiqués addressing the issue, thus undermining NATO's posture and negotiating position.

But the desire to take both deterrence and reassurance into consideration on every issue remained. Norway shared the Danish sentiment that deploying new nuclear missiles put too much emphasis on deterrence and too little on reassurance vis-à-vis the Soviets. Nevertheless, Norway accepted the propositioning of equipment for a US Marine brigade on its territory in 1981, at the same time as the transatlantic missile debate. The 1981 propositioning of Marine equipment surely constituted a shift towards deterrence in policy of restrictions on permanent foreign bases on Norwegian territory. However, the official Norwegian argument was that, in principle, the Marines' equipment did not change status quo. Reference was made to American equipment prepositioned under the 1974 treaty about collocation of air force bases.

Swedish policy was, obviously, also determined by a concern to simultaneously deter and reassure the Soviet Union. However, despite Sweden's formal non-aligned status, there was never any doubt of Sweden belonging in the Western camp during the Cold War. Indeed, it has been suggested that calibrated departures from non-alignment were one of the most important tools for Swedish foreign policy makers (Walter 2001:38). From the late 1950s onwards, through the 1960s and well into the 1970s, Sweden and the USA maintained a close navy-to-navy relationship, as described by Admiral Zumwalt.

A special relationship with Sweden that involved top secret briefings by Swedish Chiefs of Naval Operations (CNO) to U.S. CNOs, visits to Swedish classified facilities; exchange of verbal commitments as to how we would conduct strategy and tactics in the event of a Soviet attack; very low key joint training exercises. (quoted in Zakheim 1998:121)

Zumwalt recalls in particular that "we were very careful not to say too much to State (i.e. the State Department) about these activities". This Swedish "unofficial alliance" had three advantages. First, it reassured US military planners that Sweden could be counted upon in the event of a major confrontation with the Soviet Union. Robust Swedish defence spending, signalling both capability and resolve, reinforced this. Second, it allowed US policy-makers to focus on the reassurance element of Nordic security politics, a shared feature of all Nordic states, albeit shaped by varying circumstances. Third, the element of moderation in Nordic policies, created by reassurance and tacit understanding, was helpful in creating domestic consensus behind the policies of the Nordic countries. From an American perspective, it was not a bad situation to have domestic Nordic consensus backing a relatively low-key deterrence posture that persisted from one government to the next. Indeed, Washington, during the Cold War, preferred modest defence efforts from countries they could count on, rather than larger but more sporadic efforts that might jeopardise the alliance relationship.


## THE COLD WAR IN PERSPECTIVE

Looking back on the Cold War, what strikes the observer is the stability of the period. The security policy formulated in the late 1940s essentially remained in place throughout the Cold War, and, indeed, to some extent beyond. The simple explanation is that the threat posed by Soviet military trumped other concerns to such an extent that the Nordic countries perceived it in one-dimensional and unambiguous terms. That said, different geopolitical circumstances did lead to different responses to the threat. Typically, the decision to join NATO was taken by Labour governments under tight international constraints and against considerable internal opposition. The people who decided that Denmark and Norway should join a military alliance did so out of perceived necessity, not because the option in itself was desirable.

Once the decision was taken, its continued support was ensured by the continuation of the palpable Soviet threat it was meant to counter. In Norway, public support for NATO membership consistently hovered around 90 per cent. The Swedish non-alignment policy enjoyed wide support at home as well. The Finnish case is slightly different. Support for Finnish security policy was not heartfelt, because it was perceived to be forced upon the country. However, the Paasikivi-Kekkonen line became widely accepted as a necessity, albeit not a popular one. The fundamental political choices concerning security had now been made. One important consequence was that during the Cold War the security policies of the Nordic countries did not change when governments changed. Only with the end of the Cold War did security policy outcomes again become subject to real bargaining and political debate.

From a European perspective, the division of the Nordic countries caused by the East–West confrontation superficially resembles the iron curtain division of the continent as a whole. However, all Nordic countries were able to maintain a variety of the Western society model, based on a market economy and political democracy. The Warsaw pact members were not. Moreover, the Nordic countries all had the ability to exercise a meaningful autonomy in their choice of security policy. This was a fundamental liberty that the Warsaw pact members simply did not have (Dov Zakheim). The Nordic countries enjoyed such freedom because "even during the height of the Cold War, the Nordic region did not dominate American strategic thinking or concerns" (Zakheim 1998:116). One may safely assume that this was true of the Soviets as well. The Nordic countries themselves were acutely aware of this. It was an explicit objective of the policies of all Nordic countries to lower tension in the region, resulting in the reassurance measures described above. However, without a favourable geopolitical position in the first place, low-tension policy would not have succeeded. Moreover, as many have observed, the strategic importance of the Nordic region was further diminished by the Cold War.

Nordic security policy during the Cold War of course merits historical attention in itself. But there are three other reasons as well. First, some of these policies are still adhered to today. Norwegian and Danish restrictions against allowing nuclear weapons on their territory, and some of the Norwegian restrictions on military exercises in the northern reaches of the country remain in effect. Second, Nordic choices made during the Cold War still have palpable effects on today's political reality. For example, the security policies of Denmark, Iceland and Norway are still strongly influenced by the fact that they are members of NATO. Third, the different historical experiences of the Nordic countries during the Cold War shape the perceptions and indeed the decisions of security policy makers about current challenges. Sweden judges non-alignment to have served the country well, and is apprehensive about changing it. In contrast, Finland felt non-alignment as a straitjacket, and eagerly grasped the first opportunity to rid itself of an undesirable constraint.

The crumbling of the Soviet Union greatly reduced the military threat to the Nordic countries. Today, in official Norwegian and Danish security policy documents, the good news is triumphantly heralded: currently, they aver, there exists no military threat to our country! The waning of the Soviet threat means that the Nordic countries face fewer constraints, which greatly enhances their freedom of action. Finland unilaterally abolished the 1948 Treaty in 1991, taking advantage of the window of opportunity created by the collapse of the Soviet Union. In the 1960s, relations with the Soviet Union forced Finland to limit its participation in the European Free Trade Association (EFTA) to associate membership (FINEFTA). In 1994, Finland became a full member of the EU, without any reservations on future European defence and security integration. The choices the Nordic countries have made while enjoying this newly won freedom are explored in the rest of this chapter.

## THE POST-COLD WAR PERIOD IN PERSPECTIVE

Before immersing ourselves in how these changes influenced actual security policies choices of each country, let us look at the consequences of the new post-Cold War environment on Nordic security thinking. First, the structure of the international system – at least in the security sector – has changed from bipolarity to unipolarity. Second, instead of the black-and-white threat posed by Soviet military power, threats are now multidimensional and ambiguous. Third, the lessened international pressure has heightened the part played by domestic politics in the security policy choices of the Nordic countries. In contrast to the situation during the Cold War, changes in government today may indeed lead to security policy changes in the Nordic countries. Finally, the use of military force as a policy instrument, not only a defence posture, is now an issue in all Nordic states.

The USA is the only state in the world to have global military reach, and has a huge lead in military technology allowing it to safely employ military force as a viable policy instrument. As far as security is concerned, the USA is so militarily dominant that there is an emerging consensus that the world is truly unipolar. Unipolarity leads to four things (Heurlin 2004:185ff). First, there is one single international agenda, and it is determined by the superpower. Under bipolarity, there are two competing agendas, leaving space for a third, non-aligned one. All Nordic countries were interested in the latter during the Cold War, especially Sweden. In today's unipolar world, it is very difficult for small states to play an agenda-setting role, as Sweden has discovered, much to its chagrin. Second, there is a tendency to seek security with the superpower, for the simple reason that it often is the only state able to render effective security assistance. This tendency towards *flocking* is present in current Danish, Icelandic and Norwegian security policy, but is posing intriguing new challenges also to formerly non-aligned Finland and Sweden.

Third, as a consequence of *flocking*, the principle of *hard work* comes into play. During the Cold War, Denmark and, though to a lesser extent, Norway were free riders within NATO. They were both net importers of security, and, being small, with little impact on the overall balance between NATO and the Warsaw pact, it was possible for them to keep their defence contributions relatively small also. Indeed, "Denmarkisation" became a term for particularly glaring free riding (Heurlin 2004:198). Today, small countries need to be seen as doing something that is appreciated in Washington. Finally, there is more room for regionalisation. Interestingly though, the regionalisation of the Nordic area does not seem to have been favoured by this trend. Instead, there has been a certain revitalisation of the Baltic region.

## Nordic Profiles – Denmark, Finland, Sweden and Norway

### DANISH SECURITY POLICY: FROM FOOTNOTES TO WAR-MAKING

Denmark's security policy has changed radically since the end of the Cold War. As the only Nordic member of both important European security organisations at the end of the Cold War, Danish policy was formulated within both organisations simultaneously. But Denmark has used its new found freedom to almost opposite purposes in NATO and the EU. From being one of the most anti-US members of NATO, Denmark has transformed itself into the most pro-American. Denmark's decision to take part in the war against Iraq was the clearest Nordic example of the tendency of flocking. Danish Prime Minister Anders Vogh Rasmussen was even willing to extend the stay of the Danish force beyond the original June 2004 withdrawal date, and greatly enhance the force as well. The policy of the liberal-conservative government has been bitterly contested by the opposition in parliament. If the balance of power in the Danish *Folketing* is reversed, Denmark's military engagement in Iraq will be affected. Danish flocking is perceived to contribute to stability, primarily in Europe, but also beyond if the war on terrorism demands it. Furthermore, it seeks to enhance Denmark's political clout in Washington. According to the Danes, their efforts in the Baltic region contributed to former President Clinton's highly publicised visit in 1997, and strengthened Denmark's standing over all (Heurlin 2004:199).

The support for the use of force against Iraq is part of a pattern in Danish security policy, but is but one instance of Denmark's new-found willingness to use military force to forward its interests. The Danish military did, in fact, fire shots in Tuzla (Bosnia 1994), Kosovo (1999) and Afghanistan (2002). The Danish armed forces have been developed to fit this policy. In 1997, the work on reforms that would give the Danish military an expeditionary capability began in earnest. This was relatively early compared with the other Nordic countries. Danish defence policy is therefore in tune with its foreign policy.

On the other hand, Denmark was the first Nordic country to experience the drawbacks of making the military forces of a small country expeditionary while maintaining a credible defence at home. For economic reasons, the expeditionary forces needed to be integrated with those of larger countries. Denmark had planned to operate its forces together with Germany. When the German government decided not take part in the war against Iraq in spring 2003, Denmark had to rethink its military contribution. On March 21, the Danish *Folketing* decided (61 in favour and 50 against) to send a submarine, a corvette, a medical team and a small staff and communications team as the Danish support of American led military action in spring 2003.[49] In June 2003, about 370 personnel were deployed, mounting later to over 500.

In the EU, however, Denmark followed a completely different tack. By rejecting the Maastricht Treaty, Denmark opted out of European security and defence integration. Although a member of the EU since 1972, Denmark is in fact the least integrated Nordic EU member.

FINNISH SECURITY POLICY: FROM STRAITJACKET TO EUROPEAN INTEGRATION

Finnish security policy has travelled further than that of any of the other Nordic countries after the Cold War. Unlike the other Nordic countries, Helsinki knew what it wanted after 1989 and acted quickly and decisively to get it. In 1990–92, two key decisions were taken, the first of which aimed at terminating the 1948 treaty with the Soviet Union (Russia). The second concerned membership in the European Union. Both decisions had the desired result. The 1948 treaty disappeared as a constraint on Finnish security policy in 1991, and the country became a full member of the EU in 1994.

The decision-making process adhered to a long-standing Finnish pattern. Unlike the other Nordics, where security policy is subject to popular participation and domestic political constraints, there is in Finland a strong tradition for political centralisation around the office of the president. For example, President Koivisto, in his memoirs, claims personal responsibility for both of the decisions just referred to (Törnudd 2001:273–74). And the broad public support for direct, personal power over the country's foreign policy is quite unique in the Nordic area. Interestingly, during the 1990s, the centralisation of foreign policy power around the president became an issue in Finnish politics. A reform process was initiated to reduce presidential powers in favour of the parliament, the prime minister and the cabinet. It resulted in a new constitution, adopted by the *Riksdag* in 1999. The president remains supreme leader in foreign and security policy matters, nevertheless, and commander-in-chief of the armed forces. It seems that presidential power in foreign policy is a deeply embedded facet of Finnish political culture. It is still premature to judge the changes wrought by constitutional reform to Finnish security policy and its decision-making processes. Old habits die hard, and the Finnish president's power probably always owed more to personality and culture than to constitutional position.

The Finnish presidency of the European Union in autumn 1999 was tasked to implement the Cologne European Council decision from the same year to create a military crisis management system. The Finnish government rose to the occasion, ignoring national misgivings about the deepening military dimensions of the EU. This process resulted in the Helsinki Headline Goals, which included decisions on size, command arrangements and military organisation that went far beyond Finnish national goals at the time. Nevertheless, President Ahtisaari's policy did not fire domestic controversy, despite certain critical remarks in the press that the European great powers dominated the crisis management process (Wegge 2003:65).

In fact, the Finnish presidency of 1999 is typical of Finland's strategy of seeking influence in the EU by belonging to the most integration-friendly political group in the EU. Informally, close integration with the EU is seen as a measure to ensure security guarantees from the EU in order to overcome Finland's traditional concerns about Russia. Neutrality as policy and posture was immediately and fully abandoned. In January 1995, when Finland entered the EU, President Ahtisaari and Prime Minister Lipponen stated that Finland's membership meant that the country was "militarily non-allied under the prevailing conditions" (Ries 2001:216). The implication is that Finland seeks European integration in the security sector. Finland's government has in fact officially declared the end of neutrality: "Since the end of the East–West divisions, the policy of neutrality that Finland followed in the Cold War is no longer a viable action." Moreover, it was noted that "[I]n ascending to the [European] Union, Finland has not made any security policy reservations concerning its obligations under its founding treaties or the Maastricht."[50]

Finland has not applied for NATO membership. However, Finland actively participates within the Partnership for Peace (PfP) (since 1994), including defence planning. Politically and militarily Finland has moved a lot closer to NATO. Finland has systematically pursued a policy to make its military forces interoperable with NATO, by taking part not only in exercises but also in NATO peacekeeping operations. Finland has provided an engineer battalion in Bosnia and an infantry battalion in Kosovo and will join Norway in taking part in a British-led Provincial Reconstruction Team in northern Afghanistan under the NATO-led ISAF umbrella. Indeed, Finland is now as close to NATO as it is possible to come without formal membership.

Finland's rapprochement with NATO also represents continuity in Finnish security policy in the sense that it is considered too important to involve the population. Public debate of the membership issue is generally to be avoided as too dangerous, given the lack of popular support for NATO. The opinion polls during the 1990s consistently showed 10–20 per cent support for Finland joining NATO (Wegge 2003:66). International terrorism has not affected public opinion in this respect.

On the other hand, that differences in opinion within the elite may be tolerated is itself a novel development. President Ahtisaari pursued an "all doors open" policy during his presidency. When Tarja Halonen was elected president in March 2000, however, a new sense of scepticism to NATO membership became manifest at the centre of political power in Finland. The situation changed again on October 14 2001, when Prime Minister Lipponen announced that an open debate on NATO membership was required and that the issue would have to be dealt with in the next Defence Review (summer 2004). The review will in all probability mention NATO membership as a possibility, not to be pursued at the moment. As of today, no decision on NATO membership has been taken, but no one seems to doubt that a future decision to join would be accepted by the population. The constitutional reform of 1999 does not seem to have altered the way in which Finland makes its security policy decisions.

Finland's reaction to September 11 2001 has been remarkably muted. Finland has loyally abided by the European Union's joint position during the crisis, but seems to harbour reservations that have resulted in a noticeably low profile, generally trying to avoid the issue. This has been noted in Washington. The US query on September 27 2001 concerning how Finland would react to a request for overflight rights was first non-committal. Then President Halonen a few days later stated that humanitarian overflights would be permitted and military ones would be decided on a case-by-case basis. The reserved Finnish reaction at a time, marked by an outpour of sympathy and solidarity with the USA, was unusual in Europe. The fact that Sweden did not receive a similar preliminary request indicates greater American confidence in Sweden than Finland (Ries 2002:223). In contrast to Finland's low profile in the anti-terror campaign, the other Nordic countries have been among its most ardent supporters in Europe.

Unlike other Nordic and European countries, Finland's armed forces have not been part of the wave of radical reform to make them more expeditionary and professional. The Finnish army is still focused on personnel-intensive territorial defences based on conscription. More than 80 per cent of all males still undergo military training. The Finnish Act on Peace Support Operations limits the total number of soldiers serving abroad at any one time to 2000. Finnish policy makers continue to bluntly state that territorial defence is the top priority. The development of a reaction force for international operations, changing the wording in official defence planning from having "a credible defence" to having a "a credible defence capacity", points slightly away from the national territorial defence. However, the modest reform of the defence sector has not kept up with the complete and extensive re-alignment of Finland's European policies. It might be argued that this amounts to an inconsistency in Finland's security policy, but the official line is that defence is a national undertaking, augmented by international guarantees. Neither Finland's policy nor its defence planning betrays any interest in or plans for using force internationally. Finland views the use of military force as a last resort, only to be undertaken if its security policy fails.


SWEDEN: IN SEARCH OF A MISSION

Like Finland, Sweden's security policy has been completely altered by its membership in the European Union. Sweden no longer speaks solely for itself, but is now part of EU policy. Unlike Finland, however, Sweden has not embraced European security and defence integration. Sweden sought membership for economic and political reasons, not for security. The country has only reluctantly modified its neutrality policy, and as little as possible, to be compatible with EU membership. The defined objective of Swedish security policy was first altered from "being neutral" in the event of war to "aiming to be neutral" in event of war, to finally, in 2002, to "have the possibility to remain neutral" in event of war.[51] European efforts of security and defence integration during the 1990s have been met with scepticism and resistance. Sweden joined forces with the United Kingdom in resisting the inclusion of security and defence in the EU. During the Swedish EU presidency in spring 2001, extraordinary efforts were made to forward the *civilian* crisis management within the EU. Even though outside NATO, Sweden's multifaceted ties with the US have led to a policy wanting the USA to stay in Europe.

After the elections of 1995, the Social Democrats regained power in Sweden and have remained in power ever since. The Social Democratic government initially tried to revive the role as leader of the non-aligned, with a special mission among the lesser-developed nations in the world. In a unipolar international system, however, the policy was repeatedly frustrated. The adjustment from a social democratic ideal for the world to being one of many medium-sized countries in the EU has been painful. Indeed, the traditional idealistic streak in Sweden's foreign policy has fallen on hard times in the encounter with the *realpolitik* bargaining going on inside the EU. The experience seems to have caused a re-alignment of Swedish strategy and objectives vis-à-vis the EU. According to analyst Bengt Sundelius (2002:280), Sweden's security policy is currently going through a formative period.

First, there is a general movement towards an approach giving more emphasis to Sweden's own interests in its European policy. Second, there is a growing appreciation that military force might be useful. Sweden decided in favour of swift and comprehensive reform of its military in 1999–2000. Its formidable Cold War territorial defence is currently being transformed into a small expeditionary force, whose main task is to be able to take part in international military operations. In Finland, we saw that change in security policy is running well ahead of military change. Swedish military reform, in contrast, is almost outpacing official security policy. However, the change was initiated at the elite level, and has no real support in public opinion or among the electorate. This is a real constraint on Sweden's participation in international military operations. Similarly, even support for NATO membership is growing at the elite level in Sweden. For example, in autumn 2002, the Conservative Party stated that NATO membership was a future possibility. But actual Swedish membership seems a more remote possibility than Finnish membership, since only 30 per cent of Sweden's population support it and, in contrast to Finland, popular opinion will be decisive. The country has tried to preserve its relations with the US, but without abandoning its almost instinctive preference for non-alignment.

NORWAY: FIGHTING MARGINALISATION

Paradoxically, the Soviet threat that dominated Norwegian security policy for four decades also provided an answer to at least some enduring Norwegian security challenges. The High North was an area of military importance to both camps in the Cold War. The confrontation with the Soviet Union ensured that the American interest in the High North was dominated by the strategic concern of securing the sea-lanes across the Atlantic and bottling up Soviet submarine-based ICBMs as close to their bases on the Kola Peninsula as possible. Norway also had many natural allies in Europe, for example Germany who shared Norwegian concerns about a Soviet invasion of its territory. Today, Norway's allies do not view their interest in the High North through the Cold War's prism and Norway can no longer count on the US and Europe to automatically back its views of the interests involved in the High North.

Until Estonia and Latvia joined the Alliance in April 2004, Norway was the only NATO country during the post-Cold War era sharing a border with Russia. The definition of the economic zones at sea remains open, giving Norway a territorial dispute with Russia. The disputed area is rich in natural resources, certainly fish, and potentially oil and gas. Norwegian security was enhanced when the Soviet threat disappeared. But it has been accompanied by a decline in allied interest that has left Norway somewhat alone in managing its relationship with Russia.

The inherent need for allies is an important backdrop for Norwegian policy towards NATO in general and especially towards NATO's counter-terrorism policy. In fact, the fight against international terrorism is viewed as a new, much-needed mission to ensure that NATO remains a vehicle for managing collective defence, and not merely collective security. In short, Norway views the war on terrorism in the context of maintaining the transatlantic alliance. The long-term challenge to Norway is to avoid managing the relationship with Russia on its own, without allies. In a collective defence organization, support from the members is guaranteed, whereas in a collective security organization, support is subject to evaluation in each case. Also, a collective security organization tries above all to mediate conflict, whereas Norway wants backing to stand firm and prevent conflict. Norwegian security policy explicitly aims at preserving NATO as an organization providing collective defence among its members and collective security on its perimeter.

In 2001, the Norwegian armed forces were still in the process of adapting to the changed security environment after the demise of the Soviet Union ten years earlier. The Norwegian military forces had for decades been built for the sole purpose of allaying the Soviet military threat. This meant a large, territorial conscript army and an air force that could only be used in an air-to-air role, with no air-to-land capability whatsoever. Forces had very limited capacity for personnel and equipment transportation out of Norwegian territory. The transformation to an expeditionary force began in the early 1990s, but bureaucratic inertia, local interest groups and the absence of a clear threat providing a concrete goal slowed the transformation of the Norwegian armed forces down.

Most analysts see September 11 as a catalyst for the transformation of the Norwegian armed forces. It sped up change already under way, largely for other reasons. The effort to make the Norwegian military more expeditionary has two primary objectives: the first is to enhance the capability to fight wars abroad; the second is to enhance the armed forces' deployment capabilities for peace-keeping purposes. The war in Kosovo in 1999 resulted in more emphasis given to war-fighting capabilities, which was sustained and enhanced by the military needs following September 11.

The revision of NATO's strategic concept in 1999 divided political opinion about how far Norwegian forces could be deployed as part of a NATO operation. Out of area operations were vigorously opposed by a coalition stretching from the radical left wing well into the centre of the Labour Party and including important liberal groups as well. These groups shared a concern, albeit in different degrees, that NATO might become a tool for American-led interventionism. The Norwegian reaction to out of area operations mirrored the debate in most European NATO countries. NATO's new Strategic Concept from April 24 1999 – in the middle of the Kosovo campaign and NATO's only war – used the deliberately undefined phrase "the Euro-Atlantic area" to delimit the alliance's geographical responsibilities to maintain security and stability.[52]

Against this background, many anticipated that NATO involvement in military operations in the wake of September 11 would prove controversial. However, Norwegian public opinion firmly supported military action against the Taliban. The military operation that ended the Taliban regime was, of course, not a NATO operation but a joint USA–UK undertaking. But for the Norwegian politicians and public, the incontrovertible links with the September 11 attack legitimated the use of military force.

Since January 2002, Norway has contributed to two military operations around Afghanistan: the International Security Assistance Force (ISAF), and the American-led operations against Taliban and al Qaeda. On 11 August 2003, NATO took the lead of ISAF, enhancing Norwegian interests in the mission's success. Currently, Norway deploys a company (192 personnel), three staff officers, a CIMIC team and a medical unit (40 personnel) to ISAF.[53]

Concerning the operations against the remaining Taliban and al Qaeda fighters, Norway has contributed to air transport operations (with Denmark and the Netherlands) and deployed Special Forces in two rounds (January–July 2002, April–October 2003). The six F-16 fighter planes were potentially the most controversial Norwegian contribution as they carried bombs to be used to support allied forces.[54] On 27 January 2003, Norwegian fighters dropped two laser-guided GBU 12 bombs on a bunker held by former Taliban fighters now answering to Afghan warlord Gulbuddin Hekmatayar. The action cost 18 fighters their lives. This was the first time since World War II that Norwegian planes had used live ammunition against an enemy. The event passed by without stirring public opinion or affecting the standing of Norway's minority government. One can only conclude that counter-terrorism has given the

Norwegian armed forces a global role. If flying from Kyrgyzstan to bomb a target in Afghanistan is possible for a Norwegian military plane, then geography no longer is an issue in itself.

Norwegians generally remain wary of the use of force internationally, however. The Iraq question divided the political class and public opinion along familiar lines. A clear majority of Norwegians opposed the 2003 war in Iraq. There are two prerequisites for having a majority of Norwegians favour the use of force. The first is that it is explicitly and unequivocally mandated by the United Nation Security Council. The mandate for the military operation against Iraq in 2003 for example, was deemed insufficient by a majority of Norwegians. Generally speaking, pre-emptive actions directed against terrorism do not appear to be considered sufficient grounds for using military force. The second prerequisite is that a clear link to a concrete, horrific act of terrorism is established. The military operation in Afghanistan 2001 seems to have met this demand. The margin in the electorate supporting Norwegian participation in international operations is never large, and the electorate can easily turn against any given operation. Opinion follows traditional patterns. More men favour military force as part of the counter-terrorism offensive than women. The support for forward deployment of troops in counter-terrorism has more support among the politically conservative than the radical.

Thus, the controversial policy of deployment of Norwegian military forces in international operations – both traditional peace-keeping for stabilization purposes and in a war-fighting role – is Norwegian defence policy today. The policy, it is argued, is seen to enhance Norwegian security because it a) prevents terrorists from entering Norwegian territory; b) it fights them before they can do any harm; c) it disrupts and limits their training and planning for terrorist attacks. The policy is criticized for not addressing the root causes of terrorism. Indeed, an excessively militarised foreign policy may fuel resentment among the population in the area and lead to increased recruitment to terrorist organizations. The policy is often associated with the US in general and the Bush administration in particular. Norway's security policy, however, takes as its premise that the fight against terrorism requires the whole gamut of means, including the use of military force. The dilemma that resentment in the Muslim world might increase is at least ameliorated if a coalition representing the world community undertakes the military intervention rather than the United States alone. Norway has a political and moral obligation to participate in such a coalition, even though it may increase the short-term risk of terrorist attack on Norway.

The fact that the International Stabilization Afghan Force (ISAF) has become a NATO operation, whereas the coalition in Iraq is not, seems to have had little impact on Norwegian public opinion, but might be a concern at the elite level.

## Nordic Security: More Similar and More European

The strict bipolarity of the Cold War cut across the Nordic region, making these otherwise so similar and similarly inclined countries adopt widely different security policies. The obvious explanation is that the geopolitical forces worked differently in each country. Simply put, the different Nordic choices are explained by different constraints, not by different preferences. To what extent does this pattern of dissimilarity still hold true 15 years after the end of the Cold War?

Table 1  Nordic alignments during and after the Cold War

| Relationship with | Denmark | Finland | Sweden | Norway | Iceland |
|---|---|---|---|---|---|
| NATO | Founding member 1949 | PfP country since 1994 | PfP country since 1994 | Founding member 1949 | Founding member 1949 |
| EU | Member 1972, not part of military integration | Member 1994, militarily fully integrated | Member 1994, hesitant but militarily fully integrated | Non-member participating militarily when possible | Non-member |
| US | 1949–89 Footnotes 1989- Flocking | Low key member of the war on terrorism | Tacit complex web of relations | Strong bilateral relations | More positive to base |

Their security policies have in fact become more similar in the last 15 years. As far as institutional allegiances are concerned, however, the over-all picture remains one of differences dominating similarities. Sweden and Finland were non-aligned during the Cold War; both joined the EU in 1994 and have so far remained outside NATO. Denmark was one of the founding members of NATO in 1949. Denmark joined the EU as far back as 1972, but is not part of its military cooperation. Denmark is thus less integrated than are Sweden and Finland in the ongoing European security integration. Norway and Iceland, on their part, are non-members of the EU, but founding members of NATO. However, in contrast with Denmark, Norway tries to join EU security and defence operations and related activities whenever it can. The enlargement of the EU and NATO means that the Nordic countries are part of a European trend towards security integration. The Nordic pattern of alignment can be summarised as in Table 1.

As far as the post Cold War policy issue is concerned, the Nordic countries are grappling with the same interrelated issues as the rest of Europe. In a situation with multidimensional and ambiguous threats, what should one prioritise? In contrast to the situation during the Cold War, lessened international pressure allows domestic policy disagreement. Thus, changes in government today may indeed lead to security policy changes in the Nordic countries. Finally, the controversial issue of using military force as a policy instrument has exacerbated domestic political conflict, in the Nordic countries and Europe alike.

# Chapter 14: The Nordics and the EU

*Janne Haaland Matlary*

The four Nordic states dealt with in this chapter – Norway, Denmark, Sweden, and Finland – have few commonalities in their relationship with the European Union (EU). Norway remains outside the EU after three applications – in 1967 when British entry as well as Norwegian entry was vetoed by de Gaulle (Riste 2001); and in 1972 and 1994 when a referendum said no. Denmark entered along with the UK in 1973, while Sweden became a member in 1995 with a slim majority. Finland entered the EU the same year with a fair majority.[55] Thus, today, Norway and Iceland remain outside the EU, regulating their relationship with the union through a comprehensive economic agreement covering the internal market, the European Economic Area (EEA). Iceland is a special case as its main source of national income is fish. Prospective Icelandic EU membership will therefore depend on an acceptable regime for fish. The third EEA member state is Liechtenstein, a tiny state with no common interests with the Nordics. Thus, at the outset, it is clear that the Nordic states chose very different historical paths to EU membership.

But inside the EU there are also major differences between the Nordic members: Finland chose "maximum integration" as its strategy (Arter 2000), while Sweden tries to cover the whole spectrum of EU activity but is more constrained than Finland in terms of public opinion. For example, Finland easily entered the European Monetary Union (EMU), making the decision in parliament without much discussion; Sweden waited until 2003 to put the question to the public through a referendum, the outcome of which was negative. The government had analysed the implications for Sweden in great detail already in 1996 (SOU 1996:158), but the Persson Government spent seven years "maturing" the issue before daring to put it to the vote. Denmark, finally, has self-imposed derogations from the Common Foreign and Security Policy (CFSP), and is also outside the EMU; Danish public opinion remains very sceptical of integration beyond market liberalization.

Table 14.1  Referenda on the EU. Per cent in favour of membership/wider integration

|  | 1972 | 1986 | 1992 | 1993 | 1994 | 1998 | 2000 | 2003 |
|---|---|---|---|---|---|---|---|---|
| Denmark | 63.4 | 56.2 | 49.3 | 56.7 | | 55.1 | 46.9 | |
| Norway | 46.5 | | | | 47.7 | | | |
| Finland | | | | | 56.9 | | | |
| Sweden | | | | | 52.3 | | | 43.2 |

Sources: Statistics Sweden; Todal Jenssen et al. 1998; Tor Bjørklund 1997
Denmark: 1986: Single European Act; 1992: Maastricht Treaty; 1993: Edinburgh Agreement; 1998: Amsterdam Treaty; 2000: Euro
Sweden: 2003: Euro

Thus the Nordic case contains good examples of "variable geometry" ranging from economic integration without membership (Norway and Iceland); membership at the periphery (Denmark and, to some extent, Sweden), and membership with aspirations to be at the core (Finland). The ability of each state's political elite to seek further integration can be seen as a function of how constrained this elite is. As much of the scholarly literature suggests, public opinion/national identity play a key role in how the EU is seen. Whereas the political elites mostly favour more integration, Nordic publics are sceptical. Finland is an exception because the political elite traditionally is not particularly constrained by public opinion. The other factor that makes public opinion salient is decision-making through referenda. In both Sweden and Denmark it has been seen as politically important, indeed as necessary, to have the legitimacy of the referendum for major integrative moves. This variance of Nordic approaches to the EU seems surprising in light of the many common features that other chapters in this book underscore.

This article provides an overview of what seem to be the three main determinants of the EU relationship: economic factors; foreign policy, and public opinion/national identity. While the Nordics share common characteristics in terms of economic organisation – large public sector, welfare state, they also differ in important respects. Norway is a raw material producer and exporter.

Finland has had to restructure and modernize rapidly after its markets in the former USSR dried up at the end of the Cold War. Sweden and Denmark are modern industrial economies that seek to adapt to the post-industrial economy. One major thesis in the literature is that economic conditions are the major explanatory variables for the differing relationship with the EU.

Another major set of explanations relate to foreign and security policy. In this field there are fundamental differences between the Nordics in the field of security, but many similarities exist in general foreign policy, especially with regard to the UN, peace-keeping, and development aid. In terms of security, Finland has been tied to the USSR throughout the entire period of the Cold War (Arter 1999; Nyhamar in Chapter 13 in this volume), while Sweden has guarded its neutrality closely. Norway, Denmark and Iceland are NATO members. Thus, the security policies of the Nordics have traditionally been very different. Yet in areas less important for geo-politics the Nordics have displayed some common traits, particularly with regard to the emphasis on the UN, development aid, and the importance of international law. There has also been major foreign policy cooperation among the Nordics for many years, excepting the field of security. Commonly Scandinavian positions at the UN have been coordinated, and the same values have been expressed in multilateral foreign policy. As we shall see, EU membership for Sweden and Finland affected common Nordic positions at the UN, and also the close cooperation.

The third set of explanations for the different Nordic approaches centres on public opinion/national identity. This is a more complex category of variables which are hard to measure, but which seem to be very important. Constructivists like Iver Neumann underline that perceptions of "who we are" are decisive for how we define "the Other" – the EU as "the Other" is therefore defined in relation to our self-perceptions. Neumann (2001) argues that the concepts that we use to describe the EU and ourselves shape public opinion. Thus the sense of a distinct, autonomous Norwegian identity clashes with any suggestion of "union" not least because Norway was a less than equal partner in a union with Denmark for four hundred years, and an uncomfortable partner in a union with Sweden for a century thereafter. The power of the concept is real power, as he argues.

It has been very difficult indeed to "prove" the relevance of a sense of national identity as opposed to "rational" economic and/or security interests. The methodological implications here are widely debated in political science today between rationalists and constructivists. In this chapter we will only draw on one piece of empirical scholarship which shows that states with a view of sovereignty as indivisible tend to have publics that are highly sceptical to integration. The Nordic states are examples of such states.

## The First Determinant: Economic Factors

Christine Ingebritsen (1998) provides a major study of the relative importance of political economy as the main explanatory variable of the differing Nordic EU relationship. She argues that the national interests in leading sectors explain the differing EU integration: changes in agriculture, industry, and security policy, she finds, explain much of the difference. This is what makes Stein Rokkan's words true in the final analysis: "Votes count, resources decide" (Rokkan 1975:217).

There are important differences in the Nordic economies, and each government must respond to a different set of interest groups. In Norway, agriculture and fisheries account for much of the negative attitude to the EU; in Sweden large industry worked in the opposite direction. While the export structure of Finland is centred on industry and high technology, oil and gas make up more than 40 per cent of Norwegian exports. In Denmark and Sweden industrial exports dominate, while Iceland is entirely dependent on fishing (Ingebritsen 1998:117). We can therefore understand EU attitudes by analysing the political economy of each state.

Denmark has agriculture as its main export sector, and has benefited from the Common Agricultural Policy (CAP). Farmers in Denmark have been in favour of free trade, and were therefore well prepared for membership. The economic dimension has been popular, while the political dimensions of membership have not. When Denmark joined the EC in 1973, it was with a comfortable majority. Manufacturing superseded agriculture as the major export article further down the line, but it fitted well with the internal market and the emphasis on access. Both the Danish private sector and political parties remain firmly pro-EU. However, when the Danes rejected the Maastricht Treaty – officially, the "Treaty on Political and Economic Union" – by a narrow margin in 1992, it was probably related to the concept of a "political union" and, to some degree, of supra-national integration in foreign policy. The approach is pragmatic and intergovernmental, as in the UK. The final outcome of this matter was that Denmark managed to vote in favour of a so-called "national compromise" whereby the state opted out of the supra-national aspects of the Common Foreign and Security Policy (CFSP).

Norway has an entirely different economic structure with oil and gas making up the largest export segment. There is no need for membership in order to secure export markets. However, opening up markets through membership would have major consequences for both fishery and agriculture. In the referenda of 1972 and 1994 both sectors played pivotal roles. The oil revenue generates subsidies for agriculture, where income levels far exceed what CAP would provide for. This special source of income also makes for a certain insulation, not unlike a "Kuwait economy" – non-exposure to competition and concomitant temptation to postpone necessary changes in a globalising economy. Ingebritsen writes that Norwegian businesses have often relied on support from the state and have not globalized as quickly as businesses in the other Nordic states. The oil fund seems to act as a buffer, at least psychologically (ibid.:133), seeming to delay in exposure to international competition, she suggests. Norway also maintains a dispersed pattern of habitation through politico-economic measures, and inhabitants of the "peripheries" are generally more sceptical to EU membership than urbanites. For instance, the voting pattern in Norway and Sweden in 1994 was similar, but in Sweden a much larger part of the population lives in urban areas.

The oil revenue and a more sheltered economy led to a different assessment of the EU, Ingebritsen argues, adding that "[t]he immobility of the factors of production created an entirely different political and economic situation in Norway" (than in Denmark and Sweden) (ibid.:133). The fishery and agricultural interests resisted EU membership on rational, economic grounds. Agriculture would not have benefited from membership under any circumstance. As Ingebritsen says, "[t]hey had the most to lose [not least because] Norway maintains the highest level of agricultural subsidies in northern Europe" (ibid.:134). The fisheries make up a very small part of the economy, but are a key source of employment on the northern coast, and therefore remain politically very important. The "no" vote in November 1994 led to the fall-back solution, the EEA agreement, which remains Norway's formal association with the EU.

*Sweden's* larger business sector had a major impact on the EU decision. Swedish industry is well integrated internationally, and has a long international history. That business threatened to leave Sweden, and sometimes followed up the threats with action, undoubtedly put pressure on government to join the EU. Sweden's capital-intensive industry, with its larger units than Norway's and less subsidies, combined in a common front for EU membership. And because the European export markets are crucial to this industry, the internal market programme played a major role in the national debate.

Also typical of the Swedish approach was the major effort to research the consequences of membership for various segments and interests of Swedish society. The Swedish government published a mass of information and analyses on the issues in its official reports (SOUs – *Statens Offentliga Utredningar* – Swedish Government Reports). Also trade unions favoured the EU, and the pro-EU segments were well organized. In the end it was clear that a large proportion of Swedish society had joined the pro-forces in a corporatist pattern of rational and intense organization as a unified group. The referendum came out 52.3 per cent in favour of membership.

*Finland* was another joiner in 1995. The main reason for Finland was not the economy, but security. The EU was the Finnish way to integrate in the West after decades of enforced "Finlandization". But Finland also sought Western integration in the economic sphere. The long-standing Soviet market collapsed with the fall of the Berlin wall, and Finland had to re-align its economy very quickly under the threat of greatly increased double-digit unemployment figures and a steep fall in GDP. Finland had a lucky mix of raw material exports and high-tech industry, the main markets for which were and remain EU members. The Finnish elite was of one mind, it was imperative to join the EU. It was important also in order to attract foreign direct investment (FDI). And once Sweden announced its intention to join, Finland followed suit immediately. Although "Arctic agriculture" played a role on the "no" side, the sector played nothing like the significant role it had in Norway. The membership negotiations also resulted in the retention of most of the national subsidies coupled with CAP funding. The Finnish parliament ratified the results of the negotiations, and the referendum came out with a 56.9 per cent majority.

In sum, "the economic export structures and what Europe offered each state can explain why some states were more positive than others to EC membership", Ingebritsen concludes, and finds support among other scholars. Moses and Jenssen, for instance, suggest that "Norway's opposition to membership is best explained by its relative wealth and the nature of its export dependence on the EC, while Finland and Sweden are both heavily dependent on European markets and are economies in search of recovery" (Moses and Jenssen 1995:18). Ingebritsen agrees that key economic sectors explain very much in the Nordics' choice of EU relationship, arguing that although elites are constrained by public opinion, they tend nonetheless to prevail. But as we shall see in the last section, it may be that the opposite conclusion is warranted, i.e., that Nordic elites, despite their desire to join, were stopped by the domination of popular movements of the referenda process.

## The Second Determinant: Foreign and Security Policy

Other factors can be pivotal too, in addition to the economy. Also largely an elite phenomenon, foreign and security policy seems to play a key role in whether to join the EU. The NATO-affiliated Nordics have not wanted a "competing" EU security policy, and are against a gradual process of integration in this area. Denmark, as mentioned, opted out of the defence alliance in the EU and remains on the outside. Norway's interest in the EU has been purely economic (Neumann 2001). The Swedish elite likewise resisted a common security policy because of Sweden's long-standing neutrality. The Finns were in a special position, wanting a "Western rebranding" as a state, as Arter puts it (Arter 2000:691). The end of the Cold War obviously played a key enabling role for the Nordics, especially Finland. It put an end to what is known as "Finlandization", denoting one country's forced dominance by another. As Arter (1999) explains, Finnish security policy lacked the Western embeddedness of the other Nordic states.

Pedersen argues that Denmark and Sweden were influenced by German unification to such an extent that they realized that the EU now would represent a focal point also in foreign policy (Pedersen 1996). He argues that structural factors – the end of the Cold war – led to an impetus for integration in the EU for political reasons. Public opinion is rarely only shaped by economic rationality, and factors linked to identity and self-image play a key role. Widfelt (1996) notes the key importance of Swedish neutrality, an issue that played a role in the EU debate from the 1960s onwards. There is a large literature on the role of foreign policy factors, and some that argue that security plays a key role, for Norway (Sæter 1993) and for Finland (Tiilikainen 1996).

Let us look at the larger foreign policy picture. As we have noted, the security policies of the Nordics differ, and geo-political factors have constrained policy choices. The end of the Cold War obviously changed the geo-political picture beyond recognition: the threat of invasion vanished. The EU has developed a security role, and NATO has changed, both affecting the Nordics deeply. The emerging literature on the effects of "Europeanization" in this area (Rieker 2003; Ojanen 2000) shows that the EU members Finland and Sweden have sought to develop a security policy that allows them to retain a nominal neutrality without having to tackle the issue of NATO membership at home. The EU's gradual development of a security policy has influenced these neutral states, as these studies show, but these states have also been instrumental in developing EU policy.

EFFECTS OF EU MEMBERSHIP: ADAPTATION AND RESPONSES

How have the Swedes and Finns adapted to EU membership? What kinds of changes have been noted? Do they express coordinated efforts to shape EU policy? Both Sweden and Finland were neutral in the post-war period. In the Swedish case, neutrality was the government's major argument against membership. However, during a period of a mere six months the then prime minister Ingvar Carlsson changed his mind, reversing this argument in the process. Finland, too, acted quickly to accommodate membership and the end of neutrality.

After some years of EU membership, Sweden's foreign and security policy changed significantly. As Ekengren and Sundelius tell us, "[c]onstitutional issues, administrative procedures, policy processes, the prevailing logic of appropriate procedures, policies and state strategies have been greatly affected by the requirements of membership" (Ekengren and Sundelius 1998:1). However, preparations for EU membership started already in 1989, with the creation of more than 20 permanent working groups with personnel from the various ministries, but coordinated by the Ministry of Foreign Affairs (MFA). That said, the political branch of the MFA was not particularly involved, nor did the Defence Ministry (DM) take part in this adjustment process. But "there was a clear administrative and judicial drive in Sweden already underway before the 1991 application to become fully integrated" (Ekengren and Sundelius 1998:6). Finland also engineered a process of adjustment, but here it was important to de-politicize steps towards Europe. Finnish business elites adapted, and waited for the political segment to follow them.

In Sweden, the arguments against membership persisted until the abrupt turnaround of October 1990. Opposition had centred on anti-supranationality, on a fear that Sweden would lose much of its "bridge-building" role in the world, and that Sweden's foreign policy stance as the champion of the Third World would be eroded through membership (Pro. 1987/88). Prime minister Carlsson had as mentioned stated in a newspaper article at the end of May 1990 that neutrality hindered membership in the EU. But only six months later, the new security order invalidated the neutrality argument. A new foreign policy rhetoric flourished: neutrality became compatible with membership, with an emphasis now on non-alignment. In the words of the Swedish Foreign Affairs Committee, "Sweden's policy of non-alignment with the possibility of neutrality in the case of war in its vicinity remains" (Utrikesutskottets Betänkande 1991/92, UU19). When prime minister Carl Bildt took over, he stated that Sweden wanted a European identity and to influence European policy. He was stating, in fact, that a pro-active CFSP policy – in the sense of more integration – would be the Swedish stance from then on.

In Sundelius's detailed analysis of the period 1990–91, he shows how Sweden quickly acclimatized to the EU, led by market and economic forces (Sundelius 1994). The foreign policy "establishment" rewrote Swedish foreign policy in response. The term "neutrality" was erased from official rhetoric even before membership. "The transition from an image of Sweden as the committed neutral to a committed European seemed to have been fully completed well ahead of the beginning of the membership negotiations" (Sundelius and Ekengren 1997:8). This, remarks Sundelius, was in response to the European Commission's rather dim view of neutrality. This is how the EU affected Sweden then. The elites took advantage of the opening offered by the CFSP to re-adjust domestic policy. After decades of inertia, domestic policy changed almost over night.

Austria had already been told by the European Commission in an *avis* that neutrality was incompatible with membership. Both Finland and Sweden lost no time in denouncing their neutrality claims. The new policy was called "non-alignment". This meant, for Finland, minimalist neutrality; neither an alliance with the West European Union nor with NATO. Yet both Sweden and Finland became observers to the West European Union (WEU) in 1992, along with Denmark. Later in the decade we see Swedish and Finnish troops on peace-keeping operations in Macedonia under EU command in the Balkans.

Small states can be expected to favour a pro-active – in this case pro-integrationist – strategy in international politics in general, especially under the conditions of complex interdependence where the issues are economic, concern "soft power", and where issues related to territoriality in general mean less. The powers of persuasion and negotiation are not correlated with size or geopolitical position; and it follows that small states may maximise these powers in a similar manner to large states. Also, in the EU system, there are two other conditions that make pro-active participation especially attractive. One is the development towards a system of differentiated integration, the other, the important role that agenda-setting plays.

All these four factors make a pro-integration strategy desirable. Both the Finnish and the Swedish prime ministers have repeatedly voiced their desire to be pro-active in the EU after joining – as have other leaders. Former prime ministers Carlsson and Bildt both emphasised the need to be pro-active; the Finnish prime minister cited the need to participate in the inner core of the

EU as one of the main justifications – perhaps the main justification – for Finland to join the EMU (Arter 2000).

However, public opinion in the Nordic states has traditionally been strongly anti-integrationist, with the possible exception of Finland. Historical studies of approaches to Europe and the EU in the national debates show there to have been a much closer identification with the UK and the US than continental Europe in Norway and Denmark, but less so in Sweden (Riste 2001). The public remain staunchly opposed to any notion of supra-nationality or concept of political union. Economic integration is justified pragmatically, but political integration is widely resisted. In this setting it is clear that EU's role in foreign policy ought to be purely intergovernmental, as far as the Scandinavian public are concerned. We should thus anticipate initial scepticism towards wider integration efforts – pro-activism – also on the part of the Nordic elites, but that it would disappear with participation in the day-to-day processes of EU decision-making, and that one would learn very quickly that a pro-active strategy is advantageous. Finland and Sweden's periods of membership acclimatization showed that the political elite in both states adapted very quickly, though they were variously constrained by public opinion and political opposition.

In formulating a hypothesis about EU strategy in foreign policy, we can assume that the elite, which interacts with the EU, learns and internalises what it considers the advantages of a pro-integration strategy and seeks to persuade peers and the public of its benefits. However, the success here depends on the various constraints, and they vary from country to country in the Nordic region. For instance, the Danish foreign policy elite is so constrained that is has to be extremely careful in pursuing a pro-active strategy; the Norwegian elite would like to pursue a pro-active strategy but is extremely constrained by non-membership, for which it attempts to compensate by pursuing bilateral contacts and trade-offs with EU member states and maintaining a "high profile" in other European multilateral fora. The Swedish elite is also pretty constrained, but enjoys more leeway than the Danish elites. In Finland, the elite is fairly free to pursue a pro-active strategy, also in this policy area.

What we hypothesise is thus that the Nordic foreign policy elite – those persons who do business with the EU and other international actors – quickly learn that pro-activism in the EU is of particular importance, and seek to develop such a strategy further. This ties in with the experiences of other small EU states – the Benelux countries and Ireland are favourable to integration in general; only the Netherlands seem to have changed sides from a reactive to a pro-active strategy in foreign policy. Ireland has been more reluctant, yet moves in this direction are reported (Tonra 1996). The leading cause, it seems, is the interaction in the EU setting, rather than any change in foreign policy views.

We thus assume that this learning process takes place at the elite level and is not transmitted to the public at large. This may happen at a later stage, but in any case it is a process that requires much time. New foreign policy "doctrines" have to be formulated, disseminated and internalised. The new European geo-political situation is certainly one in which the post-war doctrines have to be rewritten, but here too, societies need time. It is therefore reasonable to assume that constraints in foreign policy imposed on the elite in each Nordic state have remained at a fairly constant level.

### SWEDEN: A CASE STUDY

If we select one the Nordics for a more detailed appraisal, we can get a snap-shot of what happens when domestic and foreign policy increasingly become one process. How did Sweden fare in the CFSP? Former prime minister Carlsson had stated that one purpose of joining was to make the EU a "progressive force in world affairs" (Ekengren and Sundelius 1998:20). The Swedish foreign office (FO) coordinates EU positions and all instructions to Brussels. There are weekly meetings with all relevant ministries in the coordination committee. There is an expert level group as well, which settles questions which are not resolved in the coordination committee. The bilateral politico-economic divide in the ministerial organisation has been replaced by a desk system in order to facilitate the quick lead-times in EU decision-making. The desk officers' role has been upgraded as "a direct result of the experiences of the first half-year of membership. The fact that almost every unit in the Foreign Ministry is affected by the CFSP was not realised until one worked inside this network", say Ekengren and Sundelius (ibid.:15), adding that "Quickly, EU coordination concerns became an overarching priority for the ministry as a whole" (ibid.:16).

Being in the EU is therefore not an intergovernmental issue where national and EU policy are nicely separated. On the contrary, it is increasingly one policy arena where even small states can wield considerable influence. Yet small state independence is hard to maintain in this system where the EU must arrive at one common position. A case study of the early Swedish experience as an EU member is illustrative of this dilemma. In my elite interviews with civil servants at the Swedish MFA[56] two years after joining the EU, I focused on whether they were able to be pro-active, whether they could set the agenda, and on how small states could achieve influence. I also asked how much policy power they had lost as an EU member state, and in what areas.

Several respondents emphasized that "idea power" plays a key role in the agenda-setting, and that small states with constructive proposals could influence a lot. In the literature two such cases are mentioned. One is Finland's success at launching the so-called Northern Dimension Initiative (Arter 2000) and the other the joint Swedish–Finnish proposal, also successful, to include the so-called Petersberg tasks – crisis management and peace-keeping. My interviewees stressed that good ideas can succeed even if one is a small state, but that they have to be launched at the right time – in the beginning of a policy process, and they have to be "sold" to other states at once to acquire momentum. EU decision-making processes are continuous – in foreign policy through the telex system known as the COREU system – and there is only *one* process; not at all a typical intergovernmental process. "Sweden gets a lot through, is able to set the agenda and influence it", says one respondent, "but all arguments must be in terms of objective facts, not as national interests." But the price of EU membership is that the Nordic cooperation at the UN, often with a common statement, has had to be abandoned. Also, Sweden has on occasion had to abandon national policy at the UN, to facilitate a common EU stance – a very powerful norm indeed. An individual Swedish profile disappears, and peace negotiations or national stances, said this source, are out of the question. Another respondent said that there was a lot of tacit Swedish–Finnish coordination, but that it was not advantageous to act openly as "a Nordic bloc". Instead, Sweden could show its global ambitions by taking an interest in the South. In concrete terms, this meant Swedish engagement in the Spanish-led Barcelona process. Finally, the Swedes said that since Denmark has a CFSP opt-out clause, they spent little time informing Copenhagen. The Swedish elite wants maximum integration, said this source, but is constrained by public opinion, especially in terms of the neutrality questions.

The CFSP is an instance of IT diplomacy, with direct links with the foreign ministries. The flow of telexes increased from about 4,000 immediately after its 1973 inception to about 15,000 e-mails in 1994. This is about 2–300 messages weekly. Reactions happen very quickly, one sits and waits for the reaction from the others before deciding oneself. The country with the presidency determines the agenda. The reports on the world from national ministries are available to all the others. In addition, CFSP states participate in more than 50 working groups.

FROM REACTIVE TO PRO-INTEGRATIVE STRATEGY?

There was a perception that the overall direction of European integration was "an unavoidable historical development of an irreversible nature". Swedish officials expressed the view that they had "no alternative than to follow European developments in whatever unpredictable direction they might take, and therefore had to be flexible and adaptable." It is very important to forestall developments, to anticipate what the others will do.

The Finnish Prime Minister Paavo Lipponen stated forcefully in March 1997 that it was necessary for Finland to join the EMU in order to participate in the inner core of EU decision-making as EMU would form "an inner informal core" (Agence Europe 20.3.1997). Finland needs to be proactive in order to influence, he stated. There is evidence of a much more pro-active strategy in Sweden too, according to Sundelius, "although this is still elusive" (Ekengren 2002). However, both the Bildt government and the social democrats wanted to ensure that necessary preparations were in place well ahead of membership; steps were therefore taken in advance of Sweden's 1991 membership application.

In conclusion there is evidence that both Finnish and Swedish elites appear to desire core integration, or, as we have termed it here, a pro-active role. Yet domestic factors appear to have constrained them.

## The Third Determinant: Public Opinion and National Identity

The Nordic states have always been reluctant Europeans. Despite "rational" economic interests and strong foreign policy elite aspirations to join the leading integration bloc, the European Community, later the EU, has been seen by most Scandinavians as an economic form of cooperation, and the prospect of "political union" has been met with scepticism and outright hostility. Bergquist (1970) records how the Swedes failed to conduct any discussion involving the public on the EC in the 1970s apart from certain functional, pragmatic aspects: there was never any debate on the issue of integration as such (Bergquist 1970). This finding has been seconded by af Malmborg's studies of post-war Swedish relations with the EC. There was always a negative view on integration that is non-functional and supra-national (af Malmborg 1994). Bergquist adds that there was always a dichotomy between Europe and global versus Nordic issues, with a preference for the latter in foreign policy discussions.

In Finland, the relationship to the Soviet Union meant that closer links with the EC were out of the question. It was impossible for Finland to join

EFTA, and only intensive efforts by the Swedes secured an associative membership for Finland (af Malmborg 1996). When geo-political changes made it possible, the Finns were quick to align themselves towards the EU. They joined the EEA negotiations in 1989, and moved to application for full membership in 1992. Here there was little or no domestic debate or opposition.

In Norway, the EEA negotiations paved the way for a second membership application, although not until both Finland and Sweden had tendered theirs. The Norwegian view of the EU echoed Sweden's inasmuch as it has been one of pragmatic functionalism, based on economic arguments. There has been little or no interest in the possible merits of European integration, and political union has been viewed negatively.

The Danish case is similar to the Swedish and Norwegian. Here too, the EC/EU has been viewed as a mutually beneficial economic undertaking, and the Danes were always the most reluctant participants in the foreign policy consultations, known as the European Political Cooperation (EPC). Each time there was a proposal for making the EPC more integrative, e.g., through majority voting, or more extensive in scope, through making it a political union, the Danes opposed. When the Maastricht Treaty (TEU – Treaty on Political Union) was negotiated, the Danish parliament discussed the CFSP at length, concluding that defence should not be included in the common policy; that Denmark should not be a member of the WEU; and that the CFSP should remain intergovernmental (Archer 1996). Although the Danish parliament ratified the TEU by a large majority; the subsequent referendum resulted in a rejection of the treaty by 50.7 per cent. This in turn resulted in a special concession granted to Denmark at the European Council meeting in Dublin in 1992, whereby the Danes were granted exception from union citizenship, defence cooperation, and EMU's third stage. A "national compromise" between the parties was developed, and put to another referendum, which culminated in an acceptance of the TEU with the new Danish "opt-outs". However, Denmark joined the WEU as an observer in 1992, and has participated in the CFSP. An official paper from SNU (Danish Commission on Security and Disarmament) in 1992 asked whether marginalisation in NATO was a real danger as the WEU was becoming the "European pillar" of NATO. The paper concluded that "Denmark runs the risk of weakening its membership of NATO. Denmark is close to becoming isolated on this question" (cited in Archer 1992:267).

## Conclusion

In view of the historical setting of the Nordic states, they have, for different reasons, not been aligned towards the EU and Europe. Finland was constrained in both its trade and foreign policy by its Soviet neighbour; Sweden remained neutral while pursuing a post-war foreign policy of global and Nordic engagement; Norway adopted an Anglo-American alignment, also shared by Denmark in terms of defence policy. On the one hand it therefore seems highly plausible that these states will define their "national" interests vis-à-vis the EU as minimalistically as possible – no supra-nationality in foreign policy, no defence cooperation, no integration of the CFSP, no majority voting. This will be in opposition to the positions taken by other small states in the EU such as Belgium, the Netherlands and Ireland, which goes to show that small states are indeed very different in the EU.

As Neumann argues, concepts matter: public opinion matters to the politicians. The problem with this argument is that it has been hard to establish empirically (Neumann 2001). A recent article by Koenig-Archibugi put it to the test by operationalizing sovereignty, defined as divisible/indivisible. We cannot go into the details of his method in this article, but his findings are pretty emphatic: states that view their own sovereignty in zero-sum terms – that is, states with strong mono-cultural and state-centric traditions such as the Nordics – are clearly least in favour of integration. The author takes the CFSP as his test case, a sensitive area in terms of sovereignty. Using regression analysis he finds that public opinion in Sweden, Denmark and the UK is least favourable to integration (Koenig-Archibugi 2004:163).

# Chapter 15: Comparative Perspectives on the Northern Countries

*Knut Heidar*

In comparative research scholars often pursue a "most similar systems design" and find the Nordic countries a profitable setting. This means searching for countries that vary in terms of the "dependent variable" – state form, party system, etc. – but which have broad contextual similarities. The point is to control for as many (potentially relevant) explanatory factors as possible in order to discover the effective "independent variable". This approach tries to ease the general problem in all comparative research, described as "too many variables, too few countries" (Lijphart 1971). When spotting significant differences the potential explanatory options are more easily targeted and studied in comparisons of fairly similar rather than of very different countries. One example is the old classic "why did Norway get such a radical labour movement after WWI, compared to the moderate movements Sweden and Denmark got?" Different comparative studies have pointed to likely explanatory factors like "rapid, socially disruptive industrial growth" in Norway and "the early political integration of working-class parties" in Denmark and Sweden (Lipset 1960; Lafferty 1971). The trouble with this approach, of course, is the truism that the more similarities, the less interesting and significant variations can be found among the countries studied. We would not maximize the most interesting regime type variations when selecting the Nordic countries. Often in political science, the optimal interests do not fit the optimal method – and one just has to make the best of it.

The approach in this book has not been analytical in the theoretical sense described above, more one of an "area approach" where we have looked for intriguing differences and similarities among the Nordics. In other words, we wanted to study the quarry found in the hunting grounds accessible to us, rather than seeking out hunting grounds known for the type of game we were looking for. Internal as well as external perspectives guided the choice of a Nordic area approach. The internal perspective originates with the idea of a common "Nordic-ness", a commonality founded on shared history along with the linguistic, religious and political homogeneity of the Nordic – and particularly the Scandinavian – countries. This rather deep sense of belonging to a distinct part of Europe, what we term the Nordic identity, has been based on close cultural, political and economic ties and nurtured institutionally by the post-war establishment of the Nordic Council. In a 1949 Scandinavian publication on "Nordic Democracy" (but written in the Scandinavian languages) – with forewords by the three prime ministers – the message was that the Nordic countries had reached a degree of "political maturity" which made their story well worth telling to the outside world, particularly as Cold War tensions grew (Koch and Ross 1949). This was the history of the "happy democracies", to use an expression coined by the eminent Swedish political scientist and newspaper editor Herbert Tingsten (quoted in Lane et al. 1993:196). Another book, this time in English, on Nordic Democracy, from 1981 saw the Nordic countries as making a "special contribution" to debates on democracy (Allardt et al. 1981: Foreword). It was also stressed, however, that although Norden looked "fairly homogeneous" from the outside, the differences appeared "often more clearly" from the inside (1981:2–3).

The external perspective is sustained by the history of the northern cultural periphery as a group of peaceful, harmonious countries, and cultivated in the notion of a "Nordic model". In this last chapter I shall be looking into some aspects of this Nordic model. I argue that it is a useful catch phrase, and as a rough guide to certain aspects of the politics of the region. On the other hand, recent international history has obviously caused dramatically new circumstances for the Nordic countries, most notably apparent in their different affiliations with the European Union. But the "model" as such fails if the analysis of a particular polity or distinct version of liberal democracy is what we're after. I will argue that comparative perspectives on Nordic politics are well worth pursuing, though the advent of the EU and globalisation does make "system independence" more questionable (see, e.g., Bergman and Damgaard 2000). Insofar as all these countries operate in the same environment, an environment which exposes them to forces of increasingly powerful nature, we should not expect intra-Nordic comparisons to shed much light on the causes of change.

## The meaning of "Nordic Model"

Marquis W. Childs's 1936 book *Sweden: The Middle Way* was a journalistic account of Swedish politics written for the US market (Childs 1936; 1980). Childs argued – in the midst of the depression – that the US had more political options than to choose between the fascist and the communist alternatives. Sweden exemplified "the middle way" between the two undesirable extremes. In Sweden the forces of capital and labour worked together, softening otherwise socially disruptive market forces while retaining basic political and economic freedoms. The book was an instant success. The key elements of the middle way – a strong labour movement, labour–capital collaboration, political compromise and pragmatism – became core elements of what would later be known as the "Nordic Model" (Lane 1991; Petersson 1994).

To some, the middle way was seen as a road to success, political peace and general welfare. To others, the Swedish strong-state-plus-strong-social-democracy formula was a mark of "the new totalitarians" (Huntford 1971). Rhetorical battles were waged over the Swedish (and Nordic) way with interventionists taking on free-marketers, the political left jousting with the political right. In the 1980s, when the Swedish economy slowed down and political volatility rose, the image of the successful Swedish/Nordic model faltered. The murder of the Swedish Prime Minister Olof Palme in 1986 likewise stained the image of a harmonious society. The German novelist Hans Magnus Enzensberger published several essays in the 1980s of his impressions of certain European countries, including Sweden and Norway. He wrote about a "Swedish autumn" and of Norway as being "out of step" (Enzensberger 1987). The old Swedish system was in crisis, he said, economically and politically, and Norway had turned into an artificial creation of oil-financed self-indulgence. In other words: neither could lay claim to model country status.

The literature advances several "Nordic models", each focusing on different aspects of politics and society. There are welfare models, models of wage negotiations, models of political consensus, party models, etc. General descriptions of the political systems – the particular type of Nordic democracy, like the Swedish "middle way" – are also present. The British political scientist David Arter in a recent book presented a seven-point ideal-typical picture of the Nordic model of government (Arter 1999:146–149). The points were:

1. Dominant or strong social democratic parties
2. Working multi-party systems
3. Consensual approach to policy-making

4. Consultation with pressure groups
5. Centralized collective bargaining
6. An active state
7. Close relations within political elite producing pragmatism

These characteristics made Arter ask whether the Nordic states constituted a distinctive sub-type of liberal democracy expressed by the "three Cs": Compromise, Co-operation and Consensus.

Arter builds on an extensive literature leading back to Childs (e.g., Elder et al. 1988; Lane 1991, 1993; Peterson 1994). But, like most of his predecessors, he conveys a certain ambiguity as to how distinctive the Nordics really are. It is evident that many of the apparent similarities are extracted from the Swedish case only. The tendency to build on Swedish experience is most apparent in the emphasis on the dominance of Social Democracy in party politics and government formation. This dominance continues – even today – in Swedish politics, but it is less true of the other Nordic countries.

The Norwegian sociologist Lars Mjøset suggests that if a Nordic type or model is to be established by comparative research, not only must the Nordics share the model's basic elements, the model must also be unique, that is, non-applicable to other countries (Mjøset 1992). No other countries should fit the "Nordic Model", outside the Nordic area. He concludes, however, that comparative research has only demonstrated several "Nordic peculiarities" (663), not a Nordic package of common characteristics that is exclusive to the Nordics. This – it seems – is the main problem with the "Nordic model" metaphor. The politics of the Nordic region simply do not pass the analytical test for a particular regime type. The literature is revealing on this point. When researchers anchor their work in analytical, comparative discussions of democratic systems, scholars like Lijphart often find that the Nordic countries fall into one particular subtype. In his *Democracies* the Nordic countries all end up in the group of consensual, unitary countries. However, they are also joined by Israel, Luxemburg, Portugal and Italy – among others (Lijphart 1999:248). If we focus on specific elements of the Nordic model, such as the strength of social democracy, the corporatist arrangements or pragmatic political culture, it is difficult to exclude, for example, Austria from the "Nordic model". And the consensual elements are just as strong in the Netherlands where one would also find strong elite collaboration seasoned with pragmatism. However, the cultural and social basis of politics in the Netherlands ("pillarization") is very different compared to the Nordics. In other words, the "area study approach" creates an impression that the political systems of these countries are of a similar, exclusive type, while analytical, comparative work is unable to provide the proof.

## Comparative perspectives: Persistent similarities and current trends

The comparative discussions in these chapters bear out the argument that similarities and differences are analytical constructions. All human phenomena look different the closer the observer gets to them. The low resolution of the panoramic shot gives a general view, making the major contours appear "similar" or even "identical". Only the close up can reveal the differentiating details. Comparisons require analytical efforts in creating classes of phenomena (like different types of democracy), and it is the analyst's decisions, or – rather – the analytical requirements of the theoretical perspective, that dictate the specificities of these concepts. When the Roman writer Tacitus surveyed the "northern countries" inhabited by the Germanic peoples, he saw an undifferentiated tribal area vastly different from the Roman Empire. When Childs travelled across the Atlantic Ocean to Scandinavia between the wars he found "the middle way" in a north European country that differed markedly from the capitalist US. "The middle way" was not only a descriptive term – it was a summons to act. Finally, discussions of Nordic politics from vantage points internal or external to the region are almost bound to home in on different perspectives – affecting the choice of classes or concepts for comparisons.

From a distance, the Nordics are not too dissimilar in terms of cultural, religious, language, political traits. Although all are highly secularised societies they are all marked by the legacy of Lutheran Protestantism as the state religion. While recent immigration has made them – in particular the Scandinavian countries – more multi-cultural, the dominant cultures are largely unaffected. The languages are sufficiently similar to facilitate close inter-Scandinavian connections (including with some parts of Finland). The histories of the Nordic countries are highly intertwined and they share a basically egalitarian culture. The discussions on welfare state policies (Chapter 12), the rise of broad social movements (Chapter 5) and the political parties (Chapter 3) illustrate some of the political consequences of this unified cultural tradition. All countries experienced a strong corporate system in the post-war era with high levels of state involvement in the system of collective bargaining and wage settlement (Chapter 6). All gave voting rights to women early on, and comparatively speaking women made up significant proportions of parties, parliaments and governments, especially from the 1970s (Chapter 9). The local government institutions have been strong and share similar institutional traits (Chapter 10).

Still, there is an ambiguity in most chapters in their discussions of the "commonness" of the Nordic political systems. The geo-political forces which set the nation-building stage for these systems also affected the processes involved. In and of themselves, they all crossed the democracy thresholds in fairly similar ways, but the make up and attitudes of the state-building groups differed (Chapter 1). Their economies also differed and still differ in important respects. After adopting relatively similar politico-administrative systems, their public administrations nevertheless developed differently (Chapter 2). Regional organization is structurally similar – again particularly in the Scandinavian area – reflecting the common needs of the nation-states, though historic developments have introduced individual differences here too (Chapter 11) The countries differ in their securities policies – although tending to converge more than diverge as NATO, the EU and perceptions of external threats change (Chapter 13). Relations with the EU are obviously different; some are members, others remain outside (Chapter 14). Despite these disparities and the less than uniform reality behind the Nordic model perspective, it must also be acknowledged that the Nordics themselves use the Nordic model metaphor or at least what they conceive as a fairly uniform "Nordic experience" to advertise the importance of their own home ground (e.g. Esaiasson and Heidar 2000).

The Nordic societies changed much in the late twentieth century. Like those of other industrial democracies, their economies turned more service-based and open, their politics more volatile and dependent on inter-state co-operation, particularly through the EU. Several of what were once considered traditional Nordic politics have been challenged. Generous welfare provisions have been tailed down to accommodate a tighter fiscal climate. Neo-liberalism in the wake of Thatcher's and Reagan's years in power prompted the changes and ushered in administrative reforms under the aegis of New Public Management. This notwithstanding, the Nordics retained the strong state, a tradition that has proved remarkably robust, and pragmatic policy styles have encouraged re-alignment rather than outright system change. New parties emerged in the 1970s, like the populist progress parties of Denmark and Norway and the new parliamentary green parties of Sweden and Finland. Voting became more value based, but entrenched class values still sustain the old parties, limiting scope for party change. The social movements that used to nurture political participation and bring the concerns of rural and outlying communities to the attention of national politicians have not only declined in terms of participation, they have changed, towards a more consumer-centred management approach. The strong corporate nature of wage negotiations and public policy implementation has subsided, giving way to more pluralistic forces and to increased lobby practices. Local and regional government have come under heightened pressure to streamline state policy implementation. Today, their role as arenas of local democracy is challenged. The rise of the EU and an altered security setting following the end of the Cold War have created more similarities rather than more differentiation over the past fifteen years or so. The old ways are clearly not what they were.

Changes in the wider world – with an "ever closer" European Union and a more open and interactive global community – have triggered changes. Dependency on European and global trends is, of course, nothing new in the history of the Nordics, given their security needs, seafaring traditions and reliance on international trade. Nordic economies, politics and cultures in modern times have always been closely tied to Europe and the Anglo-American community. Today's changes, however, are challenging some of the core traditional characteristics of Nordic polities – their egalitarianism and small-scale localism. There are debates, however, over the relative impact of external and internal forces. In a recent book, Barth, Moene and Wallerstein argue, for example, that the threat to the Nordic model, with its strong corporate structures and ability to produce economic equality, comes even more from internal processes than from economic globalization. The flat income structure of the Nordic societies are under pressure from the rebellion of the middle classes, the well educated, but low paid groups who are refusing to pay the high taxes necessary to finance redistribution and general welfare (Barth, Moene and Wallerstein 2003).

## The uses of Nordic comparisons

Comparative analyses fulfil two rather different purposes. They can help us understand things and they can help us explain things. Making comparisons to further understanding is not unlike the traveller who tries to understand more about himself and his culture through travelling abroad. It is by the *differences* we can judge our own experiences and understand them better. This is obviously a worthwhile approach in inter-Nordic comparisons –would the Swedes see their own parliamentarism in a different light after studying the

Danish *Folketing*? – and perhaps particularly in comparisons of the Nordics with non-Nordic countries – What could one learn about Norwegian political culture by contrasting it with that of the US? While studying the rare party type of the Nordic agrarians (Chapter 3) one may certainly query what sort of society would create this particular type with so few sister parties elsewhere (for a discussion, see Rokkan 1970: Chapter 3). On the other hand, does the lack of Christian-Democratic parties tell us something about the Nordic Protestant political culture (e.g. Madeley and Enyedi 2003)?

The explanatory comparative approach takes a different form. The point of course is to compare similar phenomena in different settings in order to discuss causal relationships, i.e. causes and/or effects. This is the theory-generating approach in comparative analysis, and it comes in two versions. First, Lijphart's study "Democracies" is an example of a *deductive explanatory* approach in comparative theory-building. On the basis of an interpretation of the democratic tradition, Lijphart develops two (later four) analytically distinct models of democracy. From this he goes on to undertake an empirical analysis of how different democracies can be grouped within his ideal types – or placed on the empirical continuum between them (Lijphart 1999). Lijphart found – as mentioned before – that the Nordics fell within the same democratic type. Another example of this approach is the one-country analysis of Norwegian democracy in Harry Eckstein's "theoretical case study" of Norway as a stable democracy. In this book Eckstein tested the general theory that congruence in societal authority structures supports stable political democracies (Eckstein 1966).

On the other hand, the *inductive comparative* approach to theory-building looks at factual differences between states as documented in the literature and seeks to develop analytical models to explain what differences it finds. A classic example is Barrington Moore's attempt to account for variation in regime types by the different historical developments of the countries in question (Moore 1966). The rise of fascist, communist and democratic regimes respectively was explained by the different strategies employed by the elites in the old agrarian societies when challenged by industrialization and a capitalist world system. Major differences among the Nordics are legion. How can one explain the different security policies, the different relations to the EU and different developments in party systems? What are the mechanisms in these societies, their histories or their external context that could explain these differences?

## The Northern Countries

When the Romans looked across their borders towards the north, they surveyed what they termed "the northern countries". These territories included much of present-day Germany, Poland and the Nordics. They were tribal areas, whose leading distinction was not being part of the Roman Empire. To non-Nordic observers today, the group of Nordic countries no doubt are distinguished by strong cultural ties and by close similarities in institutional structures and policies. The growing strength and impact of the EU and the rise of international cooperation and regulation (as engineered by the WTO agreements, for instance), have, however, shifted the balance of change-inducement from internal, intra-Nordic forces towards international and intergovernmental factors. All the Nordics are in practice bound by new EU internal economic market regulations and must abide by the decisions of EU's Court of Justice.

Inter-Nordic comparison is consequently hampered by decreasing "system independence". National polities have never been fully independent, and diffusion was clearly a likely explanatory option also in the heydays of the Nordic Council. Incidentally, they were in the 1950s and early 1960s, when public commissions travelled to Stockholm from the other Nordic capitals to learn more about how the Swedes did it. System independence is a highly problematic premise for all comparative research. It is especially so today when the EU is about to strengthen its policy-making capabilities and the World Trade Organisation stages rounds of negotiations on trade regimes. On the other hand, no observer of the EU could fail to notice the differences in member states' interests and policy approaches. They prevail in national policy approaches, and there is a striking degree of internal robustness when new policies are to be adopted and implemented. There are good reasons, therefore, to continue asking why the Scandinavian welfare arrangements remain relatively similar, how and why they differ from the continental or the Anglo-American systems, why some Nordics choose to stay outside the EU, and why women reached such a high level of political integration in the Nordic countries.

The five Northern countries are most fruitfully seen as a group of countries with similarities as well as differences. There are good reasons to study them comparatively, but these reasons should not be taken for granted.

# Notes

1   Benclux is shorthand for the countries in the Benelux Economic Union, the Netherlands, Belgium and Luxemburg, that started immediately after the end of WWII and led to a customs union and the removal of internal trade restrictions. It represented an early EU "internal market" so to speak. Switzerland was a loose military confederation of quasi-independent states from 1291, but is still a Europe in miniature with marked internal differences (language and religion), strong federalism and – a distinct citizenship identity.

2   Nation-building is the conscious effort by the state elites to create a shared "national" identity among all inhabitants of the territory controlled by the state. See for example Rokkan 1970.

3   The degree to which it reinforced existing national identities and created new ones is a matter of debate, see for example Østergård 1997 and Lunden 1992.

4   This choice is made to give more space to the old Scandinavian core of the Nordic countries and runs counter to the "Nordic ethos". The three Scandinavian countries are the closest in terms of language. One may also argue that it reflects a weakening of the Nordic dimension after the end of the Cold War (Laursen 1998:118-21). For many purposes, however – for example when discussing the relationship with the EU and the securities policies – the analysis is more interesting when at least Finland is included.

5   The governments of Estonia, Latvia and Lithuania formed a Baltic Council of Ministers in 1994, however, modelled after the Nordic Council.

6   Speaking of institutions controlling the legitimate use of force within their territory.

7   The figure is "criteria dependent," disputed and hard to calculate.

8   The following presentation of political forces in the Nordic countries is based on Heidar et al. 2000:21-24.

9   For the Norwegian discussion, see Heidar 1993.

10   The parties in Iceland – with its "Althingi" – are not included in this chapter

11   The term "borgerlig" is commonplace in the Scandinavian countries and is not used, or intended, as a foil to Marxism's working classes.

12   In the electoral systems, there are thresholds for representation to restrict entry for the smallest parties, see chapters 4, 7 and 8.

13   We present the parties along a left–right dimension with the parties of the left

on top. Some of the parties resist a simple left–right identification, notably the greens and the populist right. Some parties, although somewhat easier to place, would still strongly object to this type of one-dimensional view – notably the agrarian and Christian parties.

14    Actually the party had governed for 61 of the past 70 years, "a record without equal among democratic societies" (Madeley 2003:165)

15    However, all governments after 1971 except 1983-85 have been minority governments in Norway, see chapter 8.

16    The expression is from Elder, N., Thomas, A.H and Arter, D., *The Consensual Democracies? The Government and Politics of the Scandinavian States*, 1988. Note, however, that these authors included a question mark in their book title.

17    This absolute approach to examining class voting is relatively insensitive and somewhat problematic in that it fails to take into account the changing popularity of the various parties over time and the effect that might have on voters of all classes. We need always therefore to compare support of various classes when studying class voting. What the absolute class voting approach does offer, however, is a direct way of examining Rokkan's model.

18    The anonymized election surveys used in this chapter were drawn from the Norwegian Social Science Data Services, Danish Data Archives in Odense (DDA) (the Danish Election surveys) and the Swedish Social Science Data Service in Gothenburg (SSD) (the Swedish Election Surveys). The Norwegian Election Surveys were sourced from NSD. Neither NSD, DDA nor SSD are responsible for our present analyses and interpretation of the data .

19    These parties are the liberal, Christian and (apart from Denmark) agrarian parties and two smaller parties in Denmark.

20    The rightist parties include the Conservatives and Radical Right. In Denmark the Agrarian Liberals are also included as they belong more to the right than the centre.

21    Party choice is a nominal level variable and strictly it is wrong to use the notion "explained variance". The analyses of value orientations and party choice were performed by multinominal logistic regression and the measure for explained variance is a pseudo measure, called Nagelkerke's pseudo R2.

22    The data in this section is taken from Sivesind et al (2002). For a description of different size measures, see this main publication from the Norwegian part of the Johns Hopkins Comparative Nonprofit Sector Project (CNP) in which more than 40 countries take part. Sweden and Finland are included, but not Denmark and Island.

23    In the following that means Austria, Finland, France, Germany, Ireland, Netherlands, and UK, which are the seven EU countries in the Johns Hopkins Comparative Nonprofit Sector Project (CNP) that include religion in their 1995 figures. See Salamon et al. (1999).

24    Concerning organizational development there only exists good data from Nor-

way. However, we believe that many of the same trends are also found in the other Scandinavian countries. This section and the rest of the chapter are largely based on Tranvik and Selle (2003, 2004).

25   The "segmented state" (see Egeberg, Olsen and Sætren 1978) is in many ways a consequence of the aforementioned "corporate pluralism", i.e. the strong integration of different societal actors within different areas of public policy.

26   Increased fragmentation implies that the traditional segmentation of the voluntary sector is weakened.

27   The connection between financial integration and other forms of integration may be weakened in NPM – an emerging system that highlights "contracting", while at the same time these financial instruments are undergoing deep change. There is, for instance, a move away from more or less "free" basic grants where public authorities lay down few restrictions on how organizations spend the money towards project support where the control and implications for the organizations are much more profound (for an extensive discussion of this change, see Eikaas and Selle 2002).

28   However, we still see extensive organizational influence in certain fields even within the NPM system, particularly in foreign aid (Tvedt 2003).

29   However, many of the strictly local associations can survive with very little financial support even from their own members and are not really dependent on governmental support to survive.

30   I would like to thank, in particular, Harald Berntsen, Arvid Fennefoss, Geir Høgsnes, Ove K. Pedersen, Torger Aarvaag Stokke, Reidar Webster and Per Ola Öberg for their advice.

31   Later works within the same tradition are presented and discussed in Williamson (1989).

32   For the Norwegian case I also used a third category, *internal corporatism* where either individual posts or entire departments are "taken over" by sector professions who are ideologically close to and have regular contacts with their respective organizations. Being without comparative data from the other Scandinavian countries, I disregard this kind of corporatism here (Nordby 1994).

33   The current organization resulted from a merger of the Swedish Employers Association (Svenska Arbetsgivareföreningen) with the Swedish National Federation of Industry (Sveriges Industriförbund) in the late 1990s.

34   Any attempts to increase voters' influence on the composition of the party lists at national elections have failed in Norway. For example, May 26, 2003, the majority of the Norwegian parliament (Storting) rejected a proposal to introduce personal votes in national elections. In local and regional elections, however, this option is available (Narud and Strøm, 2004).

35   Interestingly, the importance of regional ties becomes evident when MPs' roll-call behaviour is analyzed. For most purposes, in the Nordic parliaments, the party leadership demands loyalty to the party line. On issues reflecting strong local interests,

however, the building of local or regional alliances across party lines is normally accepted (see, e.g., Bjurulf and Glans 1976).

36    Observe that the distinctions made here are not identical to the ones discussed on page 118 in reference to Esaiasson (2000).

37    The Lagting serves as a kind of upper house. On it sits one-quarter of the members of the Storting. The remaining three-quarters constitute the lower house (the Odelsting). Bills must be presented in the Odelsting first, but the consent of both "houses" is needed before a bill becomes law. Neither the Odelsting nor the Lagting have their own committee system; each standing committee has members from both. The state budget is decided by the Storting as a unicameral assembly.

38    Larger nations typically have larger legislatures. Empirical evidence suggests that the size of unicameral legislatures or the popularly elected chamber of bicameral systems tends not to stray too far from the cube root of the population. This rule fits the Danish, Norwegian, Finnish and Icelandic legislatures quite well. The Swedish Riksdag does, however, have some 140 seats more than the population cube root indicates (see Taagepera and Shugart 1989:173–83).

39    This is the case in most bicameral systems. Still, upper chambers may influence government formation and duration indirectly (see Druckman and Thies 2002), but potential effects of this kind are disregarded here.

40    Or, more precisely, the government must be tolerated by an absolute majority in the legislative assembly.

41    The last instance of a president exerting strong influence over government formation was in 1987, when president Mauno Koivisto intervened (Raunio 2004:136).

42    See Strøm (1986, 1990) for a detailed elaboration and test of this hypothesis.

43    Damgaard (1994:86) writes: "At least it is now obvious to competent observers that the parliaments of Scandinavia have not declined in recent decades. On the contrary, they have assumed increased significance."

44    A new law on local government in Norway even opened for local parliamentary democracy as an alternative to the traditional alderman model (a model in which the municipal council elects an executive committee according to proportional representation) which had prevailed earlier and which did not permit a vote of no confidence. A form of local parliamentary government had been in practice in Oslo on a trial basis since 1986 (cf. Baldersheim 1992), but by 2002 this alternative had been adopted by only one other municipality. A few other municipalities voted to change over to a parliamentary form of local government following the 2003 local elections.

45    Such partnerships, both with private and third sector actors, are not entirely new (cf. Eikås and Selle 2001). What is new is the degree of interest in exploiting such arrangements in a variety of additional areas where they are now considered feasible.

46  This chapter builds on research and reports produced jointly with Siv Sandberg, Krister Ståhlberg and Morten Øgård in connection with the project "Norden in the Europe of Regions" 1995–2001. Cf. Baldersheim, Sandberg, Ståhlberg and Øgård 2001.

47  Adapted from Baldershcim & Ståhlberg 1999. Note that the number of communes deviates slightly from those in table 10.1 in chapter 10 due to different base years.

48  Denmark: Amtsrådets økonomiudvalg; Finland: Landskapsförbundens styrelse and Ålands Landskapsstyrelse; Norway: Fylkeskommunenes fylkesutvalg; Sweden: Landstingens styrelser and Kommunestyrelserna i landstingsfria kommuner (Gotland, Göteborg, Malmö). The survey included the largest city of each region. Data collection took place in late 1997 and early 1998. A total of 1,258 questionnaires were returned, 706 from the regions and 552 from the cities. Responses from cities are not included here.

49  http://www.um.dk/udenrigspolitik/irak/vedtagelse.asp

50  *Security in a Changing World: Guidelines for Finland's Security Policy*, Report by the Council of State to the Parliament, 6 June 1995, pp. 56–57.

51  Regeringen/ Den svenske Utenriksdeklarasjonen 2002, http://www.utrikes.regeringen.se/fragor/utrikespolitik/sakret/index.htm

52  "The Alliance's Strategic Concept", press release NAC S(99)65, 24 April 1999, paragraph 48. http://www.nato.int/docu/pr/1999/p99-065e.htm

53  The facts are taken from "Norwegian Contributions to the War against Terrorism" (as of November 2003), published by the Royal Norwegian Ministry of Foreign Affairs.

54  http://odin.dep.no/fd/norsk/aktuelt/nyheter/010001-990083/index-dokooo-b-n-a.html

55  Details on EU debates and national political processes can be found in, e.g., Nelson 1993:41–63; Arter 1999:316–341.

56  I conducted in-depth interviews with a state secretary who was also one of Sweden's chief negotiators with the EU; the Europe Correspondent's assistant; a Middle East expert; the leader of the European Integration Section; a diplomat in charge of Baltic affairs and enlargement; the person in charge of policy coordination between the MFA and other ministries; the person in charge of flexible integration; and the head of the MFA long-term planning unit section. The interviews were conducted in May 1997, and are available as annotated notes. The interviewees remain anonymous.

# Bibliography

Aberbach, Joel D. and Tom Christensen (2001), Radical reform in New Zealand: crisis, windows of opportunities, and rational actors. *Public Administration* 79 (2): 404–422.

Agence Europe (1997), daily news bulletin from Brussels.

Albæk, Erik, Lawrence Rose, Lars Strömberg and Krister Ståhlberg (1996), *Nordic Local Government: Developmental Trends and Reform Activities in the Postwar Period*. Helsinki: The Association of Finnish Local Authorities.

Allardt, Erik et al. (eds) (1981), *Nordic Democracy*. Copenhagen: Det Danske Selskap.

Amin, Ash and Nigel Thrift (1994), *Globalization, Institutions, and Regional Development in Europe*. Oxford: Oxford University Press.

Amoroso, Bruno (1996), Welfare State and Developmental Models, in Bent Greve (ed.) *Comparative Welfare Systems. The Scandinavian Model in a Period of Change*. London: MacMillan Press Ltd.

Andersen, Jørgen Gaul, Per Arnt Pettersen, Stefan Svallfors, and Hannu Uusitalo, (1999), The legitimacy of the Nordic welfare states: trends, variations and cleavages, in Kautto Mikko, Matti Heikkila, Bjørn Hvinden, Staffan Marklund and Niels Ploug, *Nordic Social Policy. Changing welfare states*. London: Routledge.

Arter, David (1999), *Scandinavian Politics Today*. Manchester: Manchester University Press.

Arter, David (2000), Small State Influence Within the EU: The Case of Finland's 'Northern Dimension Initiative', *Journal of Common Market Studies* vol. 38, no. 5: 677–97.

Arter, David (2003), From the 'Rainbow Coalition' Back Down to 'Red Earth'? The 2003 Finnish General Election, *West European Politics* (26), 3:162.

Asheim, Bjørn Terje and Åge Mariussen (eds) (2003), *Innovations, Regions and Projects*. Stockholm: Nordregion. Report 2003:3.

Baldersheim, Harald and Krister Ståhlberg (1998), Perspektiv på regioner i Norden. Åbo: Åbo Akadmi.

Baldersheim, Harald and Krister Ståhlberg (eds) (1994), Towards the Self-regulating Municipality: Free Communes and Administrative Modernization in Scandinavia. Aldershot: Ashgate.

Baldersheim, Harald and Krister Ståhlberg (eds) (1999), Nordic Region-Building in a European Perspective. Aldershot: Ashgate.

Baldersheim, Harald and Per Stava (1993), Reforming Local Government Policy-making and Management through Organizational Learning and Experimentation, Policy Studies Journal 21:104–14.

Baldersheim, Harald (1992), Aldermen into Ministers: Oslo's Experiment with a City Cabinet, Local Government Studies 18:18–30.

Baldersheim, Harald, Siv Sandberg, Krister Ståhlberg and Morten Øgård (2001), Norden i regionernas Europa. Copenhagen: Nord 2001:18.

Barth, Erling, Kalle Moene and Michael Wallerstein (2003), Likhet under press. Utfordringer for den skandinaviske fordelingsmodellen. Oslo: Gyldendal.

Bennett, Robert J. (1993), Local Government in the New Europe. London: Belhaven Press.

Berglund, Sten and Pertti Pesonen, with Gylfi Gislason (1981), Political Party Systems, in Erik Allard et al. (eds), Nordic Democracy. Copenhagen: Det Danske Selskap.

Berglund, Sten and Ulf Lindstrøm (1978), The Scandinavian Party System(s): A Comparative Study. Lund: Studentlitteratur.

Bergman, Torbjörn (2004), Sweden: Democratic Reforms and Partisan Decline in an Emerging Separation-of-Powers System, Scandinavian Political Studies 27:203–225.

Bergmann, Torbjörn and Erik Damgaard (eds) (2000), Delegation and Accountability in European Integration. The Nordic Parliamentary Democracies and the European Union, Special Issue of The Journal of Legislative Studies 6:1.

Bergquist, (1970), Sverige och EEC. En statsvetenskaplig studie av fyre åstiktsriktingars syn på svensk marknadspolitik 1961–1962. Stockholm: Norstedets och søners forlag.

Bergqvist, Christina, Anette Borchorst, Ann-Dorte Christensen, Viveka Ramstedt-Silén, Nina C. Raaum and Audur Styrkársdóttir (eds) (1999), Equal Democracies? Gender and politics in the Nordic countries. Oslo: Scandinavian University Press.

Berven, Nina and Per Selle (eds) (2001), Svekket kvinnemakt? De frivillige organisasjonene og velferdsstaten. Oslo: Gyldendal Akademisk.

Best, Heinrich and Maurizio Cotta (eds) (2000), Parliamentary Representatives in Europe 1848–2000. Oxford: Oxford University Press.

Bjarnar, Ove (2001) Sanitetskvinnen 'lot allting skje i stillhet' – var det riktig?, in Nina Berven and Per Selle (eds) (2001), Svekket kvinnemakt? De frivillige organisasjonene og velferdsstaten. Oslo: Gyldendal Akademisk.

Bjørklund, Tor (2002), The Steadily Declining Voter Turnout in Norwegian Local Elections, 1963–1999, Acta Politica 37: 380–399.

Bjurulf, Bo and Ingemar Glans (1976), Från Tvåblocksystem till Fraktionalisering. Partigruppers och Ledamöters Röstning i Norska Stortinget 1969–1974, Statsvetenskaplig Tidsskrift 79:231–253.

Blom, Ida (red) (1992), Renessanse, reformasjon, revolusjon: fra ca. 1500 til i dag. Cappelens kvinnehistorie, bind 2, Oslo: J. W. Cappelens forlag as.

Bogason, Peter (1990/91), Danish Local Government: Towards an Effective and Efficient Welfare State, in Hesse, Joachim Jens (ed.), Local Government and Urban Affairs in International Perspective: Analyses of Twenty Western Industrialised Countries. Baden-Baden: Nomos.

Borchorst, Anette (1999), Equal status institutions, in Christina Bergqvist et al. (1999) (eds), Equal Democracies? Gender and politics in the Nordic countries. Oslo: Scandinavian University Press.

Borchorst, Anette, Ann-Dorte Christensen and Nina C. Raaum (1999), Equal democracies? Conclusions and perspectives, in Christina Bergqvist et al. (1999) (eds), Equal Democracies? Gender and politics in the Nordic countries. Oslo: Scandinavian University Press.

Borre, Ole and Jørgen Goul Andersen (1997), Voting and political attitudes in Denmark. Århus: Aarhus University Press.

Borre, Ole (2003), To konfliktdimensjoner, in Ole Borre and Jørgen Goul Andersen (eds), Politisk forandring. Verdipolitikk og nye skillelinjer ved folketingsvalget 2001. Århus: Systime Academic.

Boston, Jonathan, John Martin, June Pallot and Pat Walsh (1996), Public Management: The New Zealand Model. Auckland: Oxford University Press.

Braczyk, Hans-Joachim, Philip Cooke and Martin Heidenreich (eds.) (1998), Regional Innovation Systems. The Role of Governance in a Globalized World. London: UCL Press.

Briggs, Asa. (1961), The Welfare State in Historical Perspective, Archives Européennes de Sociologie vol. 2:221–258.

Brunsson, Nils (1989), The Organization of Hypocrisy. Talk, Decisions and Actions in Organizations. Chichester: Wiley.

Bäck, Henry, Gunnar Gjelstrup, Marit Helgesen, Folke Johansson and Jan Erling Klausen (2004), Urban Political Decentralisation: Six Scandinavian Cities. Leverkusen: Verlag Leske + Budrich.

Castles, Francis G. (2002), Developing new measures of welfare state change and reform, *European Journal of Political Research* vol. 41:613–641.

Castles, Francis G. (ed.) (1993), Families of Nations: Patterns of Public Policy in Western Democracies. Aldershot: Dartmouth.

Childs, Marquis W. (1980), *Sweden. The Middle Way on Trial*. New Haven: Yale University Press.

Childs, Marquis W. (1936), *Sweden. The Middle Way*. London: Faber & Faber.

Christensen, Ann-Dorte (1997), De politisk-kulturelle betydninger af køn, in Ann-Dorte Christensen, Ann-Birthe Ravn and Iris Rittenhofer (eds), *Det kønnede samfund*. Aalborg: Aalborg Universitetsforlag.

Christensen, Ann-Dorte (1999), Women in political parties, in Christina Bergqvist et al. (1999) (eds), *Equal Democracies? Gender and politics in the Nordic countries*. Oslo: Scandinavian University Press.

Christensen, Ann-Dorte and Nina C. Raaum (1999), Models of political mobilisation, in Christina Bergqvist et al. (1999) (eds), *Equal Democracies? Gender and politics in the Nordic countries*. Oslo: Scandinavian University Press.

Christensen, Tom and Per Lægreid (2001a), A Transformative Perspective on Administrative Reforms, in Tom Christensen and Per Lægreid (eds), *New Public Management. The Transformation of Ideas and Practice*. Aldershot: Ashgate.

Christensen, Tom and Per Lægreid (2001b), New Public Management – Undermining Political Control? in Tom Christensen and Per Lægreid (eds), *New Public Management. The Transformation of Ideas and Practice*. Aldershot: Ashgate.

Christensen, Tom and Per Lægreid (2002a), *Reformer og lederskap. Omstillinger i den utøvende makt*. Scandinavian University Press, Oslo.

Christensen, Tom and Per Lægreid (2002b), New Public Management: Puzzles of Democracy and the Influence of Citizens, *The Journal of Political Philosophy* vol. 10, no 3 (September): 267–295.

Christensen, Tom and Per Lægreid (2003), Coping with Complex Leadership Roles: The Problematic Redefinition of Government-Owned Enterprises, *Public Administration* vol. 81, no 4:803–831.

Christensen, Tom and Per Lægreid (eds.) (2001), *New Public Management: The Transformation of Ideas and Practice*. Aldershot: Ashgate.

Christensen, Tom (2003), Narratives of Norwegian Governance: Elaborating the Strong State Tradition, *Public Administration* vol. 81, no 1:163–190.

Christensen, Tom, Per Lægreid and Lois R. Wise (2002), Transforming Administrative Policy, *Public Administration*, vol. 80, no 1:153–178.

Clarke, Susan and Gary Gaile (1998), *The Work of Cities*. Minnesota University Press.

Crombez, Christophe (1996), Minority Governments, Minimal Winning Coalitions and Surplus Majorities in Parliamentary Systems, *European Journal of Political Research* 29:1–29.

Dalton, Russell J, Scott C. Flanagan and Paul Allen Beck (1984), Political forces and partisan change, in Russell J. Dalton, Scott C. Flanagan and Paul Allen Beck (eds), *Electoral Change in Advanced Industrial Democracies*. Princeton, N.J.: Princeton University Press.

Damgaard, Erik (1994), The Strong Parliaments of Scandinavia: Continuity and Change of Scandinavian Parliaments, in Gary W. Copeland and Samuel C. Patterson (eds), *Parliaments in the Modern World. Changing Institutions*. Ann Arbor: The University of Michigan Press.

Damgaard, Erik (2000), Parliament and Government, in Peter Esaiasson and Knut Heidar (eds), *Beyond Westminster and Congress. The Nordic Government*. Columbus: Ohio State University Press.

Damgaard, Erik (2004), Developments in Danish Parliamentary Democracy: Accountability, Parties and External Constraints, *Scandinavian Political Studies* 27:115–131.

Damgaard, Erik (ed.) (1990), *Parlamentarisk forandring i Norden*. Oslo: Universitetsforlaget.

Dekker, Paul and van den Broek, A. (1998), Civil Society in Comparative Perspective: Involvement in Voluntary Associations in North America and Western Europe. *Voluntas* 9:11–38.

Döring, Herbert (1995), Time as a Scarce Resource: Government Control of the Agenda, in Herbert Döring (ed.), *Parliaments and Majority Rule in Western Europe*. Frankfurt/New York: Campus Verlag/St. Martin's Press.

Downs, Anthony (1957), *An Economic Theory of Democracy*. New York: Harper.

Druckman, James N. and Michael F. Thies (2002), The Importance of Concurrence: The Impact of Bicameralism on Government Formation and Duration, *American Journal of Political Science* 46:760–771.

Dryzek, John S., David Downes, Christian Hunold and David Schlosberg (with Hans Kristian Hernes) (2003), *Green States and Social Movements: Environmentalism in the United States, United Kingdom, Germany, and Norway*. Oxford: Oxford University Press.

Dunleavy, Patrick (1997). Globalization of Public Service Production: Can Government be Best in the World? in Andrew Massey (ed.), *Globalization and Marketization of Government Services. Comparing Contemporary Public Sector Developments*. London: Macmillan Press.

Dunn, Delmer D. (1997), *Politics and Administration at the Top: Lessons from Down Under*. Pittsburgh, Pennsylvania: University of Pittsburgh Press.

Ebbinghaus, Bernhard and Jelle Visser (1999), When institutions matter. Union growth and decline in Western Europe, 1950–1995, *European Sociological Review* 15:135–158.

Eckstein, Harry (1966), *Division and Cohesion in Democracy: A Study of Norway.* Princeton: Princeton University Press.

Egeberg, Morten (2003), How Bureaucratic Structure Matters: An Organizational Perspective, in B. Guy Peters and Jon Pierre (eds), *Handbook of Public Administration.* London: Sage.

Egeberg, Morten, Johan P. Olsen and Harald Sætren (1978), Den segmenterte stat, in Johan P. Olsen (ed), *Politisk organisering.* Oslo: Universitetsforlaget.

Eijersbo, Niels (2000), Ændrede vilkår for politikerne i regionerne, in Mydske, Per Kristen and Per Gunnar Disch (eds), *Fem innlegg om regionkommunen og regionpolitikere i Skandinavia.* Oslo: Dept. of Political Science, University of Oslo. Report 4/2000.

Eikaas, Magne and Per Selle (2002), A Contract Culture even in Scandinavia, in Ugo Ascoli and Constanzo Ranci (eds), *Dilemmas of the Welfare Mix. The New Structure of Welfare in an Era of Privatization.* New York: Kluwer Academic/Plenum Publishers.

Eikås, Magne and Per Selle (2001), New Public Management and the Breakthrough of a Contract Culture at the Local Level in Norway, in Anne Lise Fimreite, Helge O. Larsen and Jacob Aars (eds), *Lekmannstyre under press.* Oslo: Kommuneforlaget.

Ekengren, Magnus and Bengt Sundelius (1998), The State joins the EU, in Ben Soetendorp and Hanf, Kenneth (eds), *Adapting to European Integration: Small States and the European Union.* Harlow: Addison, Wesley, Longman.

Ekengren, Magnus (2002), *The Time of European Governance.* Manchester: Manchester University Press.

Elder, Neil, Alastair H. Thomas and David Arter (1988), *The Consensual Democracies? The Government and Politics of the Scandinavian States.* Revised edition 1988. Oxford: Martin Robertson.

Elklit, Jørgen (1984), Det klassiske danske partisystem bliver til, in Jørgen Elklit and Ole Tonsgaard (eds), *Valg og vælgeradfærd. Studier i dansk politik.* Århus: Politica.

Elvander, Nils (2002), The Labour Market Regimes in the Nordic Countries: A Comparative Analysis, *Scandinavian Political Studies* vol. 25, No. 2:117–38.

Enzensberger, Hans Magnus (1987), *Akk, Europa! Inntrykk fra syv land med en epilog fra 2006.* Oslo: Universitetsforlaget. (Originally published as *Ach Europa!*, Frankfurt am Main: Suhrkamp.)

Eriksen, Knut E. (1981), Norge i det vestlige samarbeidet, in Trond Berg and Helge Pharo (eds), *Vekst og velstand*. Oslo. Universitetsforlaget.

Erikson, Robert and John H. Goldthorpe (1992), *The constant flux. A study of class mobility in industrial societies*. Oxford: Clarendon Press.

Ervik, Rune and Stein Kuhnle (1996), The Nordic Welfare Model and the European Union, in Bent Greve (ed.), *Comparative Welfare Systems. The Scandinavian Model in a Period of Change*. Houndmills: MacMillan Press.

Esaiasson, Peter and Sören Holmberg (1996), *Representation from Above*. Aldershot: Dartmouth.

Esaiasson, Peter (2000), How Members of Parliament Define their Task, in Peter Esaiasson and Knut Heidar (eds), *Beyond Westminister and Congress: The Nordic Experience*. Columbus: Ohio State University Press.

Esaiasson, Peter and Knut Heidar (eds) (2000), *Beyond Westminster and Congress. The Nordic Experience*. Columbus: Ohio State University Press.

Esping-Andersen, Gösta (1985), *Politics Against Markets. The Social Democratic Road to power*. Princeton: Princeton University Press.

Esping-Andersen, Gösta (1990), *The Three Worlds of Welfare Capitalism*. Cambridge: Polity Press.

Eulau, Heinz, John Wahlke, William Buchanan and LeRoy C. Ferguson (1959), The Role of the Representative: Some Empirical Observations on the Theory of Edmund Burke, *American Political Science Review* 53:742–56.

European Competitiveness Index (2004), *Measuring the Performance and Capacity of Europe's Nations and Regions*. Pontypridd, Wales: Robert Huggins Associates.

*European Journal of Political Research* (Data Yearbooks), successive volumes.

Fearon, James D. (1999), Electoral Accountability and the Control of Politicians: Selecting Good Types versus Sanctioning Poor Performance, in Adam Przeworski, Susan C. Stokes and Bernard Manin (eds), *Democracy, Accountability and Representation*. Cambridge: Cambridge University Press.

Flanagan, Scott C. (1987), Value change in industrial societies, *American Political Science Review* 81: 1289–1319.

Flora, Peter and Arnold J. Heidenheimer (1981), The Historical Core and Changing Boundaries of the Welfare State, in Peter Flora and Arnold J. Heidenheimer (eds), *The Development of Welfare States in Europe and America*. New Brunswick: Transaction Books.

Flora, Peter and Jens Alber (1981), Modernization, Democratization, and the Development of Welfare States in Western Europe, in Peter Flora and Arnold J. Heidenheimer (eds), *The Development of Welfare States in Europe and America*. New Brunswick: Transaction Books.

Flora, Peter (1986): Introduction, in Peter Flora (ed.), *Growth to Limits. The Western European Welfare States Since World War II.* Vol. 1. Berlin: Walter de Gruyter.

Flora, Peter (ed.) (1986), *Growth to Limits: The Western European Welfare States Since World War II. Vol. 1: Sweden, Norway, Finland, Denmark.* Berlin: Walter de Gruyter.

Foss Hansen, Hanne (1999), Den historiske arven – Danmark, in Per Lægreid and Ove Kaj Pedersen (eds), *Fra opbygning til ombygning av staten. Organisationsforandringer i tre nordiske lande.* Copenhagen: Jurist- og Økonomforbundets forlag.

Franklin, Mark N., Thomas T. Mackie, Henry Valen et al. (1992), *Electoral Change: Responses to Evolving Social and Attitudinal Structures in Western Countries.* Cambridge: Cambridge University Press.

Fritz W. Scharpf, Philippe C. Schmitter and Wolfgang S. Streck (eds), *Governance in the European Union.* London: Sage.

Gallagher, Michael and Michael Marsh (eds) (1988), *Candidate Selection in Comparative Perspective. The Secret Garden of Politics.* London: Sage.

Goldsmith, Michael and Kurt Klaudi Klaussen (eds) (1997), *Europeanisation of Local Government.* London: Frank Cass.

Goodin, Robert E., Bruce Headey, Ruud Muffels, and Henrik-Jan Dirven (1999), *The Real Worlds of Welfare Capitalism.* Cambridge: Cambridge University Press.

Græger, Nina (2003), Norway and the EU's Defence Dimension. A 'Troops for Influence' Strategy, in Nina Græger, Henrik Larsen and Hanna Ojanen (eds), *The ESDP and the Nordic Countries: Four Variations on a Theme.* Finnish Institute of International Affairs, Helsinki.

Graubard, Stephen R. (ed.) (1986), *Norden – The Passion for Equality.* Oslo: Norwegian University Press.

Green-Pedersen, Christoffer (2002), Minority Governments and Party Politics: The Political and Institutional Background to the 'Danish Miracle', *Journal of Public Policy* 21:63–80.

Grendstad, Gunnar, Øystein Bortne, Per Selle, and Kristin Strømsnes (2004), *Anomalous Environmentalism.* New York: Kluwer Academic/Plenum Publishers.

Grofman, Bernard and Arend Lijphart (2002), *The Evolution of Electoral and Party Systems in the Nordic Countries.* New York: Agathon Press.

Grønlie, Tore (1991), Velferdskommunen, in Anne-Hilde Nagel (ed.), *Velferdskommunen: Kommunenes rolle i utviklingen av velferdsstaten.* Bergen: Alma Mater Forlag.

Gustafsson, Bjørn, Rolf Aaberge, Ådne Cappelen, Peder J. Pedersen, Nina Smith and Hannu Uusitalo (1999), The distribution of income in the Nordic countries. Changes and causes, in Mikko Kautto, Matti Heikkila, Bjørn

Hvinden, Staffan Marklund and Niels Ploug, Nordic Social Policy. Changing welfare states. London: Routledge.

Gustafsson, Gunnel (1990/91), Swedish Local Government: Reconsidering Rationality and Consensus, in Joachim Jens Hesse (ed.), Local Government and Urban Affairs in International Perspective: Analyses of Twenty Western Industrialised Countries. Baden-Baden: Nomos.

Hagen, Kåre (1999), Towards a Europeanisation of social policies? A Scandinavian perspective, in Denis Bouget and Bruno Palier (eds), Comparing Social Welfare Systems in Nordic Europe and France. Paris: Mire.

Halman, Loek and Ruud de Moor (1994), Religion, churches and moral values, in Peter Ester, Loek Halmann and Ruud de Moor (eds), The individualizing society. Value change in Europe and North America. Tilburg: Tilburg University Press.

Hansen, Tore (1990/91), Norwegian Local Government: Stability Through Change, in Joachim Jens Hesse (ed.), Local Government and Urban Affairs in International Perspective: Analyses of Twenty Western Industrialised Countries. Baden-Baden: Nomos.

Hardarson, Ólafur Th. (2002), The Icelandic Electoral System 1844–1999, in A. Lijphart and B. Grofman (eds), The Evolution of Electoral and Party Systems in the Nordic Countries. New York: Agathon Press, pp. 101–166.

Harvie, Christopher (1994), The Rise of Regional Europe. London: Routledge.

Hatland, Aksel (1992), Til dem som trenger det mest? Økonomisk behovsprøving i norsk sosialpolitikk. Oslo: Universitetsforlaget.

Hatland, Aksel (1999), The changing balance between incentives and economic security in the Nordic unemployment benefit schemes. Oslo: NOVA Skriftserie 2/1999.

Heclo, Hugh (1981), Towards a New Welfare state? in Flora, Peter and Arnold J. Heidenheimer (eds), The Development of Welfare States in Europe and America. New Brunswick: Transaction Books.

Heidar, Knut (1993), Programmatic renewal in the Norwegian Labour Party: En attendant l'Europe, West European Politics 1:62–77.

Heidar, Knut and Einar Berntzen (1998), Vesteuropeisk politikk. Partier, regjeringsmakt, styreform, 3rd ed. Oslo: Universitetsforlaget.

Heidar, Knut, Erik Damgaard, Peter Esaiasson, Olafur Th. Hardarson and Tapio Raunio (2000), Five Most Similar Systems, in Peter Esaiasson and Knut Heidar (eds), Beyond Westminster and Congress: The Nordic Experience. Columbus, Ohio: Ohio State University Press.

Helander, Voitto and Karl H. Sivesind (2001), Frivilligsektorens betydelse i Norden, in Skov Henriksen, Lars and Bjarne Ibsen (eds), Frivillighedens udfordringer. Odense: Odense Universitetsforlag, pp. 49–66.

Held, David (1996), *Models of Democracy*. Cambridge: Polity Press.

Herman, Valentine and John Popc (1973), Minority Governments in Western Democracies, *British Journal of Political Science* 3:191–212.

Hermansson, Jørgen, Anna Lund, Torsten Svenson and Per Ola Öberg (1999), Avkorporativisering och lobbyism – konturerna till en ny politisk modell. Demokratiutredningens forskarvolym XIII. *Statens offentliga utredningar*. SOU: 121.

Hernes, Gudmund and Willy Martinussen (1980), *Demokrati og politiske ressurser*. Norges Offentlige Utredninger 1980:7.

Hernes, Helga M. (1987), *Welfare State and Woman Power: Essays in State Feminsm*. Oslo: Norwegian University Press.

Hesse, Joachim Jens and L.J. Sharpe (1990/91), Local Government in International Perspective: Some Comparative Observations, in Joachim Jens Hesse (ed.), *Local Government and Urban Affairs in International Perspective: Analyses of Twenty Western Industrialised Countries*. Baden-Baden: Nomos.

Heurlin, Bertel (2004), *Riget, magten og militæret*. Aarhus: Aarhus universitetsforlag.

*Historisk Statistikk 1994* (1995). Oslo: Statistics Norway.

Høgsnes, Geir and Frode Longva (2001), Decentralized Wage Bargaining: A Threat to Incomes Policy Goals or an Instrument of Flexibility, in Henry Milner and Eskil Wadensjö (eds), *Gösta Rehn, the Swedish Model and Labour Market Policies. International and National Perspectives*. Aldershot: Ashgate Publishing Limited, pp. 146–167.

Holmberg, Sören and Henrik Oscarsson (2004), Svensk Väljarbeteende, in *Allmänna Valen 2002. Del 4 Specialundersökningar*. Stockholm: SCB, pp. 132–210.

Hood, Christopher (1991), A Public Management for All Seasons? *Public Administration* vol. *69* (Spring):3–19.

Hood, Christopher (1996), Exploring Variations in Public Management Reform of the 1980s, in A. J. G. M. Bekke, James L. Perry and Theo A. J. Toonen (eds), *Civil Service Systems*. Bloomington: Indiana University Press.

Huber, Evelyne and John D. Stephens (2000), Partisan Governance, Women's employment, and the Social Democratic Service State, *American Sociological Review* vol. *65*, June:323–342.

Huntford, Roland (1971), *The New Totalitarians*. London: Allan Lane.

Ingebritsen, Christine (1998), *The Nordic States and European Unity*, Ithaca: Cornell University Press.

Inglehart, Ronald (1977), *The Silent Revolution – Changing Values and Political Styles among Western Publics*. Princeton, N.J.: Princeton University Press.

Inglehart, Ronald (1990), *Cultural Shift in Advanced Industrial Society*. Princeton, N.J.: Princeton University Press.

IPU (2004): Interparliamentary Union, Women in National Parliaments. http://www.ipu.org/wmn-e/classif-arc.htm (30 April 2004).

Janson, Florence E. (1928), Minority Governments in Sweden, *American Political Science Review* 22:407–413.

Jensen, Torben (2000), Party Cohesion, in Peter Esaiasson and Knut Heidar (eds) (2000), *Beyond Westminister and Congress: The Nordic Experience*. Columbus: Ohio State University Press.

Jenssen, Anders Todal, Pertti Personen and Mikael Gilljam (1998), *To Join or Not to Join: Three Nordic Referendums on Membership in the European Union*. Oslo: Scandinavian University Press.

Jenssen, Anders Todal, Pertti Pesonen and Mikael Gilljam (1998), To Join or Not to Join, in Anders Todal Jenssen, Pertti Pesonen and Mikael Gilljam, *To join or Not to Join: Three Nordic Referendums on Membership in the European Union*. Scandinavian University Press.

Jerneck, Magnus and Mats Sjölin (2000), Regionalisering och flernivåpolitik – Kalmar och Skåne län, *SOU 2000: 64: Regional försöksverksamhet – tre studier*. Stockholm

Johansson, Jan (1999), *Hur blir man riksdagsledamot? En undersökning av makt och inflytande i partiernas nomineringsprocesser*. Södertälje: Gidlunds förlag.

Jungar, Ann-Cathrine (2002), A Case of a Surplus Majority Government: The Finnish Rainbow Coalition, *Scandinavian Political Studies* 25:57–83.

Kanter, Rosabeth Moss (1977): *Men and Women of the Corporation*. London: Basic Books

Karvonen, Lauri (1994), Christian parties in Scandinavia: Victory over the windmills? in David Hanley (ed), *Christian democracy in Europe: A comparative perspective*. London: Pinter.

Katzenstein, Peter J. (1985), *Small States in World Markets. Industrial Policy in Europe*. London: Cornell University Press.

Kautto, Mikko, Johan Fritzell, Bjørn Hvinden, Jon Kvist and Hannu Uusitalo (eds) (2001), *Nordic Welfare States in the European Context*. London: Routledge.

Kautto, Mikko, Johan Fritzell, Bjørn Hvinden, Jon Kvist and Hannu Uusitalo (2001), Introduction: How distinct are the Nordic welfare states? in Kautto, Mikko, Johan Fritzell, Bjørn Hvinden, Jon Kvist and Hannu Uusitalo (eds), *Nordic Welfare States in the European Context*. London: Routledge.

Kautto, Mikko, Matti Heikkilä, Bjørn Hvinden, Staffan Marklund and Niels Ploug (eds) (1999), *Nordic Social Policy: Changing Welfare States*. London: Routledge.

Keating, Michael and John Loughlin, (eds) (1997), *The Political Economy of Regionalism*. London: Frank Cass.

Keating, Michael. (1988), *State and Regional Nationalism: Territorial Politics and the European State*. London: Harvester-Wheatsheaf.

*Keesing's Record of World Events*, successive years. Harlow: Longman.

Kirby, David (1990), *Northern Europe in the Early Modern Period. The Baltic World 1492-1772*. London: Longman.

Kirby, David (1995), *Northern Europe 1772-1993. Europe's Northern Periphery in an age of Change*. London: Longman.

Kitschelt, Herbert (1994), *The transformation of European social democracy*. Cambridge: Cambridge University Press.

Kitschelt, Herbert (1995), *The Radical Right in Western Europe – A comparative analysis*. Ann Arbor, Mich: University of Michigan Press.

Kjær, Ulrik and Mogens N. Pedersen (2004), *De danske folketingsmedlemmer – en parlamentarisk elite og dens rekruttering, cirkulation og transformation 1849-2001*. Aarhus: Aarhus Universitetsforlag.

Kjellberg, Francesco (1988), Local Government and the Welfare State: Reorganization in Scandinavia, in Bruno Dente and Francesco Kjellberg (eds), *The Dynamics of Institutional Change: Local Government Reorganization in Western Democracies*. London: Sage Publications.

Kjellberg, Francesco (1995), The Changing Values of Local Government, *Annals of the American Academy of Social Sciences* 540:40-50.

Klausen, Kurt Klaudi and Krister Ståhlberg (eds) (1998), *New Public Management i Norden: Nye organisations- og ledelsesformer i den decentrale velfærdsstat*. Odense: Odense Universitetetsforlag.

Klausen, Kurt Klaudi and Per Selle (1996), The third sector in Scandinavia, *Voluntas* 7:99-122.

Knutsen, Oddbjørn and Staffan Kumlin (2003), *Value orientations and party choice in five countries. A comparative study of the impact of values and the location of party voters. Research Report no. 3*. Oslo: Department of Political Science.

Knutsen, Oddbjørn (1990), The materialist/post-materialist value dimension as a party cleavage in the Nordic countries, *West European Politics* 13 (2):258-273.

Knutsen, Oddbjørn (1995), Left–right materialist value orientations, in Jan W. van Deth and Elinor Scarbrough, *The impact of values*. European Science Foundation: Belief in Government, Volume 4. Oxford: Oxford University Press.

Knutsen, Oddbjørn (2001), Social class, sector employment and gender as political cleavages in the Scandinavian countries. A comparative longitudinal study, 1970-95, *Scandinavian Political Studies* 24, 2001:311-350.

Knutsen, Oddbjørn (forthcoming), The impact of sector employment on party choice: A comparative study from eight West European countries, *European Journal of Political Research*.

Koch, Hal and Alf Ross (eds) (1949), *Nordisk Demokrati*. Oslo: Halvorsen and Larsen.

Koenig-Archibugi, Mathias (2004), Explaining Government Preferences for Institutional Change in EU Foreign and Security Policy, *International Organization* 58, Winter:137–174

Kohler-Koch, Beate (ed.) (1998), Interaktive Politik in Europa. Regionen im Netzwerk der Integration. Opladen. Leverkusen: Verlag Leske + Budrich.

Korpi, Walter (1983), *The democratic Class Struggle*. London: Routledge and Kegan Paul

Krasner, Stephen D. (1988), Sovereignty. An Institutional Perspective. *Comparative Political Studies*, 21 (1), April 1988:66–94.

Kristjánsson, Svanur (2004), Iceland: Searching for Democracy along Three Dimensions of Citizen Control, *Scandinavian Political Studies* 27:153–174.

Kuhnle, Stein and Per Selle (1992), The Historical Precedent for Government-Nonprofit Cooperation in Norway, in Benjamin Gidron, Ralph M. Kramer and Lester M. Salamon (eds), *Government and the Third Sector. Emerging Relationships in Welfare States*. San Francisco: Jossey-Bass.

Kuhnle, Stein (1983), *Velferdsstatens utvikling. Norge i komparativt perspektiv*. Oslo: Universitetsforlaget.

Kuhnle, Stein (2000), The Scandinavian Welfare State in the 1990s: Challenged but Viable, in Maurizio Ferrara and Martin Rhodes (eds), *Recasting European Welfare States*. London: Frank Cass.

Kuitunen, Soile (2002), Finland: Formalized Procedures with Member Predominance, in Hanne Marthe Narud, Mogens N. Pedersen and Henry Valen (eds), *Party Sovereignty and Citizen Control. Selecting Candidates for Parliamentary Elections in Denmark, Finland, Iceland and Norway*. Odense: Odense University Press.

Laakso, Markku and Rein Taagepera (1979), Effective Number of Parties: A Measurement with Application to West Europe, *Comparative Political Studies* 12:3–27.

Lægreid, Per (2001), Administrative Reforms in Scandinavia – Testing the Cooperative Model, in Brendan Noel (ed.), *Public Sector Reform: An International Perspective*. Houndsmill: Palgrave.

Lafferty, Willian (1971), *Economic Development and the Response of Labor in Scandinavia. A Multi-Level Analysis*. Oslo: Universitetsforlaget.

Lane, Jan-Erik (1991), Interpretations of the Swedish Model. *West European Politics* 14:1–8.

Lane, Jan-Erik, Tuomo Martikainen, Palle Svensson, Gunnar Vogt and Henry Valen, Scandinavian Exceptionalism Reconsidered, *Journal of Theoretical Politics* 5:195–230.

Laursen, Johnny (1998), Det nordiske samarbejde som særvej? Kontinuitet og brud, 1945–73, in Johan P. Olsen and Bjørn Otto Sverdrup (eds), *Europa i Norden. Europeisering av nordisk samarbeid.* Oslo: Tano Aschehoug.

Laver, Michael and Kenneth A. Shepsle (2000), Ministrables and Government Formation: Munchkins, Players and Big Beasts of the Jungle, *Journal of Theoretical Politics* 12:113–124.

Laver, Michael and Norman Schofield (1990), *Multiparty Government. The Politics of Coalition in Europe.* Oxford: Oxford University Press.

Lidström, Anders (2003), *Kommunsystem i Europa.* Malmö: Liber.

Lijphart, Arend (1971), Comparative Politics and Comparative Method, *American Political Science Review* 65:682–698.

Lijphart, Arend (1994), *Electoral Systems and Party Systems. A Study of Twenty-Seven Democracies, 1945–1990.* Oxford: Oxford University Press.

Lijphart, Arend (1999), *Patterns of Democracy: Government Forms and Performance in Thirty-Six Countries.* New Haven: Yale University Press.

Lindal, Sigurdur (1981), Early Democratic Traditions in the Nordic Countries, in Erik Allard et al. (eds), *Nordic Democracy.* Copenhagen: Det Danske Selskap.

Lindstrøm, Ulf and Lauri Karvonen (1987), Finlands färd, in Ulf Lindstrøm and Lauri Karvonen, (eds), *Finland. En politisk loggbok.* Stockholm: Almquist & Wiksell.

Lipset, Martin S. and Stein Rokkan (1967), *Party Systems and Voter Alignments. Cross-National Perspectives.* NewYork: The Free Press.

Lipset, Seymour M. (1960), *Political Man.* Garden City: Doubleday.

Lipset, Seymour M. and Stein Rokkan (1967), Cleavage Structure, Party Systems, and Voter Alignments: An Introduction, in Seymour M. Lipset and Stein Rokkan (eds), *Party Systems and Voter Alignments.* New York: Free Press.

Longley, Lawrence D. and David M. Olson (eds) (1991), *Two Into One. The Politics and Processes of National Legislative Cameral Change.* Boulder: Westwiew Press.

Lovenduski, Joni and Pippa Norris (1993), *Gender and party politics.* London: Sage Publications.

Lovenduski, Joni and Pippa Norris (2003), Westminster Women: the Politics of Presence, *Political studies* vol. 51:84–102.

Lunden, Kåre (1992), *Norsk grålysning.* Gjøvik: Det norske samlaget.

Lundqvist, Lennart J. (1998), Local-to-Local Partnerships among Swedish Municipalities: Why and How Neighbours Join to Alleviate Resource Constraints, in Jon Pierre (ed.), *Partnerships in Urban Governance: European and American Experience*. London: Macmillan.

Mackie, Thomas and Richard Rose (1991), *The International Almanac of Electoral History*, 3rd ed., Washington D.C: Congressional Quarterly.

Madeley, John T. S. (2003), 'The Swedish Model is Dead! Long Live the Swedish Model' The 2002 Riksdag Election, *West European Politics* 2003 (26), 2:165–173.

Madeley, John T.S. and Zsolt Enyedi (eds) (2003), Church and State in Contemporary Europe. The Chimera of Neutrality, Special Issue of *West European Politics* 26:1.

Malmborg, Mikael af (1994), *Den ståndaktige nationalstaten. Sverige och den västeuropeiske integrationen 1945–59*. Lund: Lund University Press.

March, James G. and Johan P. Olsen (1983), Organizing Political Life. What Administrative Reorganization Tells Us About Government, *American Political Science Review*, 77:281–297.

Marklund, Staffan and Anders Nordlund (1999), Economic problems, welfare convergence and political instability, in Mikko Kautto, Matti Heikkila, Bjørn Hvinden, Staffan Marklund and Niels Ploug, *Nordic Social Policy*. Changing welfare states. London: Routledge.

Marks, Gary, Francois Nielsen, Leonard Ray and Jane Salk (1994), Competencies, Cracks, and Conflicts: Regional Mobilization in the European Union, in Marks, Gary, Fritz W. Scharpf, Philippe C. Schmitter, and Wolfgang Streeck (eds), *Governance in the European Union*. Sage, 1996.

Martin, Lanny and Randolph T. Stevenson (2001), Government Formation in Parliamentary Democracies, *American Journal of Political Science* 45:33–50.

Martins, M.R. (1995), Size of Municipalities, Efficiency, and Citizen Participation: A Cross-European Perspective, *Environment and Planning C: Government and Policy* 13:441–458.

Matland, Richard (1993), Institutional Variables Affecting Female Representation in National Legislature, *Journal of Politics* vol. 55 no. 3:737–755.

Matland, Richard (1998), Women's Representation in National Legislatures: Developed and Developing Countries, *Legislative studies quarterly* 23 (1):109–125.

Matthews, Donald and Henry Valen (1999), *Parliamentary Representation: The Case of the Norwegian Storting*. Columbus: Ohio State University Press.

Mattila, Mikko and Tapio Raunio (2002), Government Formation in the Nordic Countries: The Electoral Connection, *Scandinavian Political Studies* 25:259–280.

Mattson, Ingvar and Kaare Strøm (1995), Parliamentary Committees, in Herbert Döring (ed.), *Parliaments and Majority Rule in Western Europe.* Frankfurt/New York: Campus Verlag/St. Martin's Press.

Meyer, John W. and Brian Rowan (1977), Institutionalized Organizations: Formal Structure as Myth and Ceremon, *American Journal of Sociology* 83 (September):340–363.

Micheletti, Michele (1991), Swedish corporatism at a crossroads: the impact of new politics and new social movements, *Western European Politics* vol. 14. no 3:144–165.

Miles, Lee (1996), *The Nordic States and European Integration.* London: Routledge.

Mjøset, Lars (1992), The Nordic Model Never Existed, But Does it Have a Future? *Scandinavian Studies* vol. 64 – No. 4:652–71.

Mønnesland, Jan (2001), *Kommunale inntektssystemer i Norden.* Oslo: Norsk institutt for by- og regionforskning. NIBRs Pluss-serie 2–2001.

Montin, Stig and Ingemar Elander (1995), Citizenship, Consumerism and Local Government in Sweden, *Scandinavian Political Studies* 18:25–51.

Moore, Barrington (1966), *Social Origins of Dictatorship and Democracy. Lord and Peasant in the Making of the Modern World.* Boston: Beacon Press.

Moses, Jonathan and Anders Todal Jenssen (1995), Nordic Accession: An Analysis of the EU Referendums. Unpublished paper quoted in Christine Ingebritsen, *The Nordic States and European Unity.* Ithaca: Cornell University Press.

Müller, Wolfgang C. and Kaare Strøm (2000), Conclusion: Coalition Governance in Western Europe, in Wolfgang C. Müller and Kaare Strøm (eds), *Coalition Governments in Western Europe.* Oxford: Oxford University Press.

Munk Christiansen, Peter and Asbjørn Sonne Nørgaard (2003), *Faste forhold – flygtige forbindelser. Stat og interesseorganisationer i Danmark i det 20. århundrede. (Magtutredningen).* Århus: Aarhus Universitetsforlag.

Mydske, Per Kristen and Per Gunnar Disch (2000), Regionkommunen i det politiske systemet, in Per Kristen Mydske and Per Gunnar Disch (eds), *Fem innlegg om regionkommunen og regionpolitikere i Skandinavia.* Oslo: Dept. of Political Science, University of Oslo. Report 4/2000.

Nagel, Anne-Hilde (1995), Politiseringen av kjønn. Et historisk perspektiv, in Nina Raaum (ed), *Kjønn og politikk.* Oslo: Tano Forlag.

Nagel, Anne-Hilde (2000), The development of citizenship in Norway: Marshall remodelled, in Sølvi Sogner and Gro Hagemann (eds), *Women's politics and women in politics. In Honour of Ida Blom.* Oslo: J.W. Cappelens forlag as.

Narud, Hanne Marthe and Henry Valen (2000), Does Background Matter? Social Representation and Political Attitudes, in Peter Esaiasson and Knut

Heidar (eds), *Beyond Westminister and Congress: The Nordic Experience*. Columbus: Ohio State University Press.

Narud, Hanne Marthe (2003), Norway: Professionalization – Party-oriented and Constituency-based, in Jens Borchert and Jürgen Zeiss (eds), *The Political Class in Advanced Democracies*. Oxford: Oxford University Press.

Narud, Hanne Marthe, Mogens N. Pedersen and Henry Valen (eds) (2002), *Party Sovereignty and Citizen Control. Selecting Candidates for Parliamentary Elections in Denmark, Finland, Iceland and Norway*. Odense: Odense University Press.

Naschold, Freider (1995), *The Modernisation of the Public Sector in Europe: A Comparative Perspective on the Scandinavian Experience*. Helsinki: Ministry of Labour.

Nelson, Brent F. (1993), *Norway and the EU: The Political Economy of Integration*. Westport, Conn.: Praeger Publishers.

Neumann, Iver B. (2001), *Norge – en kritikk: begrepsmakt i Europadebatten*. Oslo: Pax Forlag.

Nieuwbeerta, Paul (1995), *The democratic class struggle in twenty countries 1945–1990*. Amsterdam: Thesis Publishers.

Nordby, Trond (1994), *Korporatisme på norsk*. Oslo: Universitetsforlaget.

Nordby, Trond (1999), *Samvirket mellom organisasjoner og stat: Norge*. Makt- og demokratiutredningen 1998–2003. Rapportserien nr. 4/1999. Oslo.

Norris Pippa and Joni Lovenduski (1995), *Political Recruitment. Gender, Race and Class in the British Parliament*. Cambridge: Cambridge University Press.

Norris, Pippa (ed.) (1997), *Passages to Power*. Cambridge: Cambridge University Press.

Norton, Alan (1991), Western European Local Government in Comparative Perspective, in Richard Batley and Gerry Stoker (eds), *Local Government in Europe: Trends and Developments*. London: Macmillan.

Norton, Alan (1994), *International Handbook of Local and Regional Government*. Aldershot: Edward Elgar.

NOU (1992), *Kommune- og fylkesinndeling i Norge i forandring*. Oslo: Universitetesforlaget. 1992:15.

NOU (2000), *Om oppgavefordelingen mellom stat, region og kommune*. Oslo: Norges Offentlige Utredninger 2000:22.

NOU (2004), *Modernisert Folketrygd. Bærekraftig pensjon for framtida*. Oslo: Norges Offentlige Utredninger 2004:1.

Ohmae, Kenchi (1990), *The Borderless World*. New York: Harper Collins.

Ojanen, Hanna, Gunilla Herolf and Rutger Lindahl (2000), *Non-Alignment and European Security Policy*. Helsinki: Finnish Institute of International Affairs.

Olsen, Johan P. and B. Guy Peters (eds) (1996), *Lessons from Experience*. Oslo: Scandinavian University Press.

Olsen, Johan P. and Bjørn Otto Sverdrup (eds) (1998), *Europa i Norden. Europeisering av nordisk samarbeid.* Oslo: Tano Aschehoug.

Olsen, Johan P. (1983), *Organized Democracy.* Bergen: Scandinavian University Press.

Olsen, Johan P. (1988), Administrative Reform and Theories of Organization, in Colin Campbell and B. Guy Peters (eds), *Organizing Governance: Governing Organizations.* Pittsburgh: University of Pittsburgh Press.

Olsen, Johan P., Paul G. Roness and Harald Sætren (1982), Norway: Still Peaceful Coexistence and Revolution in Slow Motion, in Jeremy Richardson (ed.), *Policy Styles in Western Europe.* London: Allen and Unwin.

Olson, Olov and Kerstin Sahlin-Andersson (1998), Accounting transformation in an advanced welfare state: the case of Sweden, in Olov Olson, James Guthrie and Christopher Humphrey (eds), *Global Warning! Debating International Developments in the New Public Financial Management.* Oslo: Cappelen Akademisk Forlag.

Olson, Sven (1986), Sweden, in Peter Flora (ed.), *Growth to Limits. The Western European Welfare States Since World War II.* Vol. 1. Berlin: Walter de Gruyter.

Oskarson, Maria (1994), *Klassröstning i Sverige: Rationalitet, lojalitet eller bara slentrian.* Stockholm: Nerenius and Santerus.

Oskarson, Maria (1995), Gender gap in Nordic voting behaviour, in Lauri Karvonen and Per Selle (eds), *Women in Nordic Politics: Closing the Gap.* Aldershot: Dartmouth.

Østergård, Uffe (1997), The Geopolitics of Nordic Identity – From Composite States to Nation States, in Øystein Sørensen and Bo Stråth (eds), *The Cultural Construction of Norden.* Oslo: Scandinavian University Press.

Østerud, Øyvind (1998), Det nordiske paradokset, in Johan P. Olsen and Bjørn Otto Sverdrup (eds), *Europa i Norden.. Europeisering av nordisk samarbeid.* Oslo: Tano Aschehoug.

Östhol, Anders (1996), *Politisk integration och gränsöverskridande regionbildning i Europa.* Umeå: Statsvetenskapliga Institutionen, Umeå Universitet. Thesis.

Øverby, Einar (1996), Pension Politics in the Nordic Countries: A Case Study, *International Political Science Review* vol. 17, No. 1:67–90.

Page, Edward C. and Michael J.Goldsmith, (1987), Centre and Locality: Explaining Cross-National Variation, in Edward C. Page and Michael J. Goldsmith (eds), *Central and Local Government Relations.* London: Sage.

Page, Edward C. (1991), *Localism and Centralism in Europe: The Political and Legal Bases of Local Self-Government.* Oxford: Oxford University Press.

Paloheimo, Heikki (2003), The Rising Power of the Prime Minister in Finland, *Scandinavian Political Studies* 26:219–243.

Pedersen, Mogens (2002), Denmark: The Interplay of Nominations and Elections in Danish Politics, in Hanne Marthe Narud, Mogens N. Pedersen and Henry Valen (eds), *Party Sovereignty and Citizen Control. Selecting Candidates for Parliamentary Elections in Denmark, Finland, Iceland and Norway*. Odense: Odense University Press.

Pedersen, Mogens, Ulrik Kjær and Kjell A. Eliassen (2004), Institutions Matter – Even in the Long Run. Representation, Residence Requirements, and Parachutage in Norway and Denmark, in Hanne Marthe Narud and Anne Krogstad (eds), *Elections, Parties and Political Representation*. Oslo: Universitetsforlaget.

Pedersen, Thomas. (1996), Denmark and the EU, in Lee Miles (1996), *The Nordic States and European Integration*. London: Routledge, pp. 81–100.

Peters, B. Guy (1997), Bringing the State Back in Again. Paper presented at the Conference on Governance, Loch Lomond, Scotland.

Petersson, Olof (1994), *The Government and Politics of the Nordic Countries*. Stockholm: Fritzes Förlag.

Petersson, Olof, Sören Holmberg, Leif Lewin and Hanne Marthe Narud (2002), *Demokrati utan ansvar*. Demokratirådets rapport 2002. Stockholm: SNS Förlag.

Pierre, Jon (1998), Local Industrial Partnerships: Exploring the Logics of Public–Private Partnerships, in Jon Pierre (ed.), *Partnerships in Urban Governance: European and American Experience*. London: Macmillan.

Pitkin, Hanna (1967), *The Concept of Representation*. Berkeley and Los Angeles: University of California Press.

Ploug, Niels (1999), Cuts in and reform of the Nordic cash benefit systems, in Mikko Kautto, Matti Heikkila, Bjørn Hvinden, Staffan Marklund and Niels Ploug, *Nordic Social Policy. Changing welfare states*. London: Routledge.

Polanyi, Karl (1971), *The Great Transformation. The Political and Economic Origins of our Time*. Boston: Beacon Press.

Pollitt, C., Derek Ormond and B. Guy Peters (1997), *Trajectories and Options: An International Perspective on the Implementation of Finnish Public Management Reforms*. Helsinki: Ministry of Finance.

Pollitt, Christopher and Geert Bouckaert (2004), *Public Management Reform: A Comparative Analysis*. Oxford: Oxford University Press.

Pollitt, Christopher (1995), Justification by Works or by Faith, *Evaluation*, 1 (2):133–154.

Powell, G. Bingham (2000), *Elections as Instruments of Democracy. Majoritarian and Proportional Visions*. New Haven: Yale University Press.

Powell, Martin and Armando Barrientos (2004), Welfare regimes and the welfare mix, *European Journal of Political Research* vol. 43:83–105.

Premfors, R. (1991), The 'Swedish Model' and Public Sector Reform, *West European Politics*, 14:83–95.

Premfors, Rune (1999), Det historiska arvet – Sverige, in Per Lægreid and Ove Kaj Pedersen (eds), *Fra opbygning til ombygning av staten. Organisationsforandringer i tre nordiske lande.* Copenhagen: Jurist- og Økonomforbundets forlag.

Putnam, Robert (1976), *The Comparative Study of Political Elites.* New Jersey: Prentice-Hall.

Qvortrup, Mads (2002), The Emperor's New Clothes: The Danish General Election 20 November 2001, *West European Politics* 2002 (26), 2:205–211.

Raaum, Nina C. (1999), Women in parliamentarian politics: Historical lines of development, in Christina Bergqvist et al. (eds), *Equal Democracies? Gender and politics in the Nordic countries.* Oslo: Scandinavian University Press, pp. 27–47.

Raaum, Nina C. (2001), Norske likestillingsparadokser. Refleksjoner over kjønn, arbeid og politikk., in Nina Berven and Per Selle (eds) (2001), *Svekket kvinnemakt? De frivillige organisasjonene og velferdsstaten.* Oslo: Gyldendal Akademisk.

Ranney, Austin (1981), Candidate Selection, in David Butler, Howard R. Penniman and Austin Ranney (eds), *Democracy at the Polls.* Washington D.C.: AEI publications.

Rasch, Bjørn Erik (2004), *Kampen om regjeringsmakten. Norsk parlamentarisme i europeisk perspektiv.* Bergen: Fagbokforlaget.

Ratti, Remigio, Alberto Bramanti and Richard Gordon (eds) (1997), *The Dynamics of Innovative Regions. The GREMI Approach.* Aldershot: Ashgate.

Raunio, Tapio (2004), The Changing Finnish Democracy: Stronger Parliamentary Accountability, Coalescing Political Parties and Weaker External Constraints, *Scandinavian Political Studies* 27:133–152.

Rieker, Pernille (2003), Fra nordisk balanse til Europeisering? in Pernille Rieker and Ståle Ulriksen (eds), *En annerledes Supermakt? Sikkerhets- og Forsvarspolitikken i EU.* Oslo: NUPI.

Ries, Tomas (2002), The Atlantic Link: A View from Finland, in Bo Huldt, Sven Rudberg and Elisabeth Danielsson (eds), *The Transatlantic Link. Strategic Yearbook,* Stockholm: Swedish National Defence College.

Riste, Olav (2001), *Norway's Foreign Relations: A History.* Oslo: Universitetsforlaget.

Rokkan, Stein and Derek W. Urwin (1983), *Economy, Territory, Identity: Politics of West European Peripheries.* London : Sage.

Rokkan, Stein (1966), Norway: Numerical democracy and corporate pluralism, in Robert A. Dahl (ed.), *Political oppositions in Western democracies.* New Haven and London: Yale University Press.

Rokkan, Stein (1970), *Citizens Elections Parties.* Oslo: Universitetsforlaget.

Rokkan, Stein (1975), Dimensions of state formation and nation-building, in Charles C. Tilly (ed.), *The formation of national states in Western Europe*. Princeton: Princeton University Press.

Rokkan, Stein (1975), Votes Count, Resources Decide, in Ottar Dahl et al. (eds), *Makt og Motiv: Festskrift til Jens Arup Seip*. Oslo: Gyldendal.

Rokkan, Stein (1981), The Growth and Structuring of Mass Politics, in Erik Allard et al. (eds), *Nordic Democracy*. Copenhagen: Det Danske Selskap.

Rokkan, Stein (1987), Nasjonsbygging, konfliktutvikling og massepolitikkens strukturering, (reprint) in Bernt Hagtvedt (ed), *Stat, nasjon, klasse. Essays i politisk sosiologi*. Oslo: Universitetsforlaget.

Rommetvedt, Hilmar (2002), *Politikkens allmenngjøring og den nypluralistiske parlamentarismen*. Bergen: Fagbokforlaget.

Rose, Lawrence E. and Audun Skare (1996), *Lokalt folkestyre i klemme?* Oslo: Dept. of Political Science, University of Oslo. (http://www.statsvitenskap.uio.no/ansatte/serie/notat/1-96.html).

Rose, Lawrence E. and Krister Ståhlberg (2000), Municipal Identification and Democratic Citizenship, in Lauri Karvonen and Krister Ståhlberg (eds), *Festschrift for Dag Anckar on his 60th Birthday on February 12, 2000*. Åbo: Åbo Akademi University Press.

Rose, Lawrence E. (1990), Nordic Free Commune Experiments: Increased Local Autonomy or Continued Central Control? in Desmond E. King and Jon Pierre (eds), *Challenges to Local Government*. London: Sage Publications.

Rose, Lawrence E. (1999), Citizen (Re)orientations to the Welfare State: From Public to Private Citizens? in Jet Bussemaker (ed.), *Citizenship and Welfare State Reform in Europe*. London: Routledge.

Rothstein, Bo and Jonas Bergstrøm (1999), *Korporatismens fall och den svenska modellens kris*. Stockholm: SNS förlag.

Rothstein, Bo (1992), *Den korporativa staten*. Lund: Nordstadts Juridik.

Rule, Wilma and Joseph Zimmerman (1994), *Electoral Systems in Comparative Perspectives. Their Impact on Women and Minorities*. London: Greenwood Press.

Rustow, Dankwart A. (1956), Working Multiparty Systems, in Sigmund Neumann (ed.), *Modern Political Parties*. Chicago: University of Chicago Press.

Sæter, Martin (1996), Norway and the EU: Domestic Debate vs. External reality, in Lee Miles, *The Nordic States and European Integration*. London: Routledge, pp. 133–149.

Sahlin-Andersson, Kerstin and David Lerdell (1997), *Att lära over gränser*. Stockholm: SOU 33.

Sahlin-Andersson, Kerstin (2001), National, International and Transnational

Construction of New Public Management, in Tom Christensen and Per Lægreid (eds), *New Public Management. The Transformation of Ideas and Practice*. Aldershot: Ashgate.

Salamon, Lester M., H. K. Anheier, R. List, S. Toepler, S. W. Sokolowski and Associates (1999), *Global civil society: dimensions of the nonprofit sector*. Baltimore, MD: The Johns Hopkins Center for Civil Society Studies.

Sandberg, Siv and Krister Ståhlberg (2000), *Nordisk regionalförvaltning i förendring*. Åbo Akademi.

Sartori, Giovanny (1976), *Parties and Party Systems: a Framework for Analysis*. Cambridge: Cambridge University Press.

Schlesinger, Joseph A. (1994), *Political Parties and the Winning of Office*. Ann Arbor: University of Michigan Press.

Schmitter, Philippe C. (1974), Still the Century of Corporatism? *Review of Politics* vol. 36:85–131.

Schofield, Norman (1993), Political Competition and Multiparty Coalition Governments, *European Journal of Political Research* 23:1–33.

Seip, Anne-Lise (1991), Velferdskommunen og velferdstrekanten – et tilbakeblikk, in Anne-Hilde Nagel (ed.), *Velferdskommunene. Kommunenes rolle i utviklingen av velferdsstaten*. Bergen: Alma Mater.

Self, Peter (2000), *Rolling Back the Market. Economic Dogma & Political Choice*. New York: St. Martin's Press.

Seligman, Lester G. (1967), Political Parties and the Recruitment of Political Leadership, in Lewis J. Edinger, *Political Leadership in Industrialized Societies*. New York: Wiley.

Selle, Per (1998), The Norwegian Voluntary and Civil Sector in Transition: Women as Catalyst of Deep-seated Change, in Dietrich Rueschemeyer et al. (eds), *Participation and Democracy. East and West*. New York: M. E. Sharp, pp. 157–202.

Selznick, Philip (1957), *Leadership in Administration*. New York: Harper & Row.

Sharpe, L.J. (1970), Theories and Values of Local Government, *Political Studies* 18:153–174.

Sharpe, L.J. (1993), The European Meso: An Appraisal, in L.J. Sharpe (ed.), *The Rise of Meso Government in Europe*. London: Sage.

Siim, Birthe (1997), Politisk medborgerskap og feministiske forståelser, in Ann-Dorte Christensen, Ann-Birthe Ravn and Iris Rittenhofer (eds), *Det kønnede samfund*. Aalborg: Aalborg Universitetsforlag.

Siim, Birthe (2000), *Gender and Citizenship. Politics and Agency in France, Britain and Denmark*. Cambridge: Cambridge University Press.

Sivesind, Karl Henrik, Håkon Lorentzen, Per Selle and Dag Wollebæk (2002),

*The Voluntary Sector in Norway. Composition, Changes, and Causes.* Oslo: Institutt for samfunnsforskning.

Skjæveland, Asbjørn (2003), *Government Formation in Denmark 1953-1998.* Århus: Institut for Statskundskab, Aarhus Universitet.

Skjeie, Hege (1997), A Tale of Two Decades: The End of a Male Political Hegemony, in Kåre Strøm and Lars Svåsand (eds), *Challenges to Political Parties. The Case of Norway.* Ann Arbor: Michigan University Press.

Skjeie, Hege and Mari Teigen (1993), Kvinners inntog i topp-politikken – et uttrykk for politikkens marginalisering?, in Bjørn Erik Rasch (ed.), *Symbolpolitikk og parlamentarisk styring.* Oslo: Universitetsforlaget.

Skjeie, Hege and Birthe Siim (2000), Scandinavian Feminist Debates on Citizenship, *International Science Review* vol. 21, no 4:534–360.

Skocpol, Theda (2003), *Diminished Democracy: From Membership to Management in American Civil Life.* Norman, OK: University of Oklahoma Press.

Skocpol, Theda, Marshall Ganz and Ziad Munson (2000), A Nation of Organizers: The Institutional Origins of Civic Voluntarism in the United States, *American Political Science Review* (94), No. 3: 527–546.

Sørensen, Øystein and Bo Stråth (eds) (1997), *The Cultural Construction of Norden.* Oslo: Scandinavian University Press.

SOU (1996), *Sverige och EMU,* EMU-utredningen (Report of the Government's Expert Group) SOU:158.

Ståhlberg, Krister (1996), Finland, in Erik Albæk, Lawrence Rose, Lars Strömberg and Krister Ståhlberg, *Nordic Local Government: Developmental Trends and Reform Activities in the Postwar Period.* Helsinki: The Association of Finnish Local Authorities.

Stark, Agneta (1997), Combating the Backlash: How Swedish Women Won the War, in Ann Oakley and Juliet Michells (eds), *Who's Afraid of Feminism? Seeing through the Backlash.* London: Harmish Hamilton, pp.224–244.

*Nordic Statistical Yearbook 2003,* vol. 41 (Nord 2003:1), Copenhagen: Nordic Council of Ministers.

*Statistical Yearbook of Sweden 2003.* Stockholm: Statistics Sweden.

Steen, Anton (1981), The Farmers, the Consumers and the State: Redistribution and Conflicts in Norway, Sweden and the United Kingdom, *European Journal of Political Research* vol. 9:1–16.

Steen, Anton (1986), Velferdsstat og utjevningspolitikk, *Tidsskrift for samfunnsforskning* vol. 27:528–551.

Steen, Anton (1995), Welfare State Expansion and Conflicts in the Nordic Countries: The Case of Occupational Health Care, *Scandinavian Political Studies* vol. 18, No. 3:159–186.

Stjernquist, Nils (1996), *Tvåkammartiden. Sveriges riksdag 1867-1970.* Stockholm: Sveriges Riksdag.

Stokke, Torgeir Aarvaag (2002), Mediation in Collective Interest Disputes, in Peter Wahlgren (ed.), *Stability and Change in Nordic Labour Law.* Scandinavian Studies in Law. Vol. 43. Stockholm: Stockholm University Law Faculty.

Storper, Michael (1997), *The Regional World: Territorial Development in a Global Economy.* New York: The Guilford Press.

*Stortinget i navn og tall 2001-2005* (2002). Oslo: Universitetsforlaget.

Strøm, Kaare (1986), Deferred Gratification and Minority Governments in Scandinavia, *Legislative Studies Quarterly* 11:583-605.

Strøm, Kaare (1990), *Minority Government and Majority Rule.* Cambridge: Cambridge University Press.

Strøm, Kaare (1990a), A Behavioral Theory of Competitive Political Parties, *American Journal of Political Science* 34:565-598.

Strömberg, Lars and Tone Engen (1996), Sweden, in Erik Albæk, Lawrence Rose, Lars Strömberg and Krister Ståhlberg, *Nordic Local Government: Developmental Trends and Reform Activities in the Postwar Period.* Helsinki: The Association of Finnish Local Authorities.

Strukturkommissionen (2004), *Strukturkommisionens betænkning: Sammenfatning.* København: Indenrigs- og Sundhedsministeriet. Betænkning nr. 1434.

Styrkarsdottir, Audur (1999), Women's List in Iceland – A response to political lethargy, in Christina Bergqvist et al. (eds), *Equal Democracies? Gender and politics in the Nordic countries.,* Oslo: Scandinavian University Press, pp. 88–96.

Sundelius, (1994), Changing Course: When Neutral Sweden Chose to Join the EU, in Walter Carlesnaes and Steve Smith (eds), *European Foreign Policy: the EC and Changing Perspectives on Europe.,* London: Sage.

Sundelius, Bengt (2001), The Makers of Swedish Security Policy, in Bo Huldt, Teija Tiilikainen and Lars Svåsand (2003), *The Norwegian Progress Party: A Populist Party?* Paper prepared for the conference: Contemporary Populisms in Historical Perspective, Liguria Center, Bogliasco, Genoa, Jan. 7-10, 2003.

Taagepera, Rein and Matthew Soberg Shugart (1989), *Seats and Votes. The Effects and Determinants of Electoral Systems.* New Haven: Yale University Press.

Thomassen, Jacques (1994), Empirical Research into Political Representation: Failing Democracy or Failing Models? in M. Kent Jennings and Thomas E. Mann (eds), *Elections at Home and Abroad.* Ann Arbor: University of Michigan Press.

Tiilikainen, Tapani Vaahtoranta and Anna Helkama-Rågård (eds), *Finnish and Swedish Security. Comparing National Policies.* Stockholm: Swedish National Defence College.

Tilikainen, Teija (1996), Finland and the EU, in Lee Miles, *The Nordic States and European Integration*. London: Routledge, pp. 117–132.

Titmuss, Richard M. (1963), The Social Divisions of Welfare, in Richard M. Titmuss, *Essays on 'the Welfare State'*. London: Allen and Unwin.

Togeby, Lise (1994), Political Implications of Increasing Number of Women in the Labour Force, *Comparative Political Studies* 27: 211.240.

Tonra, Ben (1996), *Iceland, Denmark, and the Netherlands in the EPC*, Paper at ECPR Joint Sessions. April 17–22, 1994, Madrid.

Törnudd, Klaus (2001), The Makers of Finnish Security Policy, in Bo Huldt, Teija Tiilikainen, Tapani Vaahtoranta and Anna Helkama-Rågård (eds), *Finnish and Swedish Security. Comparing National Policies*. Stockholm: Swedish National Defence College.

Tranvik, Tommy and Per Selle (2003), *Farvel til folkestyret? Staten og de nye nettverkene*. Oslo: Gyldendal Akademiske.

Tranvik, Tommy and Per Selle (2004), Strong State and weaker Democracy. The decline of the Democratic Infrastructure in Norway, in Lars Tragardh (ed), *Scandinavian Volunteerism*. Forthcoming.

Tvedt, Terje (2003), *Utviklingshjelp, utenrikspolitikk og makt.* Oslo: Gyldendal Akademisk.

Valen, Henry (1988), Norway: Decentralization and Group Representation, in M. Gallagher and M. Marsh (eds), *Candidate Selection in Comparative Perspective*. London: Sage Publications.

Valen, Henry, Hanne Marthe Narud and Audun Skare (2002), Norway: Party Dominance and Decentralized Decision-Making, in Hanne Marthe Narud, Mogens N. Pedersen and Henry Valen (eds), *Parliamentary Nominations. The Case of Denmark, Finland, Iceland and Norway*. Odense: Odense University Press.

Valen, Henry, Hanne Marthe Narud and Olafur Hardarson (2000), Geography and Political Representation, in Peter Esaiasson and Knut Heidar (eds), *Beyond Congress and Westminister: The Nordic Experience*. Columbus: Ohio State University Press.

Van Roozendaal, Peter (1992), The Effect of Dominant and Central Parties on Cabinet Composition and Durability, *Legislative Studies Quarterly* 17:5–36.

Volden, Craig and Clifford J. Carrubba (2004), The Formation of Oversized Coalitions in Parliamentary Democracies, *American Journal of Political Science* 48:521–537.

Von Sydow, Björn (1991), Sweden's road to a unicameral parliament, in Lawrence D. Longley and David M. Olson (eds), *Two Into One. The Politics and Processes of National Legislative Cameral Change*. Boulder: Westwiew Press.

Wägnerud, Lena (2000), Women's Representation, in Peter Esaiasson and Knut Heidar (eds), *Beyond Congress and Westminister: The Nordic Experience*. Columbus: Ohio State University Press.

Wagstaff, Peter (ed.) (1999), *Regionalism in the European Union*. Exeter: Intellect.

Wahlke, John C, Heinz Eulau and LeRoy C. Ferguson (1962), *The Legislative System*. New York: Wiley.

Walter, Tore Egil (2001), Nordiske militære utfordringer i et svensk perspektiv. *Militærmaktseminaret 2002. Forsvaret ved et veiskille*. Oslo: NUPI.

Weaver, R. Kent and Bert A. Rockman (eds) (1993), Do Institutions Matter? Washington, D.C.: Brookings Institution.

Wegge, Njord (2003), Med Brussel som tyngdepunkt? *Norwegian Institute for Defence Studies 5*.

Widfelt, Anders (1996), Sweden and the EU; implications for the Swedish Party System, in Lee Miles, *The Nordic States and European Integration*. London: Routledge, pp. 101–116.

Wilensky, Harold L. (1975), *The Welfare State and Equality*. Berkley: University of California Press.

Williamson, Peter J. (1989), *Corporatism in Perspective. An Introductory Guide to Corporatist Theory*. London: Sage Publications Ltd.

Wollebæk, Dag and Per Selle (2002), *Det nye organisasjonssamfunnet. Demokrati i endring*. Bergen: Fagbokforlaget.

Wollebæk, Dag and Per Selle (2003), Generations and Organizational Change, in Paul Dekker and Loek Halman (eds), *The Values of Volunteering. Cross – Cultural Perspectives*. New York: Kluwer Academic/Plenum Publishers.

Wollebæk, Dag and Per Selle (2004), The role of women in the transformation of the organizational society in Norway. *Nonprofit and Voluntary Sector Quarterly*, Forthcoming.

Wollebæk, Dag, Per Selle and Håkon Lorentzen (2000), *Frivillig innsats. Sosial integrasjon, demokrati og økonomi*. Bergen: Fagbokforlaget.

Zakheim, Dov S. (1998), The United States and the Nordic Countries during the Cold War. *Cooperation and Conflict* 33:2,115–130.

# List of Contributors

*Harald Baldersheim* (PhD, LSE) is professor og political science at theUniversity of Oslo. His research and teaching interests include local governance, regionalism, and transitional processes in Eastern Europe.

*Tom Christensen* (Dr.philos., Tromso) is professor of public administration and organization theory at the Department of Political Science, University of Oslo. He has researched and lectured on central civil service, public reform and organization theory.

*Knut Heidar* (PhD, LSE) is professor of political science at the University of Oslo. He has researched and lectured on political parties, political elites and West European politics in general.

*Oddbjørn Knutsen* (Dr.philos., Oslo) is professor of political science at the University of Oslo. His research interests are in the fields of comparative politics with a special focus on Western Europe, political sociology and electoral behaviour, value orientations and ideology, and methodology and statistics.

*Janne Haaland Matlary* (Dr.philos., Oslo) is professor of political science at the University of Oslo. Her field of research is international politics, mainly security affairs and European integration. She was Norwegian state secretary of foreign affairs 1997–2000.

*Hanne Marthe Narud,* (Dr.polit.) is professor of political science at the University of Oslo. Her main fields of research are voters, parties, parliaments and political representation.

*Trond Nordby* (Dr.philos., Oslo) is professor of political science at the University of Oslo. He has written several books and lectured on political parties, administration of health, corporatism and parliamentary systems.

Tore Nyhamar (Dr.polit., Oslo) is a senior researcher at the Norwegian Defence Research Establishment. His research interests include security policies and diplomacy, in particular the effects of terrorism on US-European relations and on American security policies.

Nina C. Raaum (Dr.polit., Bergen) is associate professor of political science at the Department of Comparative Politics, University of Bergen. She has researched and lectured on political participation, gender and politics and comparative politics in general.

Bjørn Erik Rasch is professor of political science at the University of Oslo. He has researched and lectured on theories of democracy, voting procedures, electoral systems and parliaments.

Lawrence E. Rose (PhD, Stanford University) is professor of political science at the University of Oslo. He has also previously taught at Stanford University and the University of Virginia in the USA. He has undertaken research relating to local government and politics throughout both Eastern and Western Europe with special emphasis on the role of citizens.

Per Selle (Dr.polit., Bergen) is professor of comparative politics at the University of Bergen. He has researched and lectured on the welfare state, social capital/civil society, voluntary organizations and environmental politics.

Anton Steen (Dr.philos., Oslo) is professor of political science at the University of Oslo. Main fields of interest are theories of public policy-making, post-communist elites and democratization, the welfare state, ethnic integration.

Tommy Tranvik (PhD, Bergen) is a researcher at the Stein Rokkan Centre, University of Bergen. He is working on issues related to the political use of the Internet, local government and civil society in Norway.

# Index